LONDON RECORD SOCIETY
PUBLICATIONS

VOLUME XXI
FOR THE YEAR 1984

THE LETTERS OF
JOHN PAIGE, LONDON
MERCHANT,
1648–1658

EDITED BY
GEORGE F. STECKLEY

LONDON RECORD SOCIETY
1984

SBN 90095221 0

ACKNOWLEDGEMENTS

The Editor wishes to thank James Farnell for introducing him to the Paige letters. Editorial work was assisted by a generous grant from the Program for Editions of the National Endowment for the Humanities and by a travel grant from the Faculty Research Fund of Knox College.

Phototypeset by
Wyvern Typesetting Ltd, Bristol
Printed and bound in Great Britain
at The Pitman Press, Bath

CONTENTS

ABBREVIATIONS

Sources

All works cited are published in London unless otherwise stated.

A.H.N.	Archivo Histórico Nacional, Madrid
A.H.P., S.C.	Archivo Histórico Provincial, Santa Cruz de Tenerife
B.L.	British Library
C.C.M.E.I.C.	*Calendar of the Court Minutes of the East India Company*, ed. E. B. Sainsbury (Oxford, 1922–38)
C.S.P.D.	*Calendar of State Papers, Domestic Series*
C.	P.R.O., Court of Chancery
C. 105/12	P.R.O., Chancery Masters' Exhibits, C. 105/12, Clerke *et al.* v. Paige
C. 110/151	P.R.O., Chancery Masters' Exhibits, C. 110/151, Best v. Turner
C.J.	*Journals of the House of Commons*
E. 190	P.R.O., Exchequer, King's Remembrancer, Port Books
Ec. H. R.	*Economic History Review*
exam.	Examination in the High Court of Admiralty
Firth and Rait	*Acts and Ordinances of the Interregnum*, ed. C. H. Firth and R. S. Rait, 3 vols. (1911)
H.C.A.	P.R.O., High Court of Admiralty
M.C., Inq.	Museo Canario, Las Palmas de Gran Canaria, Inquisición
n.s.	new style
P.R.O.	Public Record Office
PROB 11	P.R.O., Prerogative Court of Canterbury, Registered Copy Wills

Weights, measures, monetary units

cwt	hundredweight
D	ducat
hhd	hogshead
kt	quintal
lb	pound
m	mil
R	*real*, Spanish
t	ton

INTRODUCTION

Origins of a London merchant

The letters published here were written by the London merchant John Paige in the years 1648 to 1658. They were used in an accounting between Paige and one of his trading associates, William Clerke, and form part of a larger Master's exhibit in Chancery which includes accounts, invoices, bills of lading, and letters written by Paige's other trading associate, Gowen Paynter.[1] The exhibit, taken as a whole, may well constitute the most complete documentation that is extant for any London merchant of the Interregnum. And in addition to casting some light on London's business conditions during those years of political experiment and commercial war, Paige's letters reveal the mind and methods of a young merchant who dispatched ships to five continents, counselled the government on matters of trade, and would serve for many years as a director of the East India Company.

John Paige's own activities in the 1640s and 1650s nicely represent the larger features of London's trade in the seventeenth century. Before 1640 traders in Spanish wines had participated in the import boom which had made the City a centre of conspicuous consumption.[2] And Paige's main business at mid-century was the importation of a luxury wine from Tenerife in the Spanish Canaries. From 1660 to 1700 the most significant development in London's foreign trade would be the growing re-export of Asian and American goods.[3] And Paige was already in the 1650s not only an importer of wines but also an East India merchant and a broker of American fish, sugars, hides and dyestuffs. If the middle two decades were years of commercial growth in London, even while the export of English cloth may have declined, it was because the City's trade was, like Paige's, based on elements both old and new.[4]

1. C. 105/12.
2. F. J. Fisher, 'The development of London as a centre of conspicuous consumption in the sixteenth and seventeenth centuries', Royal Hist. Soc. *Trans.*, 4th ser., xxx (1948), 37–50.
3. R. Davis, 'English foreign trade, 1660–1700', *Ec. H. R.*, 2nd ser., vii (1954), 150–4.
4. Statistics of the receipts from customs and excise during the Interregnum are found in M. B. Ashley, *Financial and Commercial Policy under the Cromwellian Protectorate* (Oxford, 1934), 56–7, 68–9. According to D. C. Coleman, the rising trend in customs receipts from 1643–58 confirms a high rate of growth in English overseas commerce during the 1640s and 1650s (*The Economy of England, 1450–1750* (Oxford, 1977), 134–5). But R. Davis (*The Rise of the English Shipping Industry* (1962), 11) and J. P. Cooper ('Social and economic policies under the Commonwealth', in *The Interregnum: the Quest for Settlement*, ed. G. E. Aylmer (1972), 123–5) emphasise the obstacles to commercial growth during the Interregnum. Statistics indicating a depression in the market for woollen cloth from 1648 to 1653 are found in D. W. Jones, 'The "Hallage" receipts of the London cloth markets, 1562–c. 1720', *Ec. H. R.*, 2nd ser., xxv (1972), 585–7.

Information about his origins and business associates, as well as the pattern of his trade, might indeed tempt us to identify Paige as one of the influential 'new merchants' of the revolutionary decades, men who were at once interlopers on the preserves of the old chartered companies and also serious entrepreneurs in the newer American trades. These merchants, of whom Maurice Thomson is taken as the pre-eminent example, have been described as typically republican in politics, Independent in religion, and militantly expansionist in their commercial programmes. It is argued that they played an important role in the radical politics of the 1640s and that they helped to design key economic measures of the commonwealth, notably the Navigation Act of 1651.[5] And Paige, a young Canary merchant who joined Thomson in trading ventures and petitions, was at least familiar with these activists and their programmes.

Like most of the 'new merchants' Paige was a Londoner only by adoption. His migration from Stoke Fleming in Devon, where he was born in about 1627, was one instance in an established pattern of mobility which had had consequences for London's trade.[6] The Thornes of Bristol and the Hawkins family of Plymouth, pioneers in the Canary trade, had sent their sons to London in the sixteenth century.[7] And if the City's share of the Spanish trade grew faster than that of the outports in the seventeenth century, it was in part because the Lants, Boones, Warrens and other contemporaries of Paige had brought their knowledge of the Spanish trade from West Country towns to London.[8]

Paige was first sent to London, after an apprenticeship in Tenerife, by his master, Gowen Paynter. Paynter, another West Countryman, was the fifth son in a family of traders and sea captains from Dawlish. He had been a factor at Tenerife in the 1630s for three London merchants, John Paynter, probably his older brother, and Robert and Richard Lant, sons of an Exeter mayor and leading City merchants in the Spanish trade. With John Lambell, the Lants' first cousin, Gowen Paynter received ships at Tenerife and re-laded them for London. By the 1640s he was a professional factor who acted for several London and Bristol merchants and needed the help of apprentices (**128**).[9] Paige, it appears, entered

5. J. E. Farnell, 'The Navigation Act of 1651, the First Dutch War and the London merchant community', *Ec. H. R.*, 2nd ser., xvi (1964), 439–54; R. Brenner, 'The Civil War politics of London's merchant community', *Past and Present*, no. 58 (1973), 53–107.

6. PROB 11/397/81, Will of John Paige. The ages Paige gave when examined in the Admiralty Court suggest that he was born in 1627. W. Letwin documents Paige's later association with Sir Josiah Child (*The Origins of Scientific Economics* (1963), 24, n. 45, 26, n. 47) but confuses Paige with his cousin John Paige who was the merchant and sometime mayor of Plymouth (e.g. **5a**, **37**, **46**, **81d**, **96d**).

7. G. D. Ramsay, *English Overseas Trade During the Centuries of Emergence* (1957), 136; P. S. Crowson, *Tudor Foreign Policy* (New York, 1973), 23–4.

8. Davis, *Ec. H. R.*, 2nd ser., vii, 150, n. 3.

9. C. 105/12, J. Paige to W. Clerke, 16 March 1648; PROB 11/306/185, Will of Gowen Paynter; H.C.A. 13/72, exam. of Gowen Paynter, 5 Aug. 1658, 13/53, ff. 27, 107, 13/55, f. 22, 13/56, f. 155, 13/57, f. 200, 13/62, exam. of Edward Bullocke, 28 June 1649; C. 105/12, Account by Robert and Richard Lant of goods sent to Andrew Cox and Gowen Paynter, 13 July 1641; *Deposition Books of Bristol, 1643–7*, ed. H. E. Nott (Bristol Rec. Soc., vi, 1935), 160; *Deposition Books of Bristol, 1650–4*, ed. H. E. Nott and E. Ralph (Bristol Rec. Soc., xiii, 1948), 91; *Merchants and Merchandise in Seventeenth-Century*

Paynter's service at Tenerife in about 1642 and sometimes travelled as a supercargo on ships to London before becoming a permanent resident of the City in late 1648. By then he was twenty-one years old and ready to assume the role of London wholesaler in his master's wine trade (**1, 7b**).

As Paige was becoming the London factor for Paynter in 1648, he was also transacting business for one of Paynter's associates in Tenerife, William Clerke. The second son of Samuel Clerke, doctor of divinity and absentee master of Wyggeston's Hospital, Leicester, William was born at Kingsthorpe, Northamptonshire, in 1620. He was apprenticed to Richard Lant of London and by the 1630s had been sent to assist his master's agents in Tenerife. Taken captive by Turks as he was sailing from Palma in the Canaries to London, Clerke was not yet ransomed from Algiers when his father was making out a will in early 1641. By May, however, he was free and living in the Lants' parish of All Hallows Barking, and by 1645 he was again in Tenerife where he lived with another factor of the Lants in a house described by Inquisition officials as decorated with pictures of Greek philosophers, bare-breasted women, and, inexplicably, the King of Sweden.[10] Three years later, as these letters begin, both William Clerke and Gowen Paynter had broken their association with the Lants and were consigning wines to John Paige at London (**10**).

Paige, as a factor, received commissions of only two per cent from Clerke, but he was anxious to have his patronage (**22b**). He was aware that Clerke sent wines to other London merchants and had relatives who could handle his affairs in the City.[11] To impress Clerke that he had quickly established his name among London's traders, Paige wrote in 1649 and 1650 that it was no longer necessary to address letters to him under cover of another merchant's name for his own was known on the Exchange (**10, 25a**). And though he had rented lodgings during those years in the parish of St Mary at Hill, by early 1651 he had married Katherine Paynter, his master's daughter, and had taken a house in the parish of St Helen, probably the residence in Bishopsgate Street which he was leasing as late as 1677 from his fellow Canary merchant, John Bewley (**26a, 31c, 66b, 118**).[12] The location was convenient. At nearby St Helen's

---

Bristol, ed. P. McGrath (Bristol Rec. Soc., xix, 1955), xvii. Giles Paynter, a shipmaster mentioned in the letters, was Gowen's brother (e.g. **31c, 32, 40b, 47c**).

10. PROB 11/186/61, Will of Samuel Clerke; *Visitation of Northampton, 1681*, ed. H. I. Longden (Harleian Soc., lxxxvii, 1935), 50–6; *A History of Leicestershire*, iv, ed. R. A. McKinley (Oxford, 1958), 401–2; H.C.A. 13/57, ff. 198, 300, 303; Archivo Municipal de La Laguna, R-X, lv, Representaciones al Cabildo, i. 73; *Catalogue of Original Manuscripts of the Inquisition in the Canary Islands*, ed. W. de Gray Birch, 2 vols. (1903), ii, 563–5. William's younger *brother George Clerke* (b. 1624) was also apprenticed to a London merchant, resided at Lisbon, and returned in 1651 to trade at London where he had some dealings with Paige (e.g. **24, 47b, 48, 52b, 60b, d, 63d**). A *cousin George Clerke* from Willoughby in Warwickshire also became a London merchant and figures briefly in Paige's letters (e.g. **10, 12a, 14, 16–17**). *Leonard Clerke*, a merchant of West Country origins, was apparently not a relative of the Northampton and Warwickshire Clerkes (C. 6/146/43; PROB 11/381/165).

11. See above, n. 10.

12. H.C.A. 13/63, exam. of John Paige, 24 April 1650; *Inhabitants of London in 1638*, ed. T. C. Dale (1931), 114; PROB 11/348/96, Will of John Bewley; *Little London Directory of 1677* (1863).

the young merchant worshipped with men who would be his lifetime business associates. His typical working day might have taken him to the Custom House where he could check the weights of goods he had imported or the destinations of his competitors' ships (**40b**, **58a**) or to Doctors' Commons where he might hear testimony before the Admiralty Court (**78a**). Closer to home, he could stop at the hall of the Merchant Taylors, whose company he would join, transact business at the Ship Tavern in Bishopsgate Street, or walk the Exchange to deal with underwriters at the Insurance Office and to gather the latest foreign and domestic news, the 'timely advice'—'the main of all business'—which he reported to his principals in Tenerife (**9**).

The structure of trade with the Canaries
The rhythm of Paige's business activity and correspondence was set by Tenerife's vintage and London's social season, for the principal item imported from the Canaries was a sweet, white malmsey which held a special attraction for the City's elite. Paige also regularly sent price quotations from London and the continent for a variety of American goods, dyestuffs, hides, tobacco and sugar, all of which were available at the Canaries and accounted for a large share of the cargoes which he imported at London. The difficult task for English merchants was to balance such importation of wines and American goods by exporting merchandise of equal value to the Canaries. Paige shipped English manufactures from London, worked with his West Country contacts to send fish, and with his correspondents on the continent to ship wheat and linens. But he was also enticed into sending ships along exotic routes in quite dangerous ventures to find goods which would sell for 'ready money' in the Canaries. This was necessary because the wine from Tenerife's narrow northern slopes was to discriminating Londoners what Madeira would become in the eighteenth century, and the Canarian winegrowers could extract ever higher prices, paid largely in cash, from Paynter, Clerke and the other resident English merchants.

To enjoy the best market at the peak of London's social season, the Canary merchants wanted their rich cargoes home 'at Christmas, which is all in all for wines'.[13] In January 1646 the Thames was so full of ice when the vintage fleet arrived two weeks late that the masters would not venture up river from Gravesend. Two veteran merchants nevertheless ran 'the great hazard' of hiring a lighter and running 60 pipes amid the ice to the Custom House. They might have feared that the unfortified and delicate malmsey would grow eager by being too long on board (**39a**, **66c**, **71b**) and require 'mending' with good Malaga wines (**50**). But they could

13. C. 110/151, J. Turner to R. Wilson, Sr and M. Bradgate, 8 June 1647, n.s.; Fisher, Royal Hist. Soc., *Trans.*, 4th ser., xxx, 43. For general comment on the Canary wine trade, see A. Bethencourt Massieu, 'Canarias e Inglaterra: el comercio de vinos (1650–1800)', *Anuario de Estudios Atlánticos*, ii (1956), 31–144, and G. F. Steckley, 'The wine economy of Tenerife in the seventeenth century', *Ec. H. R.*, 2nd ser., xxxiii (1980), 335–50.

also anticipate that their risks would bring rich rewards for 'there was never such a want of Canary wines' in London.[14]

And so it was at Christmas that Paige usually faced payment of customs and freight for wines (**47d**) and then prepared to renew the cycle. The Canary merchant might begin buying merchandise in February or March if a large outward cargo were intended (**17, 30a, 84c**). But if the ship carried little and went directly to Tenerife for the vintage, it was usually freighted by 1 July to accomplish the three- to four-week passage in late summer and to lie in the dangerous roadstead Puerto de la Cruz off the northern coast of Tenerife. There the ship might remain for up to three months, taking in 30 to 40 half-ton pipes of wine on days when northerly winds did not force the crew to put out to sea in order to save ship and limb.[15] And on the way home the sailors might face experiences like those of the *Susan*'s crew in December 1651 when 'dark and dirty' weather forced them to cut the mainmast by the board and jettison the boat and gun (**50**).

But merchants like Paige, Paynter and Clerke risked their capital and hired others to risk their lives because the rising demand for Canary wine in London brought ever higher prices and attractive returns in the first half of the seventeenth century. Only 585 pipes of Canary wine were taxed at London in 1595.[16] But the single wine import book preserved from the middle decades of the seventeenth century shows that almost ten times that much, at least 5,508 pipes (2,754 tons), was taxed in the twelve months ending on 25 December 1644.[17] And the vintage fleet of 1644 (about twenty-four ships) can be compared with Paige's references to the number of shipmasters hired for later vintages to get a rough estimate of the Canary wine imported in 1649–55. With two exceptions, Paige's reports indicate a fleet of twenty or more ships, and this suggests that in 1650 and again in 1654–55 the amount of Canary wine taxed annually at London was comparable to the 5,500 pipes of 1644. In 1649 the importation may have been well above this figure because Paige listed forty ships with a total capacity of 6,490 tons (12,980 pipes) which had been freighted for the vintage (**128**). On the other hand, the importation from 1651 to 1653 may have fallen below 5,000 pipes. In 1651 English merchants agreed to limit their purchases at the Canaries in an effort to force down wine prices (**52b**). In the autumn of 1652 Paige reported only twelve ships freighted for the vintage, the fleet initially turned back to London after the Dutch victory off Dungeness, and the war discouraged factors at Tenerife from buying wines (**63d, 73a**).[18] But an annual importation during peacetime of 5 to 6,000 pipes (and perhaps considerably more than that in 1649) compares favourably with the average of 5,033 pipes calculated from import books of the 1630s and 5,522 pipes

---

14. C. 110/151, Accounts of trade between R. Best and J. Turner, 1642, and R. Best to J. Turner, 10 and 13 Jan. 1646.
15. Ibid., J. Turner to R. Wilson, Sr and M. Bradgate, 21 April 1647.
16. E. 190/9/7.
17. E. 190/43/3. One folio is missing from a period of heavy importation, and one can suppose that the actual importation taxed was close to 6,000 pipes.
18. C. 105/12, Paynter to Clerke, 15 Jan. 1653, n.s.

from those of the 1660s.[19] Londoners' consumption of a luxury wine seems not to have been much affected by civil war and political change.

Price data from the period confirm the buoyant demand. Richard Best, a London wholesaler, sold Canary wine during the years 1640 to 1647 for £16 to £19 per pipe. And even in years when Paige was reporting a vintage fleet of unprecedented size (1649–50) and expecting twenty new merchants in the trade (1650–51), prices moved well over £20, by early 1652 to £30 per pipe (**11a, 13a, 22d, 29, 30a, 51a–b, 52a, 53c, 59b**). The onset of war allowed Paige to sell at nearly £36 in 1653 (**68a, 80**), but prices over £30 per pipe were common from the late 1650s to the 1680s.[20]

In order to impress Clerke that he could obtain the best prices on the London market, Paige compared his own success with that of the pre-eminent wine merchant of the mid-seventeenth century, Rowland Wilson, Sr. (**6, 9, 39b**). Wilson and his partner Martin Bradgate (**27b**) had been involved in the Canary wine trade as early as 1615.[21] It appears that Henry St John had traded with them from time to time, and these three merchants, who also dealt in Iberian and French wines, accounted for 21 per cent of the Canary taxed at London in 1644.[22] Their chief factor at Tenerife, John Turner, was shipping over 1,100 pipes of wine annually from 1645 to 1647, so that the partners probably continued to import about 20 per cent of the Canary at London in the late 1640s.[23] Indeed Paige feared in 1651 that Wilson and company were determined to engross all of the best wines and was convinced at other times that Turner would use every trick, including the interception of letters, in order to confound his competitors (**22c, 23b, 30a**).

Paige himself probably imported at most about 200 to 300 pipes of wine a year in the late 1640s and early 1650s, only a fraction of that handled by Wilson and company, and Clerke shipped little malmsey to Paige in 1654–6. In those years Clerke did buy a volume of *vidueño*, the drier and inferior Canary, which he intended to sell in Barbados, Ireland or Bristol. But Paige did not expect success in any of those markets. Other merchants intended to supply Barbados where beverage Madeira was

19. Steckley, *Ec. H. R.*, 2nd ser., xxxiii, 342. The average for the 1660s is computed from data which include the importation figures for 1667 when the taxation of Canary wine at London was drastically affected by the formation and then dissolution of the Canary Company. When the number for that year is not used, the average for the decade becomes 7,705 pipes.

20. Prices are found at C. 105/12, in the letters of Paynter to Clerke, 1658–61 and in various Admiralty and Chancery cases from 1654–90.

21. E. 190/18/2.

22. E. 190/43/3. Wilson was also a chief importer of Iberian and French wines as well as an important Guinea and East India merchant (J. W. Blake, 'The English Guinea Company, 1618–60', *Belfast Natural Hist. and Phil. Soc.*, 2nd ser., iii (1945–6), 22, 27; *Seventeenth Century Economic Documents*, ed. J. Thirsk and J. P. Cooper (Oxford, 1972), 511–12; *C.C.M.E.I.C., 1640–3*, 61, *1650–4, passim*). Brenner identifies him as one of the 'new merchants', but is not always careful to distinguish him from his son, Rowland, Jr, the politician (R. Brenner, 'Commercial change and political conflict: the merchant community in Civil War London' (unpublished Ph.D. thesis, Princeton University, 1970), ff. 281, 381, 497).

23. C. 110/151, *passim*. Turner's letters, preserved as part of a master's exhibit in the Chancery case of Best v. Turner, were written from Tenerife in the 1640s and have been used extensively here to illuminate the pattern of trade at the islands.

already a staple of the market (**91b**, **93b**, **99b**).[24] The West Country took, by Paige's estimate, only about 100 pipes of Canary a year (**89d**). And when vintage ships were forced by weather into western ports or directed against Paige's advice to Dublin, the London factor arranged to bring the wines to the City (**65**, **66c**, **102**).[25]

So the Canary trade at mid-century was not really one of an Atlantic empire, nor did it serve even an English national market. There is some evidence that the wine was traded in the provinces, but Macaulay was probably right to doubt that the squirearchy could regularly have afforded choice Canary, and it was apparently Paige's practice to sell only the inferior wines to those who drove 'a country trade' (**50**).[26] In his drinking song, 'On Canary', the royalist Alexander Brome praised the effect of the wine on the drinker ('Though an abbess he court/In his high shoes he'll have her'), but he also saw the trade as an urban phenomenon:

> 'Tis this that advances the drinker and drawer:
> Though the father came to town in his hobnails and leather,
> He turns it to velvet and brings up an heir,
> In the town in his chain, in the field with his feather.[27]

Ranter poets numbered Canary among the delights of their heaven on earth, but surely a good many more sober citizens of London consumed their share and the growing metropolis took well over half of Tenerife's malmsey from the time Paige became a Londoner until the end of the seventeenth century.[28]

Paige also dabbled in the sugar trade and quoted London prices for whites from Palma in the Canaries (e.g. **5b**, **17**, **22a**, **53c**, **64b**). But he recognised that the Canarian product had been eclipsed in Europe by sugars from Brazil and Barbados (**31b**, **106a**). In fact Clerke sent his assistant Henry Hawley from Tenerife to Barbados where he trucked *vidueño* wines for sugars that were delivered to Amsterdam (**25b**, **28**, **31a**, **35**, **40a**, **42**, **44**), and all three parcels of sugar which Paige received at London from the Canaries were American in origin (**103**, **106a**, Table 1 below).

In addition to wines and sugars, the consumer goods of an ever richer metropolis, Paige imported such raw materials as dyestuffs and hides. Though he could find no vent for Canarian orchil, a purple dyestuff (**26b**, **31b**), he quickly sold American cochineal imported via the Canaries (**22a**,

24. C. 105/12, John Paige [of Plymouth and cousin of John Paige, London], Barbados, to W. Clerke, 24 Aug. 1661; M. Lister, Barbados, to H. Oldenburg, 27 June 1675, *The Correspondence of Henry Oldenburg*, 10 vols, ed. A. R. and M. B. Hall (1965–77), x, 373, no. 2690.
25. Cf. H.C.A. 13/62, 28 June 1649.
26. B. Whitelocke, *Memorials*, 4 vols (Oxford, 1853), i, 436; T. S. Willan, *The Inland Trade* (Manchester, 1976), 133–45; T. B. Macaulay, *The History of England from the Accession of James II*, 6 vols, ed. C. H. Firth (1913–15), i, 311; H.C.A. 13/73, exam. of Capt. Peter Bimewijsent, 25 Feb. 1659.
27. *English Poets*, ed. A. Chalmers, vi (1810), 657.
28. C. Russell, *The Crisis of Parliaments* (1971), 363–4; Steckley, *Ec. H. R.*, 2nd ser., xxxiii, 343.

TABLE 1. *Goods sold at London by John Paige for the account of William Clerke*

Year Ship	Wine/pipes	American goods, etc.	Net sale in £s	
1649 *Samuel*	11		155	
Blessing	79		1,189	
1650 *Blessing*	71		1,205	
Elizabeth	87		1,414	
Constant John		Rosewood, campe- chena, indigo		736
1651 *Swan*		Indigo, cochineal		429
1652 *Matthew*		Campeachy wood, cochineal		429
Susan	43		351	
1653 *Blessing*	80		1,625	
Turned-out	30		562	
1654 *Matthew*		Brazilian sugar		43
1655 *Peter and Anne*		Hides, campechena, sylvester		1,692
?*Agreement*		Campechena		56
1656 *Plough*		Brazilian sugar		16
Mary	10		80	
		Silver plate		87
		West Indian sugar, sarsaparilla		662
		Brazilwood		12
			£6,581	4,162

Source: C.105/12, Account of Paige with Clerke, 1648–56.

40b, 52a). And his accounts with Clerke reveal that imports of American goods from the islands accounted for about 40 per cent of their trade by value (Table 1 above). John Turner, Wilson's agent in the Canaries, preferred to deal in American dyestuffs and hides rather than in wines because, 'God sending [them] home, a man shall find what a man embarked and may keep them and stay for a market'.[29] And this relative durability also allowed for a natural rhythm in the trade. Ships which had hurried to London in December with the first wines could return to Tenerife for West India goods in the spring when there was more leisure to load, provided that the proper licences had been obtained from Canarian officials (**9, 22a, 26a, 39a, 59a, 85**).

The Judge of the Indies granted permission to export American goods from the Canaries, Paige told the Admiralty Court in 1650, so long as the merchants paid the usual duties and returned a certificate proving that

29. C. 110/151, J. Turner to R. Wilson, Sr and M. Bradgate, 5 Nov. 1646, n.s. American goods accounted for 27 per cent of the trade between Turner and Richard Best from 1639–42 (ibid., Accounts between Turner and Best).

they had sent the goods to a country at peace with Spain.[30] While Paynter lived at Orotava in the heart of Tenerife's lush vineyards, Clerke lived near the bureaucrats at the capital city of La Laguna where he could apply for the necessary papers and also ship the American goods which lay down the hill at Santa Cruz, the port most frequented by West Indiamen (**82, 84a–b**).[31] But Paige's testimony had been necessary in 1650 because the Captain General of the Canaries, Don Pedro Carrillo de Guzmán, had imprisoned Englishmen, Clerke among them, on charges that included the illegal export of American goods. London merchants, including Paige, petitioned the Council of State to protest that this prosecution violated the Anglo-Spanish treaty of 1645, and Don Pedro was soon replaced as Captain General (**9, 15, 19a**).[32] But again in 1654 Paige's principals feared that Canarian officials would embargo hides which they wished to export from Palma, and Paige worried that such rigour would 'undo the [West] Indians and cause them to forsake the Islands, which will be a great hindrance unto that trade' (**84b, 96e, 99b**).[33] Clerke nevertheless continued to send American goods to London in 1655 and 1656 even after he had nearly ended his trade in wines.

To be sure, Paige tried to discourage the export of some American goods from the Canaries. Ginger, which came to London directly from Barbados, was not worth insuring (**63b, 91b**). Indigo came in such quantity from the East Indies that Paige paid cellar rent for nearly a year before he could dispose of his stores (**22a, 26a, 40a–b, 60d, 101**). But cochineal was quite another matter. Composed of dried insect carcasses, this brilliant red dyestuff would be used for centuries to colour the coats of English soldiers and was second in value only to silver as a Mexican export.[34] And while Paige might ordinarily trust ship captains to see his imports weighed at the Custom House, he went in person to verify the cochineal. One chest sold in 1650 for £222, and a single barrel in 1652 for £182 (**22a, 40b, 52a**).[35] However, Paige had to keep his partners informed about the market trends of even this valuable commodity. Abundant supplies via Cadiz of sylvester and campechena, the wild and inferior varieties, could depress the market for cultivated cochineal mesteque, even though a pound of this quality dyestuff, by the salters' estimate, would 'strike a better colour and go further than 4 lbs of campechena' (**91a**).[36]

Indeed, Paige learned to be constantly alert to the prospects for large importations of all American goods via southern Spain. In December

30. H.C.A. 13/63, exam. of John Paige, 24 April 1650; cf. exams of William Bulkley, George Webber and Edmond Cowse, 20 April 1650.
31. C. 105/12, Paynter to Clerke, 6 Jan. 1649, n.s.; F. Morales Padron, *El comercio Canario-Americano (siglos XVI, XVII y XVIII)* (Seville, 1955), *passim*.
32. *C.S.P.D., 1650*, 105, 109. The petition is found at B. L., Add. MS 32, 093, f. 367.
33. C. 105/12, Paynter to Clerke, 29 Jan. and 22 March 1654, n.s.
34. J. H. Tremenheere, 'The Empire', *Quarterly Review*, cxv (1864), 355; R. Lee, 'American cochineal in European commerce', *Journal of Modern History*, xxiii (1951), 205.
35. C. 105/12, Paige's account with Clerke, 1648–56.
36. J. Hellot confirms this ratio in *The Art of Dyeing Wool and Woollen Cloth* (1789 ed.), 148. See also S. Fairlie, 'Dyestuffs in the eighteenth century', *Ec. H. R.*, 2nd ser., xvii (1964–5), 488–510.

1648 he reported a London price of 14s per pound for Varinas tobacco, and in June 1649 advised that at 13s it was the only American commodity worth sending from Tenerife (**1**, **2**, **5a**, **6**). But after the galleons had arrived at San Lucar, the price fell to 5 or 6s per pound in late 1649, and Clerke, who had acted on Paige's earlier advice, was caught holding a parcel (**10**, **12a**). Thereafter Paige often reported the latest speculation about the great Spanish fleets and the effect of their arrivals on the London market for American goods (**31b**, **58a**, **59b**, **94b**, **96c–d**, **101**, **110b**, **117**).

Only the prices of American hides, imported via the Canaries from Caracas, Havana and Santo Domingo, suffered no sharp decline at London during the period. John Turner had considered them a staple item if they came well enough cured for the London tanners, and Paige thought hides 'the staplest' of American goods because they could be sold for cash while other goods, including wines, were frequently sold on credit (**40a**, **46**, **56a**).[37] He predicted that the arrival of 4,000 hides in 1653 would not lower the price a farthing; and after he had sold a cargo in 1654 at 10d per pound, the highest price quoted in the letters, he declared that 10,000 hides would not satiate the London demand (**58a**, **73c**, **83b**, **85**, **87**, **89a**, **91a–b**, **92**).

The prices which Paige quoted for hides and other American goods were drawn from continental as well as London markets. Campeachy wood shipped via the Canaries had regularly been re-exported to the continent by London merchants because an import licence had been necessary in England before 1650.[38] And even after the London price for the dyestuff had risen in 1654 to more than twice the first cost at the Canaries, Paige also reported French quotations, perhaps because the English tariff was so high (**26b**, **49**, **79–80**, **81c**). He had correspondents in Amsterdam, Middelburg, Antwerp, Nantes, Le Havre, Rouen, Lisbon, Bilbao, Cadiz and San Lucar (e.g. **40b**). He sent his employers bills of rates especially from the French and Dutch cities and issued warnings when the lists could not be trusted for having been 'toned' with overstated quotations (e.g. **5b**, **6**, **7b**, **9**, **61e**, **77c**, **84b**). He finally sent Clerke's indigos to Lisbon (**48**), looked especially to Rouen and Nantes as markets for hides and dyestuffs (e.g. **40b**, **89a**, **90**, **96c**, **112**, **117**) and could suggest Genoa as the best alternative when ginger was a drug on the London market (**82**).

The Canaries did not always, however, provide American goods at the lowest prices. Paige justified his investment in a cargo of tobacco imported from Cadiz in 1654 by observing that the prices of American goods in Spain were 20 per cent cheaper than at the Canaries (**90**, **91a–b**). And there were even better terms in the American trade for those who sent their ships direct to the source as Spain proved unable to maintain an imperial monopoly. Both John Turner in 1646 and William Crosse in 1721 discouraged silent participation in American voyages with Canarians who, they warned, gave 'lame accounts' and were typically men of no

37. C. 110/151, J. Turner to R. Wilson, Sr and M. Bradgate, 19 March 1646, n.s.
38. H.C.A. 13/53, f. 435, 8 Dec. 1637; *C.S.P.D., 1636–7*, 154, 403, *1640–1*, 369; *C.J.*, vi, 426.

integrity.[39] Perhaps the risk was no greater when Englishmen sent ships on their own. They could use the Canaries as staging points for their assault on the Spanish colonial monopoly.[40] And Paige's interest in the game must have heightened as he watched his Devonshire cousins, the Stephens, his correspondent at Antwerp, John Shaw, and his friend George Jennings all successfully penetrate the Spanish markets in America for tobacco, hides and dyestuffs (**57, 110b**).[41] Later, when his wine trade was interrupted by war, Paige himself risked investment in a voyage to the West Indies.[42]

Paige drew upon London sources to supply the household needs of his principals. From his own parish he sent Thomas Leigh when Clerke needed an apprentice (**47a, 48, 52b, 60d, 62, 64b**).[43] In London he paid the wife of Clerke's cook, William Phillips, and the apothecary who concocted pills for Clerke's stomach. He found Turkey carpets and Russian couches in the emporium of the metropolis and contracted in Westminster for a coach upholstered in scarlet and silk which had been ordered by a wealthy Canarian.[44] But Paige's invoices show that he had to exploit international as well as provincial markets to find items which would bring the cash needed by his partners at the Canaries to buy wines and American goods (Table 2 below).

Fish accounted for the largest share of his exports by value, and he shipped the same varieties recommended to Canary merchants in the late sixteenth century, a few barrels of red herring, several hundred hogsheads of pilchards bought in Plymouth, Fowey and Falmouth and picked up by ships outbound from London, but especially cod contracted in England and loaded in Newfoundland (e.g. **11a, 13a, 15, 17, 22d, 81a, 81c, 106b**).[45] Pilchards were sent to arrive in the Canaries for Lent. The rhythm of the Newfoundland trade allowed for convenient delivery of the cod during Tenerife's vintage. For example, the *Blessing*, a ship of 65 tons, loaded 1,409 quintals of dryfish at St John's, Newfoundland, in September 1651 and, after a voyage of fifty-six days, had delivered her cargo to Paynter at Puerto de la Cruz, Tenerife, by 14 November.[46] Though Paige had earlier been unable to sell wines to the royalist governor of Newfoundland, Sir David Kirke, he had contracted for part of the *Blessing*'s fish from Kirke's brother John at London, and the rest from West Country merchants, including his cousin John Paige at Plymouth (**13a, 37, 39b, 43, 49**).[47] Similar contracts for cargoes on the

---

39. C. 110/151, J. Turner to Archibald Fer, 4 June 1646, n.s.; P.R.O., Colonial Office 388/23, W. Crosse to the Lords Commissioners for Trade and Plantations, 3 Aug. 1721.
40. H.C.A. 13/59, f. 703, 13/61, exam. of Raphe Langely, 13 May 1648, 13/62, exam. of John Browne, 7 Feb. 1648, 13/63, ff. 413–14, exam. of John Cotterell.
41. H.C.A. 13/59, ff. 468, 508, 514, 13/65, exam. of Thomas Riveley, 15 Jan. 1652.
42. See below, p. xxxiv.
43. *Registers of St. Helen's Bishopsgate*, ed. W. B. Bannerman (Harleian Soc. Reg. xxxi, 1904), 23.
44. C. 105/12, Paige's account with Clerke, 1648–56, and invoices of goods sent to Clerke.
45. 'A special direction for divers trades', in *Tudor Economic Documents*, ed. R. H. Tawney and E. Power (1924), iii, 204.
46. M.C., Inq., visita de la Fé, 14 Nov. 1651.
47. C. 105/12, Paige's invoices.

TABLE 2. *Goods exported by John Paige, London, for the account of William Clerke, Tenerife, 1648–1656*

To Tenerife	Value		% of cargoes to Tenerife
Newfoundland fish	1,148		33.0
Pilchards	307		9.0
Herring	23		.5
TOTAL FISH		1,478	42.5
Miscellaneous cloth	289		8.5
English woollens	205		6.0
Linen	80		2.5
TOTAL CLOTH		574	17.0
MISCELLANEOUS (guns, coach, tackle, etc.)		562	16.0
Wheat from Middelburg	298		8.5
Wheat from England	175		5.0
TOTAL WHEAT		473	13.5
PIPESTAVES		312	9.0
FOR CLERKE'S HOUSE		72	2.0
TOTAL to Tenerife		3,471	100.0
To Bilbao, Newfoundland fish		501	
To Safi, assorted goods		332	
To Guinea, assorted goods		841	
TOTAL CARGOES		£5,145	

Source: C.105/12, Paige's account with Clerke, 1648–1656, and invoices of goods shipped. Paige's commissions have been subtracted from the totals he gives.

Matthew in 1650 and the *Mary* in 1655 confirm that a City merchant of Paige's origins could co-operate with Devon men in a trade which had sometimes caused conflict between Londoners and West Countrymen.[48]

Wheat would account for more than 13.5 per cent of outbound cargoes to Clerke if the quantity delivered by the *Elizabeth* in 1650 were known. In the late summer of that year the merchants at Tenerife had ordered grain, suggesting Danzig as a source. But Paige was advised that it was too late for a ship to escape westward through the Sound before there was ice in the Baltic and that wheat at Amsterdam and Nantes was dear. Within ten days he had freighted the *Elizabeth*, laded an assorted cargo of birding pieces, German and Polish linens, calicoes and Spanish iron, and had cleared her for Safi in Barbary. There the supercargo Richard Jewell traded for wheat which sold well at Tenerife (**23a, 26a**).[49] When the price at La Laguna soared to over three times the legal maximum in 1651, Paynter was ready to 'try all the ports without the Straits', and Paige reported from London that 'every man hath order' for corn (**37**).[50] This

48. G. Cell, *English Enterprise in Newfoundland, 1577–1660* (Toronto, 1969), *passim*.
49. C. 105/12, Paige's invoices.
50. Ibid., Paynter to Clerke, 13 Feb. and 11 May 1651.

time the *Matthew* was unable to get a cargo at Barbary, but Paige called for his correspondent at Middelburg to load the *Blessing*, and Henry Hawley, Clerke's assistant who had carried the proceeds of Canary wines from Barbados to Amsterdam in sugars, returned to Tenerife on a second ship laden with wheat (**39b, 44, 48**). As the Canarian wheat crisis continued into 1652, Paige directed the *Blessing* to Morbihan in France. There his agent John Holle loaded seventy tons and provided a bill of lading falsely dated at Plymouth to save Clerke and Paynter from trouble over contraband French goods (**61a**).[51] But when the French authorities prohibited further shipments because of drought, Paige and Clerke's brother George found a way, despite statutory restrictions, to ship 200 tons from Faversham on the *Agreement* and *Constant John*, and Paynter and Clerke sent the *Elizabeth and John* to the Azores for wheat (**61d, 63d, 64c, 65**). Paige reported the shipment of a thousand tons from Amsterdam to Tenerife in 1658. And again in 1660–1 and 1676–7 English merchants helped to alleviate, and no doubt profited from, food shortages which were caused in Tenerife not only by pests and weather but also by the continuing appropriation of scarce arable land to meet the demand for the island's luxury wine (**127a**).[52]

Canarians had less critical need in their warm climate for the most famous English export of the early modern period, but Paige's shipments of woollen textiles (6 per cent by value of all cargoes sent to Clerke) were unrepresentative of total traffic to the Canaries. English woollens accounted for 24 per cent by value of all the merchandise which John Turner sold at the Canaries in 1646 and 39 per cent of the total imports at Tenerife's busiest port in 1694.[53] Paige's shipment of '6 ends of goods' suggests the character of his cloth trade which shows no growth despite what he described as a twenty per cent decline in textile prices at London during the Dutch war (**64c, 107**). He sent a few Colchester bays, the type of new draperies which had given English merchants entry into Mediterranean markets, and he had orders for traditional Hampshire kersies (**46, 94a, 96a, 107**). But he shared John Turner's opinion that 'the multiplicity of sortments cause sales' in the Canaries.[54] And even the small sample found in Paige's invoices—fustians, silk druggets, mohairs, damaselas, medusas, calicoes, Welsh cottons and plains—proves that the merchant could find in London a veritable bazaar of cloth.

Paige's London invoices understate the quantities of linens which Paynter and Clerke received at Tenerife because most of these were shipped directly from Nantes by Paige's correspondent, John Holle, especially while the Dutch war interrupted the flow of German and Polish goods to London. Linens were required in the Canaries for uses which

51. C. 105/12, bill of lading and invoice, 28 May 1652; *C.S.P.D., 1651*, 268, 403.

52. C. 105/12, Paynter to Clerke, 10 Sept. 1660. From Jan. 1676 to April 1677, at least 34 English ships carrying wheat entered Canarian ports (M.C., Inq., visitas de la Fé). For the encroachment of viticulture on land devoted to cereal production in Tenerife, see Steckley, *Ec. H. R.*, 2nd ser., xxxiii, 339.

53. C. 110/151, Account of J. Turner and W. Throckmorton with R. Wilson, Sr and M. Bradgate, 1642–8; A.H.P., S.C., Hacienda, 9/1, Libro de entrada, 1694, Puerto de la villa de la Orotava [Puerto de la Cruz].

54. C. 110/151, J. Turner to R. Wilson, Sr and M. Bradgate, 8 June 1647, n.s.

ranged from sacking to fancy shirts and especially for re-export in quantity to Spanish America.[55] And in the absence of a competitive English industry, Paige and his partners tolerated high French prices and repeated threats of embargo to supply roans, creas, dowlas and tregars (e.g. **7a, 34, 40b, 67b, 84c, 89d, 91a, 94a**). They ran the greatest risk, however, at the moment of importation when Tenerife's officials could either enforce the latest *cédula* against contraband French goods or happily accept a bribe to overlook them (**9**).[56] It was apparently the importation of French linens, as much as indiscretions in exporting American goods, which led to Clerke's imprisonment in 1650 and to the London merchants' petition complaining of prosecutions by the Captain General (**15, 19a, 20, 25b**).[57] This official was soon replaced, but not before the English merchant Robert Breton had left his trade at Tenerife to take up residence in Madrid in order to obtain licences which would allow Canary merchants to import French goods (**21, 43**).[58] The American demand for French linens had convinced Spanish officials to regulate, rather than prohibit, the traffic and to raise revenue by selling permits.[59] And when Clerke was imprisoned again in 1656 for having imported contraband linens, it was apparently because he had not given Breton time enough to send the appropriate papers (**89e, 91a, 116–17**).

The most audacious of Paige's and Clerke's dealings in contraband was their importation of black slaves into Tenerife from Guinea. The slave population of the Canaries was never apparently as large as one might have expected, given the earlier phase of sugar production and the proximity of the slave markets. Even in Las Palmas, the capital of Gran Canaria where sugar cultivation had been intensive, slaves accounted for just over 6 per cent of the registered births in the seventeenth century. But there were complaints about the growing number of blacks imported by foreign merchants. There is evidence that Englishmen managed such traffic before and after Paige's venture. And this is not surprising since some of the earliest promoters of the English Guinea Company were also Canary merchants, notably the Londoners George Rookes, Humphrey and John Slaney, William Cloberry, and Paige's rival, Rowland Wilson, Sr.[60]

55. N. B. Harte, 'The rise of protection and the English linen trade, 1690–1790', in *Textile History and Economic History*, ed. N. B. Harte and K. G. Ponting (Manchester, 1973), 74–5; P. Lindeström, *Geographia Americae*, trans. Amandus Johnson (Philadelphia, 1925), 43, 61; C. 110/151, J. Turner to R. Leigh and R. Ryves, 2 March 1646, n.s., invoice of goods shipped on the *Island Merchant*, 7 Sept. 1646, n.s.; C. 105/12, invoice of goods laden by J. Holle on the *Blessing* at Nantes (falsely dated at Plymouth, 21 June 1649).

56. C. 105/12, Clerke's account with Paynter, 21 July 1649, n.s.; H.C.A. 13/71, ff. 506–7, exam. of Humphry Henchman.

57. See above, n. 32.

58. H.C.A. 13/72, exam. of Richard Baker, 20 July 1658, and of David Stephens, 23 July 1658.

59. H. Taylor, 'Trade, neutrality, and the "English Road", 1630–48', *Ec. H. R.*, 2nd ser., xxv (1972), 252–3.

60. E. Sánchez Falcón, 'Evolución demográfica de Las Palmas', *Anuario de Estudios Atlánticos*, x (1964), 337; L. de la Rosa Olivera, 'Catálogo del Archivo Municipal de La Laguna', *Rev. de Hist. Canaria*, xiv (1948), 74; H.C.A. 13/62, *ex parte* J. Hedges and R. Shute, 6 Feb. 1649. For Rookes see H.C.A. 13/48, ff. 335, 534, 13/49, ff. 31, 273, 300.

Londoners trading in slaves had to be wary of officials at Tenerife who were ready to confiscate such cargoes after 1640 as contraband coming from rebel Portuguese dominions, and Clerke proceeded cautiously in 1650 by commissioning Richard Baker, Breton's partner at Madrid, to obtain a licence which would allow the entry of 300 blacks (**25b**). Paige sent the £324 which Baker thought the licence would cost, and went about providing a slaver's cargo of coloured beads, Swedish iron, copper bars, Sheffield knives, German linens, and distilled drink.[61] He hired Richard Jewell to go as supercargo and persuaded him to take an assistant who spoke Portuguese (**31b, 40c, 47b**).

But in the summer and autumn of 1651 the business became the most 'vexatious' Paige had ever been assigned. After £1,000 was invested in outward cargo, Baker at Madrid could not obtain the licence (**44**). When Paige tried to freight a new ship of 200 tons for the voyage, the owners refused his offer of £160 per month (**40c**). And although he was delighted to hire the *Swan*, a 300-ton ship with thirty-two men and twenty guns, at the rate of £150, he was shocked when the captain, William Pyle, who had signed the charter-party, refused to begin the voyage. Paige attempted to enforce his contract in the Admiralty Court where, on 23 July 1651, the captain protested that he had not been informed of the ship's destination before the charter-party was sealed. But Paige produced witnesses who testified that he had indeed described his plans to Pyle at the Ship tavern in Bishopsgate Street and had even mentioned the shackles he had bought for the slaves' hands. Next Pyle objected that the voyage was excessively dangerous. He argued that Guinea was an enemy dominion, that the 300 slaves might 'rise and cut the throats' of the crew, that the Canarian officials could confiscate the ship for carrying contraband, and that, in any case, Paige was not a member of the Guinea Company. Paige had suspected that Captain Pyle had been set to this obstruction by unnamed members of the Guinea Company, perhaps including Rowland Wilson, Sr, but he was vindicated when two captains who were present in court told the judges that they themselves were fitting out ships for Guinea and that 'divers others which were not of the Guinea Company did usually set forth ships to the said River of Gambo'. So Pyle scrambled for a final plea: the thirty sailors hired for the voyage had forsaken the ship on learning of her destination. But after a long debate, the judges ordered Pyle to find a new crew and have his ship ready for departure from Gravesend within fifteen days (**42, 46, 47a–b**).[62]

Despite his victory at law, Paige did not force Pyle to command the ship after Pyle's wife appealed against the 'unhealthy' voyage. He agreed to the promotion of Henry Pulman from chief mate to captain. And the *Swan*, accompanied by a thirty-ton pinnace for negotiating the African rivers, left the Downs for the Gambia, Gold Coast, and Bight of Benin on

---

For Cloberry and the Slaneys see J. W. Blake, 'The farm of the Guinea trade', in *Essays in British and Irish History*, ed. H. A. Cronne *et al.* (1949), 86–106, and E. 190/27/4, 28/7, 30/5, 32/7, 35/1. For Wilson see above, n. 22.

61. Cf. *Acts of the Privy Council, Colonial, 1613–80* (Hereford, 1908), no. 505; C. 105/12, Paige's invoices, 2 Sept. 1651.

62. H.C.A. 13/44, ff. 305, 307–8.

8 September 1651. Paige complained that he had had no rest for ten weeks; he worried that with cargo, insurance and freight there was over £3,000 invested. But he also boasted that he had hired the *Swan* at the cheapest rate ever for a Guinea voyage; and he anticipated that she would reach Tenerife in five months with a rich cargo of 300 slaves, £1,500 in beeswax, elephants' hides and ivory (**46, 47a–b, 61e**).

Nothing was heard of the ship for a year. The monthly charges for freight mounted. Paige worried that he would be 'laughed at by many upon the Exchange' who had taken note of the voyage. He tried to unload his share in the business on Clerke (**48, 50, 53c, 58b, 61b, 64a**). And when the first news finally reached Paige in September 1652, it must have confirmed his worst fears. To be sure, the voyage had begun propitiously when the supercargo had traded less than £1,200 in goods for 200 slaves, wax, gold, ivory and elephants' hides. But Jewell died as the ship left the river Gambia, and then Captain Pulman and the merchant assistant both perished before the *Swan* had reached the Bight of Biafra. The master's mate, John Carnaby, took command, but the ship was 'staved upon the sand' at Rio del Rey and 'was utterly lost'. Carnaby sent thirty of the surviving slaves to Tenerife on the pinnace, sold the rest cheaply to other English ships, and then fled with the gold and the *Swan*'s remaining cargo to Barbados. At London Paige was left with a difficult insurance claim to negotiate, the demands of shipowners for over £900 in freight due, and threats from the widows of fourteen seamen who had perished on the voyage that they would come with their children to his doorstep to appeal for their husbands' wages (**63a**).[63]

While he conceded the widows' case for wages, payable by the shipowners, Paige was determined to resist the shipowners' claims against him for freight (**63a, 64**). But he was ignorant of the Admiralty Court's rule that 'freight is the mother of wages'. And when the judges ordered that wages be paid and civil lawyers advised that the court would force him to pay freight, Paige looked for another way out (**77a, 78b**).[64] He had successfully dealt with the *Swan*'s insurers by entertaining them 'at tavern', convincing them to concede the proceeds from the nineteen slaves who had reached Tenerife alive and to abate only 13 per cent of the total policy (**66a**).[65] And the same strategy worked with Captain Pyle, spokesman for the shipowners. Paige 'got him in the mood', perhaps again at the Ship tavern, and persuaded him to take £40 for cancelling a charter-party on which freight of £900 was due (**78b, 81b**).

There were still problems. William Berkeley, an alderman and underwriter, had died a bankrupt before paying £200 of the *Swan*'s insurance. Carnaby was in Barbados with the merchants' gold (**74, 77a, 78b, 84b, 89e**). But the human tragedy of the *Swan*'s voyage seems never to have troubled Paige. The protests from seamen's widows had been predictable: 'those kind of people will not understand reason' (**63a**). And even when he considered his capital, and the potential there had been for

63. H.C.A. 13/66, exams of John Vale and Nicholas Straw.
64. H.C.A. 3/45, f. 420, 12 Aug. 1653.
65. Clerke was selling slaves in Sept. 1652 for about £20 each (C. 105/12, Clerke's account with Paynter, 1641–54).

financial disaster, Paige congratulated himself on having kept the loss within acceptable bounds (**81b**).

Imbalance, regulation, and war

Paige paid the bills for voyages to Guinea, Barbary and Newfoundland. He sold wines on credit and held dyestuffs which did not sell. He complained from time to time that he was short of cash and might be forced to draw upon the 'usurer's bags' (**27b**, **44**, **49**, **60a**, **105**). And yet his accounts and letters suggest that he borrowed only once in a decade of trading (**45**, **47d**). This record reflects in fact a chronic problem which may have worsened in the 1650s: imbalance in the Canary trade. Because his principals in Tenerife could not sell quantities of English goods which equalled in value the wines and American goods they exported, the London factor, who sold hundreds of pipes of expensive wines but bought relatively little for outward cargoes, must have been periodically awash with cash.

Canary merchants, including Paige, Paynter and Clerke, sought to resolve this problem of imbalance by organisation and self-regulation. But other serious problems of the 1650s lay beyond their control. War with the Dutch imperilled their capital and complicated the daily tasks of Paige at London. War with Spain eventually sent Paynter and Clerke scurrying from the Canaries and forced the three merchants to rebuild their trade on new foundations.

A pipe of malvasía was selling at Orotava in the 1650s for the equivalent of nearly £14, a price perhaps 40 per cent higher than that of the previous decade. And if we can assume that the roughly 5,500 pipes which came annually to London accounted for 60 per cent of the shipments northward, the rest made up of American goods, English merchants would have had to sell each year about £3 worth of fish, wheat and cloth for every resident of Tenerife just to balance the trade.[66] They must have fallen far short of this in most years. John Turner in Tenerife advised his London partners in 1646 that cloth prices had fallen by 15 per cent and warned against sending more goods.[67] Clerke gave Paige no encouragement to send pack-goods in 1651 (**34**). Ships were sometimes dead-freighted to the vintage.[68] And wheat crises like that of 1651–2 gave Londoners rare and fleeting opportunities because the markets for grain and fish could be easily glutted, leaving the merchant with perishable merchandise. Consequently English factors in the island had to pay cash,

66. This assumes a population of 40,000–45,000. A census in 1678 showed 49,112 (J. de Viera y Clavijo, *Noticias de la Historia General de las Islas de Canaria*, 3 vols (La Laguna, 1950–2 ed.), ii, 781.) William Petyt exaggerated the importation of Canary wine and hence the imbalance in *Britannia Languens* (1680) (*Early English Tracts on Commerce*, ed. J. R. McCulloch (Cambridge, 1952), 419). But the statistics published by Whitworth demonstrate that a serious problem persisted even after wine imports had begun to decline at the end of the century (C. Whitworth, *State of the Trade of Great Britain* (1776), sec. ii, 3; Steckley, *Ec. H. R.*, 2nd ser., xxxiii, 342). Prices at Tenerife can be found at C. 105/12, Paynter's account with Clerke, and in various Admiralty Court examinations from the period.

67. C. 110/151, J. Turner to R. Best, 17 June 1646, n.s., and to R. Wilson, Sr and M. Bradgate, 30 Nov. 1646, n.s. and 21 April 1647, n.s.

68. M.C., Inq., Visitas de la Fé, *passim*.

as a rule, one-third in money for most West India goods and perhaps as much as one-half for cochineal and superior wines.[69] Their cash was undoubtedly spent quickly, and Paige remembered from his years at Tenerife that a factor there seldom held anything but unsold goods and uncollected accounts (**27b**, **63c**, **94b**).

On the other hand, as he went about selling Paynter's and Clerke's new wines at London in December and January, Paige must have become the steward of a respectable capital, perhaps £3,000 to £4,000.[70] But unable to keep it employed by investing in large cargoes for Tenerife, he had to find some way to put money in the hands of Clerke and Paynter. Canary merchants had solved this problem in the conventional way at least since 1559 when Thomas Nichols, who could not sell enough English goods in Tenerife to pay for the sugars he exported, drew on his London agents by bills of exchange.[71] And Clerke likewise paid for about 40 per cent of the goods he exported in the 1650s by drawing bills which were ultimately paid in London by Paige (Table 3 below).

But even this solution was more complicated than it appeared. Canarian winegrowers rarely needed credits in London but often instead wanted purchasing power in peninsular Spain. And the Englishman in the Canary trade had to accumulate credits in the peninsula against which he could draw, hence Paige's references to merchants who were making 'great preparation' for Tenerife's 'next vintage via Spain' by shipping cod to Bilbao or pack-goods to San Lucar (**21**, **32**).[72] Paige on occasion

---

TABLE 3. *Account of John Paige's income and expenditure as London factor for William Clerke, 1649–1656*

	Received from £	*Paid to* £	*Balance* £
Goods shipped	10,743	5,145	5,598
Freight	399	756	(357)
Insurance	120	719	(599)
Shares in ships	378	294	84
Bills of exchange	250	4,278	(4,028)
Miscellaneous	1,283	1,084	199
Interest		6	(6)
Paige's commissions		281	(281)
	£13,173	£12,563	£610

Source: C.105/12, Paige's account with Clerke, 1648–56

---

69. C. 110/151, J. Turner to R. Cocke, 1 March and 30 April 1646, n.s., to R. Wilson, Sr and M. Bradgate, 10 and 14 June 1646, n.s., to Richard Leigh, 27 Nov. 1646, n.s., and to S. Wilson, 7 Aug. 1647, n.s.

70. Rowland Wilson, Sr, the foremost London wholesaler of wine, was perceived as the kind of merchant who could 'at a pinch lay down £20,000 for a bargain' (T. Violet, *True Narrative of Som Remarkable Proceedings* (1653), 95).

71. A. Cioranescu, *Thomas Nichols* (La Laguna, 1963), 18.

72. The London factor might even remit money to the peninsula which could be drawn against to pay Canarian winegrowers. Paige sent a few hundred pounds for Clerke, but Turner in one instance called for his London partners to prepare for the Canarian vintage by sending £5,000 to San Lucar (C. 110/151, J. Turner to R. Wilson, Sr and M. Bradgate, 5 Dec. 1646, n.s.).

encouraged such designs (**81c**). But it was difficult at times to find a winegrower who would sell his wines, as Diego Pereyra did to Clerke in 1651, for bills drawn against accumulated credit in Spain. He might literally demand cash on the barrel head. Thus it was rumoured that Wilson and company intended to sell large cargoes of English goods in San Lucar and carry pieces of eight to Tenerife (**30a**).[73] But it was also possible to find individuals other than winegrowers who, in exchange for a bill drawn on Seville, would supply the local Canarian coinage.[74] Canarian officials needed to remit monies to Madrid, so John Turner drew bills for the royal *audiencia* in 1645 and Thomas Hart bid for the right to remit 20,000 Ds (c. £5,500) which were owed the King as the *donativo* of 1647. And while Paynter worried about the usual risks of dealing with seventeenth-century tax collectors, 'great men who do value themselves of the King's money to keep it in their hands a long time with one trick or other', Clerke was bidding in 1651 for the contract to remit part of the Canarian tithes to the peninsula by bill of exchange in order that he might receive in the islands 4,500 Ds (c. £1,238) in Canarian coinage with which he could buy wines or American goods.[75]

Paige's cash, then, was periodically drawn down as he accepted and paid Clerke's and Paynter's bills of exchange. Clerke drew about 55 per cent of the exchange he needed via Spain, and Paige paid the sixty- to ninety-day bills to the accounts of Abraham Lee of San Lucar or Arthur Ackland and Richard Davies of Bilbao. Most of the remaining bills paid by Paige were of ninety to 120 days and drawn in favour, or at the direction, of English merchants at Tenerife from whom Clerke had obtained cash when he could not exchange English goods for the wines and dyestuffs he exported.[76]

The boldest attempt by English merchants to deal with this persistent imbalance in the trade was their formation of the Canary Company, a chartered monopoly, in 1665. But Paige's letters of 1651–2 record an earlier effort by the traders, including Paige, Clerke and Paynter, to resolve the problem through regulation. Their assumptions were no doubt similar to those of a speaker who defended the Canary Company's charter before the Lords in 1666:

> [A]s this sort of wines (which we bring from the Canaries) is only to be had in the Canaries . . . so is there no other country (besides England) in which these wines are (to any considerable quantity) vended. . . . [W]hilst we trade thither in a loose and promiscuous way (that is, every man for himself) they have an advantage on us by raising their wines to what value, and to sell them for ready money or barter them for what kind of commodities, they please. . . . But . . .

73. C. 105/12, Paynter to Clerke, 12 Jan. 1651, n.s. Because English factors faced the persistent problem of finding cash with which to buy wines, it is difficult to accept V. Morales Lezcano's allegation that they caused deflationary pressures in the islands by their extensive smuggling of silver (*Síntesis de la historia económica de Canarias* (La Laguna, 1966), 25).
74. Archivo General de Simancas, Estado, 2981, Don Miguel de Salinas a su Magestad, 20 May 1663, n.s.
75. C. 110/151, J. Turner to R. Wilson, Sr and M. Bradgate, 24 Jan. 1646, n.s., and 7 June 1647, n.s.; C. 105/12, Paynter to Clerke, 11 May 1651, n.s.
76. C. 105/12, Paige's account with Clerke, 1648–56.

this trade may be so regulated as to turn to the advantage of this nation. . . . If the men of England do so unite and hold together that one shall not outbid another, that they will only give in exchange for those wines the commodities of their own growth . . . then must the Islanders part with their wines upon our reasonabler terms or else they must keep them to their own loss.[77]

Action upon such assumptions was motivated in the early 1650s as much by events in London as by winegrowers' demands in Tenerife. The wholesale price of Canary wine in London had been rising even faster than its cost in Tenerife, allowing profits of 33 to 50 per cent on some shipments (**12b**, **14**). But the Vintners 'met at their hall' to consider the rising prices and threatened in 1650 to fix a maximum for Canary at £21 per pipe (**14**, **17**, **22a**, **27a**). At that rate, the first cost in Tenerife plus freight, insurance, handling, and taxes would have allowed little margin to the wholesaler. And 'if ever the Vintners' had wanted 'the upper hand', their opportunity came in early 1651 when Paige estimated that there were 1,500 pipes of Canary unsold in the merchants' cellars and warned Clerke and Paynter that they must 'beat down the Islanders in price' or send no wines (**30a**, **37**, **39a**).

Before the vintage the English factors in Tenerife had agreed to limit both the price they would pay for wines and the quantity they would buy. Paige feared that Rowland Wilson, Sr's political connections might allow his company to ignore the pact; but apparently the English merchants honoured the agreement and left the Canarians with wines in their cellars (**49**, **52b**). The wines Clerke shipped as his share were poor, prompting London Vintners to call Paige 'the Canary scavenger'. But Paige also reported that 'all men that walk the Exchange' approved the regulation of the trade, and he joined other London merchants in asking the Council of State to enforce the agreement by allowing only merchants of the pact to import Canary wine (**50**, **51b**, **52b**).[78] Apparently the plan was rejected. Paige never mentions merchant regulation after the spring of 1652, and his fear that the large vintage fleet of 1653 would raise prices 'higher than last year', suggests that unrestrained market forces were once again determining prices at the Islands (**76b**). When the failure of regulation coincided with Clerke's purchase of bad wines and the *Swan*'s misadventure, Paige and Clerke nearly ended their wine trade (**50**, **56b**).

Clerke sent only ten pipes of wine to Paige after 1653, but it may have been the onset of war as much as the failure of regulation that discouraged him. Paige was almost always worried about some threat at sea—the Irish, Rupert, the French, the Turks, or Jerseymen, to whom Clerke lost a cargo in 1650 (e.g. **1**, **4**, **26b**, **27b**, **32**).[79] And just as a treaty with Portugal seemed imminent, the English provoked the Dutch by insisting on the Navigation Act (**51a**, **53b–c**, **56b**). Paige sent the act in duplicate to his partners, but when the intent of the English diplomats became clear, he warned Paynter and Clerke to send all their ships for London and predicted that trade must end as not one ship in ten would escape the

77. Bodleian Library, MS Clarendon 92, Notes of an argument made before the House of Lords in defence of the Canary Company, f. 266.
78. *C.S.P.D., 1651–2*, 99.
79. H.C.A. 13/65, exam. of Alexander Robinson, 17 July 1651.

enemy (**58a–b**). However, his pessimism vanished as the war began. He anticipated a quick and glorious victory and, despite dangers in the Channel, looked forward to big shipments of wine in January 1653. The *Blessing* arrived in February, after a stop in Falmouth, and Paige sold her wines at what he called the 'unprecedented' price of £35 13s 4d per pipe. He hoped for an unusual spring shipment on the *Mary*, and even when it seemed that all the northern nations would join the Dutch, Paige was confident that the English naval forces would 'bang them soundly' and 'ruin their trade' (**62**, **63c**, **64c**, **66a**, **68a–b**).

But just as he was reporting news that his ship the *Agreement* had captured a Dutch prize, Paige began to learn the hard lessons of commercial war. The *Golden Star*, which he had sent from Plymouth with rye, was captured and taken to Nantes (**72**). The *Elizabeth and John*, which was carrying wheat from the Azores to Clerke and Paynter, was seized off Tenerife and then burned by her Dutch captors after they had set the crew ashore.[80] The war also changed the London merchant's habits of freighting and insuring ships. Before the war Paige had sometimes invested in ships for himself and his principals. He had bought shares in the *Blessing* until he owned with his principals and the master nine-sixteenths of the seventy-ton ship. With majority control, he was determined 'to vex the other owners by sending the ship where I want' until they sold him the remaining shares (**19b**, **20**, **25b**, **27b**). But during the war Paige became disenchanted with ownership when he could not get £20 for a quarter part of the *Blessing*, and later he advised Clerke that it was better to freight ships because it was too dangerous to own both vessel and cargo and one could command even a hired ship if it were 'well tied in [the] charter-party' (**89c**).

The war also forced him to hire larger ships. The average capacity of the seven which Paige freighted before the hostilities, and for which an estimate is known, was 119 tons. He had preferred to hire them by time charter even though he considered that freight accumulating by the month, rather than per voyage, was like 'a continual moth' (**7a**, **11a**, **16**, **40a**, **53a**, **c**).[81] But the four ships which the merchants were using during the war, and for which estimates are available, averaged 168 tons, a capacity Paige considered too large for the Canary trade when peace returned (**94a**). He complained during the war of higher freight rates and poorer service, noting that the price of cordage and seamen's wages had risen 50 per cent, that owners might refuse to man the ship fully or to have it ready in the Downs by a specified date, and that most would let only per voyage, not, as he preferred, by the month (**67a**, **71c**, **77c**, **81d**, **82**, **83a**).

Finally, the Dutch war altered Paige's habit of insuring ships, already, 'a thing of more difficulty to perform than other businesses' (**22b**). Before the conflict he had never paid more than 5 per cent to insure any of the eight voyages from Tenerife to London for which there are records. But as the Navigation Act was being published in November 1651 the

---

80. H.C.A. 13/67, exams of Thomas Waight and Thomas Grey, 2 May 1653.
81. The charter by ton limited the number of days allowed for lading, and because this was an operation of unpredictable duration in Tenerife's roadstead ports, it could result in costly demurrage (Davis, *Rise of the English Shipping Industry*, 166–7).

underwriters asked 12–15 per cent (**63b, d**). Later they quoted 60 per cent for a voyage from the Canaries to Genoa and back, and 10 per cent for the short passage from Falmouth to London (**66b–c**). And while Paige admitted that good Canary would bear a rate of 15 per cent (**63b**), his accounts show that none of the cargoes solely owned by Clerke was insured during the war.[82]

When Paige did attempt, with some initiative, to protect his principals' investments during the hostilities, he was frustrated by the uncertainty of legal remedies. He learned that there were Dutch men-of-war lying off Tenerife just as the *Elizabeth and John* was carrying wheat from the Azores to Clerke and Paynter. Though Paige had no interest in the cargo and no orders from Tenerife, he quickly got £1,200 underwritten in his employers' names. And after the ship was burned by the Dutch, he followed the usual procedure by producing the captain and another witness in the Admiralty Court to verify the loss. But to Paige's astonishment they testified under oath that the wheat lost was his, not Clerke's and Paynter's, and thereby, either through 'ignorance or perfidy' contradicted and invalidated the insurance policy (**67b, 76a, 77a, 78a, 81a**).[83]

Despite such setbacks Paige continued to describe English victories in arrogant detail and even rationalised that Dutch control of the Straits would raise the price of good Canary. But he grew gloomier when he saw 'little hopes of peace' and recounted his difficulties in freighting ships (**76b, 77b–c, 80, 81d, 83b**). And even when he could send the articles of peace to Clerke and Paynter (**84c, 85**), any relief on his part was premature. The partners were yet to lose a third ship to the war. The *Agreement*, which had earlier taken a Dutch prize, was herself seized en route from Tenerife—after the peace was signed but before it was to take effect (**87–8**).

As Paige learned of this loss at the end of one war, he was reporting the details of Cromwell's western design and, effectively, the beginning of a conflict which would nearly end his trade (**85, 87, 89f, 91b**). He had long feared a rupture with Spain and now warned his principals to 'prepare for a storm' and to get their estates out of the islands by exporting West India goods and wines (**94b, 95**). But Clerke and Paynter remained confident that they could stay for the vintage of 1655 even after the Spanish ambassador had left London, thirty English merchants had fled the peninsula and others had suffered violent reprisals at Tenerife (**99b, 100b, 105, 106b, 107**). Paige sent his partners tonnage in four ships, but before the last of these, the *Prosperous*, had left the Isle of Wight with fifteen other vessels bound for the Canaries, news of the Spanish embargo reached London. Matthew Smith, master of the *Prosperous*, ignored Paige's orders not to sail, and when the ship arrived at Tenerife, the embargo had been in effect there for nearly a week (**108a**). The English merchants ordered Smith and other masters in the road off Orotava to

82. C. 105/12, Paige's account with Clerke, 1648–56.
83. This may have been due to carelessness on the part of Paige or his lawyer. The interrogatories drafted for witnesses on behalf of both the insurers *and* Paige described the wheat as 'for the account of John Paige' (H.C.A. 23/18/318).

leave the island, whereupon they sailed to Madeira took on the colours of neutral states, and the *Prosperous* returned among them to Tenerife flying the flag of Hamburg. Some of the ships were laden with wines after a special fee was paid to the Captain General, but the *Prosperous* sailed for London with nothing in the tonnage hired for Clerke's account. Paige was nevertheless forced to pay freight after the Admiralty Court had awarded the seamen their wages and had referred the freight issue to arbitrators.[84]

Meanwhile Paige's principals were beginning to suffer at the hands of Canarian officials. The Captain General, Don Alonso Davila y Guzmán, apparently took bribes from Clerke and Paynter and then confiscated their goods and credits anyway, perhaps including some of the wines which Clerke had intended to ship on the *Prosperous*. Seven other merchants, including Arthur Ingram who would later become the governor of the Canary Company, assessed their losses through reprisals at over £13,000.[85] And fearing further hostile acts, Clerke and Paynter sent home their assistants, Leigh, Standish and Hawley in December 1655 (**111a**).

When the assistants arrived in England, Paige was complaining of English actions against the Spanish. He described Cromwell's plan to regulate wine prices as 'of greater prejudice and loss to the poor merchants than the embargo in Spain' (**110b, 112**). A decision to revive Henrician powers of price control had been taken in May, a proclamation was published in July, and a wholesale limit of £26 per pipe was proposed in December 1655, which, Paige reported, caused wine prices to fall by 50 per cent. He joined other Londoners who asked for a suspension of the prisage. Their petition, which Paige himself could have written after his recent experience with the *Prosperous*, complained that some merchants had large stocks of Spanish wines which they had been able to import only after paying 'gratifications' to Spanish officials, while others had lost their estates by the embargo and that at great cost their ships had returned dead-freighted.[86] The Vintners were, of course, protesting that the proposed price ceiling was too high; but after another petition, Paige and his friends won delays in the effective date of regulation, first to Michaelmas and then to 1 December 1656 (**114–15, 117**).[87]

Paige assumed that the price control would prevent Clerke from paying more than 20 Ds per pipe, less than half the recent prices in the Canaries, but still he sent pipestaves in two ships and skilfully directed the wartime voyage of the *Mary*. When this ship was turned away from Bilbao with her cargo of Newfoundland fish, Paige hired a Dutch crew, sent her to Tenerife, and consigned the cargo under the names of Antwerp merchants (**93a, 95, 99a, 100b, 103–4, 108a, 109, 110a**). The deception

84. H.C.A. 3/46, ff. 464–5, 476, 478, 492, 545, 13/71, ff. 59–61, 107, 179, 23/18/331.
85. Viera y Clavijo, *op. cit.*, ii, 600–1; C. 105/12, Paige's account with Clerke, 1648–56; H.C.A. 13/72, exams of W. Lee, G. Webber and R. Wilde, 18 June 1657, 13/74, exam. of A. Ingram, 20 June 1664.
86. *C.S.P.D., 1655*, 151; *Tudor and Stuart Proclamations*, 2 vols, ed. Crawford (Oxford, 1910), ii 369, no. 3056; P.R.O., State Papers 18/102/7, 5 Dec. 1655.
87. *C.S.P.D., 1655–6*, 80, 93, 102, 128–9, 147; J. Thurloe, *State Papers*, 5 vols., ed. T. Birch (1742), iv, 396–7.

worked.[88] But Paynter had to receive the fish because Clerke was in prison, apparently for importing French goods without the proper licence (**116–17**). Clerke managed somehow to return West India goods to Paige on the *Mary*, but though he survived another imprisonment and stayed with Paynter for the vintage of 1656, the two sent no more wines. They arrived at Plymouth with other merchants just before Christmas 1656, and a second 'fleet' of Englishmen escaping the island was under sail (**118**).[89]

When the three merchants returned to the Canary trade, it was by different approaches. Clerke found himself in Plymouth at the end of 1656, threatened by angry creditors, and without his books which Canarian officials had confiscated. Paige advised him to come to London 'where you may be as private as you please—no place like unto it', and then helped him to escape the City for Antwerp in January 1657. When Clerke's flight was bruited on the Exchange, his creditors were angry (**118–20**), but he had gone to the continent not only to escape debts but also to obtain Spanish permission to return to the Canaries. He had advice that an agent in Flanders could get licences 'passed by the *Consejo* in Spain', and Paynter hoped that with such protection Clerke and he would be free from both insurance charges and the Judge of the Contraband (**120, 122**).[90] Clerke's mission eventually took him to Madrid in 1657 where he may have solicited the aid of English royalists. In the same year Hyde drafted a commission of consulship in the Canaries for those merchants who opposed Cromwell and awarded it to Leonard Clerke, a West Country merchant who was not apparently related to William. Both Hyde and Bennet heard appeals for aid from other merchants, including John Shaw, Paige's correspondent at Antwerp, and Francis Millington, soon to be Paige's partner in the Malaga trade. But Bennet, who resented the pressures of these merchants, warned from Madrid that Philip IV could not be expected to grant such protection to Protestants. And when he reached the Spanish capital, Clerke himself may have heard this advice from the exiled courtier. In any case he openly embraced Roman Catholicism while at Madrid and then returned to Tenerife in the late summer of 1659 carrying licences which gave him 'considerable freedom' in his trade.[91]

The trade to which he returned was fraught with wartime difficulties, which Paige and Paynter in London had already discovered. Paige had initially doubted in 1657 that Blake had intelligence of the Spanish *flota*'s approach to Tenerife (**123–4**). But English ships arrived at London with confirmation that the general had burned the treasure fleet in Santa Cruz harbour, that English captains had been given the rack by angry Canarians, and that the prices of West India goods had been driven to prohibitive levels (**125a–b**). While the Naval Commissioners rewarded

88. Such deception was practised by other English merchants trading to Tenerife during the war (H.C.A. 13/72, exam. of Domingo de la Cerda, 6 July 1658, 13/73, exam. of Peter Bimewijsent, 25 Feb. 1659).
89. C. 105/12, Paynter to Clerke, 13 July and 25 Aug. 1656, n.s.
90. Ibid., Paynter to Clerke, 15 Aug. and 14 Sept. 1657.
91. *Calendar of the Clarendon State Papers*, 5 vols, ed. O. Ogle *et al.* (Oxford, 1872–1970), iii, 301, 352, iv, 76, 291, 405, v, 737; C. 105/12, Paynter to Clerke, 15 Oct. 1659.

Blake with a pipe of Canary wine, Paige and Paynter found that their former friends at Tenerife refused to receive their goods and that French ships were supplying the Canaries with an abundance of linens (**125b, 126**).[92] They complained that the price regulation which was renewed by Parliament in June 1657, together with new taxes imposed in the same month, amounted to a prohibition of the trade (**125a, 126**).[93]

London middlemen like Paige and Paynter could easily have assumed at the beginning of the war that the Canary trade would end or that, at the least, they would be displaced from it. In 1656 Paige himself had reported the story that a junta of eight Canarian winegrowers and merchants had bribed the Captain General to expel the English (**120**). Four of the eight listed by Paige had regularly shipped wines to Iberian Jews who had settled in London. For example, Balthazar de Vergara Grimon, one of Tenerife's richest growers, and his relatives, Christóbal de Alvarado Bracamonte and Benito Venia y Vergara, had sent wines since the early 1640s to the most prominent of Jewish merchants in London, Antonio Fernandez Carvajal, and, after Fernandez's death in 1658, to the Francias, also Jewish merchants.[94] Other Londoners, including Rowland Wilson, Sr, managed to continue in the wine trade only by employing Canarians who were members of the junta identified by Paige.[95] After Paynter at London had watched these merchants import the Canarian vintages of 1657–8, he concluded that 'the Jews and Spaniards' had 'all the privilege of the trade'.[96] And as the letters end in 1658, Paige and his father-in-law had left the wine trade because, as Paige wrote, 'those [Canarian] rogues which do our business cheat us and take all the gains to themselves' (**127a**).

The two Londoners were able to continue as brokers of West India goods, but now only by risking what they had thus far avoided: direct trade with Spanish America. And driven to such adventure—now during

92. *C.S.P.D., 1656–7*, 521.

93. Firth and Rait, ii, 1057, 1123, 1187; *C.S.P.D., 1657*, 380. The debate over renewal of price regulation is reported in T. Burton's *Diary*, 9 vols, ed. J. T. Rutt (1828), ii, 202. Prices quoted in Admiralty cases of the period suggest that the regulation was not effective.

94. H.C.A. 13/59, f. 51, 13/72, exam. of Gonzalo Bais, 13/75, ff. 562, 592; C. 110/151, J. Turner to R. Wilson, Sr and M. Bradgate, 5 Dec. 1646 and 8 June 1647; L. Wolf, 'The First English Jew', Jewish Hist. Soc. of England *Trans.*, ii (1894–5), 14–46; H. Beinart, 'The Jews in the Canary Islands: a re-evaluation', ibid., xxv (1977), 65–7.

95. M.C., Inq., xxxv–22; H.C.A. 13/73, exam. of P. Bimewijsent, 25 Feb. 1659, exam. of Richard Casby, 1 March 1659. John Rowse received wines from Nicholas Alvarez (ibid., exam. of John Casby, 25 June 1659). Wilson and company turned their business in the islands over to Pedro Fernandes (C. 105/12, Paynter to Clerke, 23 April 1661).

96. The Canarian Don Lorenzo Balcarsel first promised Paynter consignments of wine in 1659 and then gave the business instead to a Jewish merchant, Diego Rodriguez Arias (C. 105/12, Paynter to Clerke, 2 March 1659, 3 Sept. 1660, and 30 Jan. 1661). Paige and Paynter no doubt supported the petition to Parliament of 15 Feb. 1659 which asked for a prohibition against Spanish wines and fruits for the duration of the war because Spanish agents in the trade had found ways 'to engross the whole advantage unto their own hands, some under the notion of Jews'. The petitioners noted that such a stoppage would 'endanger' the Spanish king's interest in the Canary Islands 'in regard those Islands have nothing to procure them a subsistence but their wines, nor any other nation to vend them but the English' (*To Parliament, the Humble Petition of Merchants trading to the Dominion of the King of Spain* (1659)).

a state of war—they were anxious to describe it as an innovation of national importance. 'Debarred' from a wine business which, they later wrote, had 'supported [their] families', they decided 'to experiment a trade into the Spanish West Indies' where 'none had formerly been driven by any English'. They had, of course, known several Englishmen who had profited from direct trade, but Paige and Paynter found the exaggerated rhetoric necessary to save their own design from catastrophe. With four other merchants they had sent the ship *Hope*, disguised as Spanish, from Amsterdam in 1657. A Spaniard, Juan Lopez, acted as captain at Trinidad, Cumana, Truxillo and Honduras, where less than £3,000 in English cloth and continental linen was exchanged for indigo, sarsaparilla and hides worth £12,000 on the London market. But a Dutch sailor, hired at Cumana where he was 'starved and eaten up by mosquitoes', became a 'quarrelsome, lewd and wicked fellow' on the homeward voyage. He threatened to kill three of the crew; and, after the disguised ship was taken as a Spanish prize by an English warship, he testified in the Admiralty Court that the *Hope* was indeed owned by Spaniards and that papers verifying this had been thrown overboard. It was now that Paige, Paynter and the other investors petitioned Richard Cromwell for the ship's release, claiming that they, the true owners, 'had opened a way to trade in [the Spanish West Indies] which otherwise must be left to the Dutch and other foreigners'.[97] But it was several months before the ship and cargo were released. And, because the *Hope*'s effective disguise had prompted action by the English warship, the Admiralty judges assessed the merchants for court costs.[98]

Dissolution

While ownership of the *Hope* was still in dispute in early 1659, Paynter asked Paige for an accounting of their partnership which had lasted fourteen years. Paige replied with 'base words and wished the ship [had] sunk' which had brought his father-in-law home from Tenerife. Paynter moved out of his son-in-law's house in Bishopsgate Street and complained that he and Paige communicated only in letters, 'like two lovers—[wanting] only the friendship'. The older merchant had lost his books to the Canarian officials and could not document his claim that he had sent Paige £50,000 in goods from the Canaries since 1647 and that his son-in-law had fraudulently made over bills of exchange to his own use. It was rumoured that Paige had failed to keep his books in order, and, in the event, merchants who arbitrated the account determined that Paige owed his former master £7,000. Of this there was still about £2,000 outstanding in 1660 when Paynter preferred a bill in chancery against his own son-in-law.[99]

From London Paynter had in the meantime resumed his trade in

97. H.C.A. 15/7, Petition of Gowen Paynter, John Paige *et al.* to Richard Cromwell, 7 Feb. 1659.
98. Ibid.; H.C.A. 13/72, exam. of Simon Blaeu, 28 Jan. 1659, 13/73, exam. of Juan Lopez, 11 Feb. 1659, of Peter Aylward, 21 Feb. 1659, and of Patrick Betts, 16 April 1659; H.C.A. 15/7, Appraisement of goods on the *Hope*, 20 April 1659; H.C.A. 3/247, 21, 24, 31 March, 1, 8, 20 April, and 28 May 1659.
99. C. 105/12, Paynter to Clerke, 7 Sept. 1659 and 10 Sept. 1660; C. 10/93/116.

pilchards, wheat and wine, but now only with Clerke who had returned to Tenerife in 1659. Paynter even wrote enthusiastically to Clerke of a plan to deliver 200 black slaves at £20 per head which, he thought, could be sold at Tenerife for £50 each.[100] But before he could act Paige's role in another Guinea design, Paynter was dying, and in his will he attempted to settle matters with Paige, whom he called the most 'perverse fellow' he had ever known. Paynter assigned to his daughter Katherine the debt of £2,000 owed by her husband and then ordered Paige as executor to buy land for his family with the money.[101]

William Clerke was also dead before his account with Paige was settled. Paige had found one excuse after another for not totting up the books, writing in 1658 that the London winter had been so bitter that 'no man could endure to sit and write an hour' (**26a, 31c, 66c, 73c, 77b, 100b, 124, 127b**). At least three of Paige's later trading partners would find it necessary to force settlements from him in Chancery, and Sir Samuel Clerke initiated proceedings in 1681 to recover the debts owed to his younger brother's estate.[102] William Clerke had traded for about twenty years after his return to Tenerife in 1659. He had married the daughter of a Canarian winecooper and had twice survived process by the Inquisition, once for having said that there was really no difference between the English and Roman religions, and later for speculating, in allegedly blasphemous terms, that heaven was a place where one is free from work.[103] At his death sometime in the late 1670s he left a young daughter. And on the child's behalf, Sir Samuel complained in Chancery that Paige had never given his brother an account and had gone about the Exchange exulting that he owed Clerke nothing, that the Spanish had taken Clerke's books, and, later, that in any case the statute of limitations had run. Sir Samuel alleged that Paige owed £10,000; Paige finally produced an account which showed his debt at £610.[104] Paige's numbers may have been the kind which the laggard merchant, according to Lewes Roberts, 'mumbles' up when finally forced to acquit himself. And the final Chancery decree of 1685 may have resolved nothing. It ordered that Paige settle with Clerke's executors after more papers had been received

100. C. 105/12, Paynter to Clerke, 22 May, 3 Sept. 1660, 23 April, 20 July, 31 Aug. 1661, to Clerke and Thomas Cowling, 22 May 1660; C. 6/237/95.
101. C. 105/12, Paynter to Clerke, 31 Aug. 1661; PROB 11/306/185, Will of Gowen Paynter.
102. C. 5/537/37, Richard Pendarvis and Francis Millington v. John Paige; C. 5/90/70, Gilbert Smith v. John Paige; C. 6/237/95, Samuel Clerke *et al.* v. John Paige.
103. M.C., Inq., clxvi-22, El fiscal de S. O. contra Guillermo Clerque; A.H.N., Inquisición, 1824, núm. 11, William Clerque. When Clerke died is unclear. His brother alleged that it was in 1677 (C. 6/237/95). But other evidence suggests that he was still alive in 1678 (*Catalogue of the MSS of the Inquisition*, ed. Birch, ii, 860–1).
104. C. 6/237/95, 10/214/79, 33/259, 78/1083. The balance of the account with Clerke shows £510, but there is an error of £100 in addition. Beyond this, the account seems to accord, except in a few particulars, with the information in the letters. Paige's most serious omission seems to have been the settlement from insurance on the *Swan*. Sir Samuel produced an account (also found at C. 105/12) which William Clerke had apparently created from rather dim recollections after the Spanish officials had taken his books in 1656. The values are given in round 100s of pounds, and entry after entry is worded conditionally.

from the Canaries, but it has not been possible to determine if such an accounting ever took place.[105]

If Paige had profited from the use of Clerke's money for nearly thirty years and from the way his account with Paynter was settled, he had not done so by capitalising a larger trade in Canary wines. He kept his hand in the business after the war and for the rest of his active life but imported only fifty to sixty pipes a year, mere dabbling when compared, for example, with Robert Breton's 600 pipes a year in the same period. Paige continued to import a small volume of Iberian wine, but he was developing other interests after the Restoration, especially in the Asian trade.[106]

He had already been involved in at least four East India voyages during the 1650s. That of the *Katherine*, a ship in which Paynter, Clerke and he owned shares (**25b**, **52b**, **61e**, **77c**), brought Paige into contact with Maurice Thomson. Thomson had plans for reorganising the eastern trade, and in partnership with him Paige would later be transformed from a mere shipowner to an active India merchant. After voyages to the Canaries and state service during the Dutch war, the *Katherine* was hired by the East India Company in February 1654 to sail to the Coromandel Coast and bring home all that she could stow as the last carrier for the United Joint Stock. Paige, whose partners at Tenerife had just lost a ship to the Dutch, was probably one of the *Katherine*'s owners who wanted assurances of safe conduct from the Hollanders even on 2 May, two days before the peace was to take effect. To satisfy the owners, Maurice Thomson acted for the Company and applied to the Dutch ambassadors. They replied that the peace was signed, that they had never granted a safe conduct to anyone, and that to do so would dishonour Dutch shipmasters. But apparently Thomson's efforts quieted the *Katherine*'s owners. The ship sailed, returned safely, and in the summer of 1655, just as the Spanish war was about to disrupt his Canary trade, Paige was pleased with his first income—freight payments—from Asian traffic (**106b**).[107]

His first endeavours as a merchant to the East were less successful. In September 1654 he had signed Maurice Thomson's petition which called for a freer Eastern trade in which individuals might send private adventures independent of the Company. Then he joined Thomson and Thomas Canham in such a voyage. They hired the *Golden Cock*, a ship of 85 tons owned by Richard Ely and Paige's cousin John Paige of Plymouth, and set her out in November for Bantam. The ship stopped at Tenerife for the vintage and had delivered wines safely to Bantam by August 1655. There she was freighted by the Company to carry pepper from Sumatra to Bantam, but in October 1656 was leaking so badly from worm damage that she was scuttled in the Jamboaye River. And in November 1657 Paige's own cousin was suing him, Thomson and

---

105. L. Roberts, *The Merchants Map of Commerce* (1677 ed.), 34; C. 78/1083.
106. C. 5/90/70; E. 190/50/3, 52/3, 73/3, 81/2, 88/1, 97/1, 105/5, 118/7, 119/6, 126/3, 137/8, 144/4.
107. *C.C.M.E.I.C.*, *1650–4*, xix, 302–3, 305, 308, 310–11, 315, *1655–60*, 38, 50. *The English Factories in India, 1618–84*, ed. W. Foster and C. Fawcett (Oxford, 1906–1955), *1651–4*, xxxiv–v, xxxviii, 277–8, 304.

Canham in the Admiralty Court to recover the value of the ship and freight due.[108]

Paige had also invested with Thomson in the *Jonathon*, another ship sent independently of the Company in June 1654. Like the *Golden Cock*, it was employed in the eastern carrying trade but was prevented by five Dutch warships from returning to Bantam from Coromandel. And this brought Paige and Thomson into the Admiralty Court as plaintiffs seeking compensation from the Dutch East India Company.[109]

Part ownership of the *Katherine* involved Paige in at least two more voyages during the 1650s. The second of these, from 1659 to 1661, was so profitable that it allowed the Company to distribute a 20 per cent dividend, the first paid on the New General Stock.[110]

India ventures had brought Paige into close association with the chief radical among London merchants of the 1640s. Maurice Thomson envisaged an English commercial empire which would be established aggressively on all continents and in which the old and narrower chartered companies would give way to national monopolies of trade.[111] And few merchants could have acted more consistently than Paige in ways that were compatible with such goals. In his first decade as a Londoner he had interloped with impunity on the Guinea Company's charter, had hailed English victories in a commercial war with the Dutch, had sent the *Hope* to violate the Spanish monopoly in America and other ships to the East Indies independently of the chartered English company. But whether he was conscious of any broad imperialistic programme is unclear. He had been commissioned by his principals to deal in slaves. He had become interested in the India trade only after the Company had hired a ship in which he owned a small share. And the voyage of the *Hope* was, after all, less a matter of aggression than of stealth.

In any case, there is nothing from which to complete a portrait of Paige as a new and revolutionary merchant—no evidence to link his economic activities with religious or political radicalism. Of his religious practices we can know only that his children were baptised at St Helen's.[112] About politics during the years of revolution he was consciously reticent: 'In these dangerous times', he wrote, 'it's good for men to be circumspect and cautious of what they say' (**15**). And there are suggestions of political conservatism, if anything, in his letters to Tenerife. He viewed with gloom the execution of Charles I which Thomson and other merchants had helped to effect (**5b**). The letter in which he had first reported the dissolution of the Long Parliament is missing (**76b**). And perhaps he had commented there in the manner of a 'new merchant' who had been politically active. But his dealings with the royalist Kirkes, with Shaw and Millington who were anxious before 1660 to gain the protection of Charles Stuart, indeed his association with Clerke, who easily embraced

108. H.C.A. 13/72, exam. of John Edwards, 13 Nov. 1657, 24/113/58.
109. *C.C.M.E.I.C.*, *1650–4*, xxii, 323, *1655–9*, 35, 71, 164, 268; H.C.A. 13/73, exam. of Henry Dacres, 16 Feb. 1659.
110. *C.C.M.E.I.C.*, *1655–60*, 86, 268, 303, 307, 309, *1660–3*, xx, 122, 129, 133, 137.
111. Farnell, *Ec. H. R.*, 2nd ser., xvi, 445.
112. *Registers of St Helen's Bishopsgate, passim*. Paige's wife Katherine gave birth to ten children from 1652 to 1669. Three survived their father.

Roman Catholicism and whose brother's lands had been sequestrated by parliament in 1644, hint at something other than puritan radicalism.[113]

What can be said with more confidence is that Paige flourished after 1660. He was elected a 'committee' of the East India Company in 1663 along with Thomson and three other trading acquaintances who figure in these letters. And though he had his differences with the Company from time to time, he served as a committee, with only one brief interval, for the next twenty-three years, rented the great vault in Crosby House, and in 1679 was dealing in Company stock worth over £12,000.[114] He was a court assistant of the short-lived Canary Company in 1665–6, served on the Council of Trade from 1668 to 1672, and as first warden of the Merchant Taylors' Company in 1687. Sir Joseph Williamson, the courtier whom Paige supported politically and advised on East India matters, recommended him to Sir William Petty as 'a very considerate merchant'. And if, as seems unlikely, he had earlier been a republican, Paige was not perceived as one in 1687 when, in the charged political atmosphere of that year, he was appointed by royal commission to serve as a London alderman.[115]

The West Country apprentice who had married his master's daughter, had sent ships from London to five continents in the 1650s, and had settled accounts with his partners when compelled by the law, died a retired Tory director in December 1689. He left a handsome estate including a coach, chariot and horses. He also left a son John (1656–1711) who survived the perils of his infancy mentioned in these letters (**125b**) and moved down the street from his father's place of business to become an early director of the Bank of England.[116]

A Note on Editorial Method
The exhibit at C.105/12 includes 148 letters written by John Paige. For this edition we have eliminated those which are trivial or repetitive and have also cut a number of such passages from the letters retained. The collection includes both original letters in Paige's hand and copies by his clerks, for he often enclosed in his current letters copies of the most

113. *Calendar of the Committee for Compounding, 1643–60* (1889–92), pt. 2, 1451–2, pt. 4, 2418–20.
114. *C.C.M.E.I.C., 1654–79, passim*; J. R. Woodhead, *The Rulers of London, 1660–89* (1965), 125.
115. C. A. J. Skeel, 'The Canary Company', *English Hist. Rev.*, xxxi (1916), 534; C. M. Andrews, *British Committees, Commissions and Councils of Trade and Plantations* (Johns Hopkins Univ. Studies in Hist. and Pol. Science, ser. xxvi, nos. 1–3, 1908), 93; C. M. Clode, *The Early History of the Merchant Taylors' Company*, 2 vols (1888), ii, 349; *C.S.P.D., 1667*, 443, 445, 449, 453, *1667–8*, 392, 470, *1673*, 496, 577, *1673–5*, 18, 45, 126, *1675–6*, 557; A. B. Beaven, *The Aldermen of the City of London*, 2 vols (1908–13), i, 7. Roger North alleged that the Council of Trade from 1668 through the early 1670s was dominated by 'leaders of the fanatic party in the City' (*Examen*, 1740, 461–2). William Letwin can find such men especially among the merchant members of the Council, but he offers no evidence to link Paige with the politics of non-conformity or parliamentary opposition (Letwin, *Origins of Scientific Economics*, 22–9). And his political association with Williamson during the same years suggests that Paige was a supporter of the court party.
116. PROB 11/297/181, Will of John Paige; W. M. Acres, 'Directors of the Bank of England', *Notes and Queries*, clxxix (July–Dec., 1940), 58.

recent ones he had sent.[117] We have used the copies to provide the text where the originals are damaged, and where the original is not extant, have transcribed from the copy.

Letters **1–117** were addressed by Paige to Gowen Paynter and William Clerke jointly or to Clerke individually in Tenerife. Letters **118–27** were addressed to Clerke at the locations indicated. Letter **104** is dated from Dover; all others are dated from London, with the exception of a few letters (**110–17**, **126–7**) written in London during the war with Spain which Paige falsely dated from Amsterdam and signed in the name of his correspondent there, John Schanternell.[118]

Letters written from Tenerife by Gowen Paynter and John Turner and cited in the Introduction are dated in the new style as indicated by 'n.s.'. Paige himself probably reported in the new style the dates of those letters which he had received from Tenerife or the continent, but it has not been possible to confirm this. All other dates, those of Paige's own letters and those given in editorial comment, are in the old style, except that 1 January is taken as the beginning of the year.

Salutations, dismissals and Paige's signatures have been omitted. Spelling, punctuation and place-names have been modernised, contractions expanded, and a few scribal errors silently corrected. Words added to the text as well as editorial explanations are enclosed in square brackets. In four letters, which are noted, a few words are supplied and bracketed where the manuscript is damaged but Paige's intent is reasonably clear. Personal names have been standardised by using, wherever available, the spellings given by the individuals when they signed various documents, principally examinations in the Admiralty Court.

Paige made some use of Spanish words and his own pidgin Spanish, e.g. verbs with Spanish roots and English endings. Most of these we have translated, leaving a few technical terms which are clarified in the Glossary, Appendix C, along with technical terms in English, commodities, weights, measures, and monetary units.

117. The book into which Peter Browne and other scribes copied Paige's letters was apparently not exhibited in the Chancery case and is unfortunately not extant (H.C.A. 13/72, exam. of Peter Browne, 23 June 1658).
118. This tactic of deception was commonly practised by Canary merchants during the war (H.C.A. 13/72, exam. of Domingo de la Cerda, 6 July 1658, 13/73, exam. of Peter Bimewijsent, 25 Feb. 1659).

LETTERS OF JOHN PAIGE, 1648–58

(P.R.O. C. 105/12)

1. to William Clerke   26 Dec. 1648
These serve to give you notice of my safe arrival here in company with Mr
Farr some 10 days since. Canary wines prove indifferent well in general. I
have sold the most part [Garvis] Russell's lading [on the *Elizabeth Ann*]
at £19 and £19 5s per pipe and doubt not but to dispose of the rest at ditto
rates. Here is news of the arrival of 10 Canarymen this day in the Downs,
whereof Mr Toope is one and Capt. Cheny, Mr Jenkins and several
others. Mr Payne is in Plymouth.

 I have not as yet received any letters from you or Mr Paynter since my
being here, which makes me the briefer at present. Only according to
promise shall give you an estimate as near as I can how prices of West
India goods are here at present: hides, 7½d [intended 6½d, cf. **2**] per lb, but
in Lisbon a good commodity, being many shipped from hence; logwood
worth £15 10s per t; West India sugars worth £6 10s per cwt; fine grana
worth 32s per lb; Varinas tobacco worth 14s per lb and none expected
from San Lucar. Per Capt. Pyle I shall write you more at large and send a
bill of rates, who is now at Gravesend and stops in Plymouth to take 400
hhds pilchards for Mr Robert Lant. There is one Mr Showers, which Mr
Lambell loaded, sunk in sea coming home. ...

 [P.S.] I have received a joint letter from you and Mr Paynter per which
take notice you have freighted Mr Barber [the *Blessing*] per month.
Concerning insurance, I shall follow your order in effecting it at as cheap
rates as I can. The times are at present very dangerous for Irish [men-of-
war are taking merchant ships, cf. **2**], which will be a means to make me
do it with expedition. ...

2. to William Clerke   8 Jan. 1649
Yours of 20 Dec. per the *Samuel* [Capt. Matthew Wood] have received
with the 11 pipes of wines which came ashore this very instant. The
Rambla wines prove white and green; the Orotava vintage proves
extraordinary rich but high colour. The wines, give them their due, prove
well, and so I doubt not but shall give you a good account of them. Now
my last unto you was per small vessel of Mr Paynter's of 26 Dec. via
Falmouth, where I wrote you somewhat brief concerning the insurance
on the *Blessing* [Capt. Barber]. I have £300 underwritten with much ado
at 6 per cent for yours and Mr Paynter's accounts from thence [Tenerife]
to Nantes, and tomorrow I am promised shall have the rest, £700, done at
ditto rate. The times are so dangerous at present that scarce any man will
underwrite a policy, being many ships of late taken by Irish men-of-war
and the coast of France is as dangerous as ours at present. After I hear of

1

her arrival at Nantes, shall insure the £1,000 backwards [to Tenerife] for Mr Paynter's and your accounts in half.

I cannot send you any bills of rates at present. I writ into France but the post is stopped through the new wars there between the Queen Regent and her subjects. Paris is at present strongly besieged by the Queen's army. What the event will be I know not. From Holland I do expect one daily, and here there are none made of late. But, however, I shall give you an estimate of what goods is worth here per advice. Ginger a good commodity, worth at present £4 per cwt; logwood from Campeche worth £15 per t; Varinas tobacco worth 14s per lb; hides worth 6½d per lb. Mr [Stephen] Slaney told me he sold those hides which you sent him in Capt. Pyle at aforesaid rate and cleared 10 per cent by them, as he says. Fine grana mesteque worth 32s per lb; campechena and sylvester a very drug. West India sugar worth £6 10s per cwt; Palma sugar worth £7 10s per cwt. In my last I wrote you of the prices of all, and since little difference, only 1d per lb in hides, which was a mistake in putting 7½d for 6½d. Your wines in Capt. Cheny are not yet landed, neither Mr Slaney's in Payne. ...

3. to William Clerke   20 May 1649
... These serve to give you notice of the arrival of Mr Barber [the *Blessing*] at Nantes, who I hope by this time may be dispatched for Tenerife with linens and staves. I shall write you at large by Mr Sidrake Blake who may be ready with this ship. ...

4. to Gowen Paynter and William Clerke   25 May 1649
I have received yours, 28 Jan., via Nantes which came to my hands about 20 days since by conveyance of Mr John Holle, by which I understand of the arrival of the *Blessing* [Capt. Barber] there, though somewhat long. She was given over for lost by the insurers here. I had £1,000 underwritten for your accounts according to order at 6 per cent, with much ado. Per advice from Mr John Holle I suppose by this time Mr Barber may be near ready to go for Tenerife with linens and pipestaves. The sum of your cargazon I know not but do expect advice from Mr Holle daily. When received, shall make insurance for your accounts. I have the policy ready drawn and they ask no less than 10 per cent from Nantes to Tenerife, which, for ought I see, the profit of your goods will not afford to give such a premium. However, I shall get what possible I can insured, but I think it will be little under abovesaid rate. The times are now very dangerous, and insurers will hardly underwrite upon any ship under 16 or 18 guns. Ten days since there was a ship of London, 14 guns, taken at her coming out of Nantes by one of the Prince's [Rupert's] frigates, so by that you may see the coast of France is very dangerous. By Gilbert Crane I doubt not but shall be able to give you a further account of this business, who may be ready within this 12 days. ...

5. to William Clerke   28 May 1649
a. I have received yours, 21 Dec., with the 11 pipes of wines by the *Samuel*, Matthew Wood master. The Rambla wines proved white and green, but the Orotava wines proved the richest Canaries that ever came

to England, by all vintners' reports, insomuch that many men were afraid to buy them, saying you had put molasses in them and that they were not natural from the grape. And truly, for my part, I never tasted such wines. I kept them until this month, being could not have a considerable price for them; and seeing the time of racking were at hand, and worser markets daily, I sold them at £20 5s per pipe ready money, one with the others. They made 10 pipes filled up within a gallon. Your wines in Capt. Cheny proved like those you sent me, rather whiter. Give them their due, they were the best wines that came to London this year, and so I make no question but you will have the best price made good to your account. Likewise Mr Stephen Slaney's wines proved well in Payne. Mr St John's, Mr Wilson's, Mr Bradgate's proved well; sold at £19 10s per pipe. Other small parcels proved indifferent, but abundance of high-coloured and foul wines this year.

Wines at present a very drug except extraordinary good. Sherry wines proved very well this year and likewise Malagas, and great quantities came home from those places. But I fear next year will come very few by reason the sickness is very hot at Cadiz and San Lucar, and now of late is come into Malaga and Seville, upon which our Canary principals here do begin to lay load. Ergo, Sidrake Blake goes as full as he can stow, and Steward hath 200 bales, and Crane, I suppose, may bring above 250 bales more. Doubtless if the sickness should continue in those places, Canary wine must needs be a great commodity next vintage, but now our vintners are grown so curious in their tastes that none but rare wines will serve their terms. What wines you send for your own account, I would wish to send those that are very good, although you send the less. In the Island a ducat or 2 you make a great difference, but here betwixt ordinary and very good wines there is above £4 or £5 per pipe.

I have written you in brief by Mr Peter Steward and sent you copy of my letter per Capt. Pyle; likewise I have written you and Mr Paynter by this ship concerning your Nantes business, to which refer you. I pray ask of Mr Paynter to see my cousin John Paige's letter of Plymouth wherein he writes of the delivery of my letters unto Capt. Pyle for you and Mr Paynter. I received a copy of yours 15 Feb. The original, I suppose, came in Mr. Mallen who is taken by the Prince's [Rupert's] ships in company with Mr Thomas, a ship of 28 guns which came from San Lucar worth £40,000, both being carried into Ireland. Likewise I received yours of 3 March, accidentally. I pray hereafter let the direction of your letters be of some other man's hand, being yours is known here by all our Canary merchants, and there are some which shall go nameless that do envy that you make use of me, so I am afraid they will intercept my letters.

5b. Per advice, Varinas tobacco worth 14s per lb; ginger worth £4 per cwt; logwood worth £15 per t; West India sugar worth £6 15s per cwt; grana mesteque worth 35s per lb; campechena and sylvester a drug; indigo of the best worth 4s to 4s 6d per lb; Palma sugar worth £7 15s per cwt; hides worth 7d and 7¼d per lb, in France worth 12 *livres*, in Holland worth 8d per lb. As the times are now few merchants govern themselves by bills of rates being they do tone [i.e. overstate the prices] ere 8 or 10 per cent.

At present little news and that is bad. I make no question but you have

3

heard ere now of that fatal blow which was struck 30 Jan. last. Our gracious King was beheaded at Whitehall, to the disgrace of all our nation and the undoing of a flourishing kingdom that was. I here send you a book called 'The King's Meditations' [the *Eikon Basiliké*] which he wrote before his death. It is worth your reading, I think as good lines as ever you beheld with your eyes. Likewise I send you the whole narrative of his trial, sentence and speech on the scaffold. I shall be the briefer because I intend to write you by Mr Crane who may be ready 10 days hence. ...

6. to William Clerke   30 June 1649

... I do here send you an English bill of rates per which you see how prices of commodities do govern here at present. Varinas tobacco is the only commodity to get money by here, worth 13s per lb. Hides worth 7d per lb. Likewise I do send you a bill of rates from Amsterdam which I received last post and another from Rouen where I find that hides are a good commodity. Caracas hides worth 16 to 17 *livres* per hide which is a good price, such as there may money be gotten by it.

Here are many ships freighted and freighting for the vintage, I mean for the Canaries. Malaga is so much infected that few ships will go there, and [to] San Lucar there goes none. The sickness is very hot in Seville; per advice from thence there have died 30,000 within this 8 weeks' time. The like hath not been known. Amongst all there came news yesterday of the death of our friend Mr George Cony and 3 English merchants more of Seville, and several more very sick of our nation. The Lord comfort them and cease that heavy judgement. The sickness is in all the country towards Madrid, and some say it begins there, which I cannot say of a certain. But it's a miracle that they did escape. Mr Richard Baker went from hence five days since for Madrid by land. Mr Leonard Clerke told me his correspondent was failed there, I take it Mr Smith. If you have any credits for any part of Spain, as I make no question you have, I would wish you as a friend to be very cautious how you draw your bills, for it would be a difficult thing to get acceptance in these perilous times.

For matter of your Nantes business I refer you to my general letter which I send you by this conveyance. If you and Mr Paynter can procure Diego Benitez' wines this year, it will be a fit parcel to load Mr Barber [the *Blessing*]. I know there will be many look after them because they proved so well this last year, better than Mr Rowland Wilson's and Mr St John's by 20s per pipe. In what I can serve you here shall find me as ready as any friend you have. ...

7. to Gowen Paynter and William Clerke   30 June 1649

a. ... [Y]esterday I received a letter of 28 June from Mr John Holle [at Nantes] wherein he writes me Mr Barber [the *Blessing*] was then there waiting for a wind to carry him away, which God send it to carry him to his desired port in safety. I have blamed Mr Holle in several letters why he did not dispatch Mr Barber away sooner because he was on monthly pay. His answer to me was that the master could not fit the ship sooner, which if it appear so it's reason he should abate you. I wrote Mr Holle to make a

4

protest. I know not where he did or no. Likewise the ship was embargoed at Belle-Île 10 days.

I here send you Mr Holle's letter which came to my hands 6 days since; likewise 2 notes, the one for damage and the other for freight paid him there; likewise an obligation of Mr Barber's for 9,200 *Rs* which he took of Mr Holle upon *bomaria* [bottomry]. Here goes a copy in English, which I caused to be translated. Now I here send you the invoice of what goods Mr Holle hath shipped aboard aforesaid ship and for your accounts in equal halves, it amounting unto 20,169 *livres*, 9 *sous*, 9 *deniers*, whereof Mr Holle writes me there is 1,500 *livres* for his account. You may please to take notice that I have insured on ditto ship for your accounts in equal halves £1,200 sterling at 5½ per cent with much difficulty. The 1,500 *livres* goes on aforenamed insurance; be it for Mr Holle's or your account, to me it's all one. By the names of the linens I can scarce know where all be proper, but for the major part I am persuaded that you have a pretty good cargazon. The bill of lading I have received, but shall keep that myself in case of loss, which God forbid. However, the policy is made very authentic, and I have the ablest men in London underwritten it, which may serve for your comfort.

7b. Mr Holle writ me hath sold your hides at 11 *livres* per hide, which is a very poor rate considering French money. By the bill of rates which I send you from Rouen, may see that the same commodity is worth above 20 per cent more. If you send another ship for France now or next spring, send her for Nantes and New Haven [Le Havre], which is the port of Rouen, where Mr Holle hath a very honest man to his correspondent by name David Conguard. To tell you truly, I know no design so hopeful, only I would wish you to have a ship of better force, which I shall freight upon 2 words advice if you like the design.

If at any time they write you the price of corn from France, the only way to make a right calculation is thus: you must note that their tons are different measure, so commonly they reduce it into Winchester measure, which is every bushel 8 gallons and every hanneck is 14 gallons just, by a measure which I brought from Tenerife last year. I am confident if you do not fall on to this trade, here are several that will. Our Canary principals do much envy that their factors, as they call them, should trade deeper than they and so much slight their employments. As I know you do not care for any man's, those words came from men's mouths which have formerly employed you both, and now, for what I perceive, would be glad you would accept of their business again. I leave you to judge. The men shall go nameless because I love peace. ...

8. to Gowen Paynter and William Clerke   5 July 1649

I have written you at large per this ship, to which refer you, and sent you copy of all your Nantes business which Mr John Holle remitted me. I received a letter by the Amsterdam post, which came to my hands this very instant, wherein have advice of the arrival of 2 Hollanders there from Canaries just at the post's coming away, so that no man hath any letters come over.

Here came yesterday letters from Malaga and Seville per post, dated 12

June, wherein they write that in 8 weeks there have died 30,000 people of the plague in Seville; and whereas it was somewhat ceased in Cadiz and San Lucar, it now increases again. From Malaga per advice there die 400 per day and that both at Malaga and Seville there die many thousands for want of food. A hen is worth from 30 to 35 *Rs*, and an egg is worth 14 *cuartos*. By this you may judge the dearth. It is too true, for I saw several letters of what I write you, else should not have given credit to it. For San Lucar there goes no ships that I hear of, so that we are like to have no sherry sacks home this year, and I question where they have people left to vintage the wines. And for Malaga, as yet I know of but 3 ships bound there, men being very fearful to adventure, whereas formerly there used to be freighted 40 sail by this time. So that in all probability Canary wines will be a great commodity here, and I question not but the Islanders will make you pay accordingly. This I thought good to give you 2 words advice whereby you might be the better prepared against vintage. Upon this news our Canary principals are much encouraged this is a year to make them. I wish it may prove so. Here are freighted and freighting abundance of ships for the vintage. I make no question but you will have some of the Malaga chinches [i.e. wretches], being they are frightened from thence by reason of the sickness. Madrid as yet is clear, but very much feared, being several towns near it infected. Likewise it begins to come into Portugal, it being at Faro already. Your credits this year for any part of Spain are dangerous to draw as the times govern now.

I hope by this time Mr Barber [the *Blessing*] is safe arrived with you. I have insured £2,000 on him for your accounts in equal halves at 5½ per cent, with much ado, and £400 for Mr Paynter's particular account. Here is news of the death of Mr George Cony and 4 English merchants more of Seville. Per Mr Chalke [the *Mary*] I shall write you more at large. As yet no news of the galleons' arrival from Indies. They make account here that all the West India goods will come for Tenerife. No news from Mr White. I fear he is miscarried. ...

[P.S.] This letter goes by the Dover post to be sent aboard Mr Crane.

9. to William Clerke   1 Sept. 1649

Your welcome lines, 1 Aug., received yesterday via Nantes, where Mr Steward is arrived and consigned to Mr John Holle, as he [Holle] wrote me. If Sidrake Blake come there, as Mr Paynter writes me is, that place will be overlaid with India goods for a long time. I am very glad to hear Mr Barber [the *Blessing*] is safe arrived [at Tenerife] and that his goods came so seasonable a time, although cost you a little extraordinary for his quick dispatch, yet I question where those that come after will come off on better terms.[1] Mr John Holle and some friends here have freighted a ship of 150 ts, she being now at Gravesend and goes for Nantes to load linens and so for Tenerife to load West India commodities, and back again. The partners here would willingly give over the voyage since Steward's arrival, but I think it's too far gone. Mr Holle hath written me several letters to come in for a part. I have written him I like not the design because they cannot procure West India goods for Nantes linens, and secondly the ship will come in the worst season of the year for disposing of the goods, being vintage time, and likewise for the procuring of West India goods.

I perceive you intend Mr Barber shall come home with the first wines, which will be very well if prove good wines. I doubt not but to sell them for your most advantage as well as the best of them all, for as hitherto I have a very good fame with the vintners, and not of the ordinary, but of the best in London; and I know at the same price they had rather buy of me than of old Rowland Wilson, provided that my wines be equal with his, which very few men's were last year except your own.

I take notice you have a good parcel of West India goods by you which you intend to keep by you until next spring, which is better than to send it here, being at present will not turn very well to account. What will be hereafter I know not. What offers shall advise you of the needful per every conveyance I know of; the like shall desire from you. What you intend to have done, give timely advice, which is, as you well know, the main of all business. I here send you an English, Holland and French bill of rates, to which refer you. Likewise I here send you the Parliament act [of 28 Aug. 1649] for making all French wines contraband in England, which act hope will help somewhat towards the sale of our Canaries next year.

Mr Richard Lant is now in the West Country getting Toope's lading of pilchards, striving very much to have the first, but all will not do. God sending Mr Chalke [the *Mary*] well, I hope he will get the start of them all, he being now dispatched, staying only for a fair wind, which God send him. The others' pilchards are not yet all bought, they being very scarce and extraordinary dear, worth 8s 6d per m besides charges.

Here enclosed I send you a list of what ships are to load at vintage [Appendix A]. Whosoever's lot it will fall out to, I know not, but I am confident some will bring *vidueños*, for *malvasías* there will not be ⅔ part to load them, in my opinion. ...

1. In his accounts at 21 July 1649, Clerke listed a payment of 4,000 *Rs* (c. £125) to Capt. General Pedro Carrillo de Guzman for 'the good dispatch of the *Blessing*'. Cf. **15**, **19a**, **20**.

10. to William Clerke   8 Nov. 1649

I received yours, 1 Aug., per Mr William Cowes and likewise another via Bilbao of 23 Aug. under covert Mr George Clerke, which letter he sent me at Exeter, but the seal broken up. He tells me it was a mistake, which is his excuse. Hereafter you may do well to send my letters under no man's covert in regard I am sufficiently known. I perceive Mr Barber [the *Blessing*] is gone for the Barbary Coast. I wish he may return in time to be one of the first ships with wines. Per advice the vintage at Malaga and Jerez prove very bad both in quantity and quality, and there is no likelihood of any permission for French wines to be brought here as yet. I received a letter, 12 Oct., from our friend Mr Richard Baker of Madrid, who writes me that the sickness is ceased in Cadiz, San Lucar and Seville and the galleons arrived very rich. Here is abundance of Varinas tobacco come; not worth at present 5s per lb and like to be lower.

I wonder in all your letters you have not given any order for insurance homeward on Mr Barber. I shall be loath to exceed your order; yet if I hear our Channel be dangerous, I shall have something done for you, being conceive it is forgotten by you, otherwise your letter miscarried.

I doubt Sidrake Blake will be gone before this come to Nantes, which makes me the briefer, desiring you to be referred unto the joint letter which I write Mr Paynter and yourself per this via. I am very glad Mr Paynter and you consign your goods all under one mark. It is far better for you and more ease to me.

11. to Gowen Paynter and William Clerke   16 Jan. 1650
a. Yours of 23 Aug. via Bilbao have received. Thereby perceive by yours you are intended to drive a trade in partnership, which in my opinion will be very well for you both. In regard of the dangerousness of these times, I hold it not good for one man to have a whole ship for his own account.

Yours, 18 Nov., per the *Blessing* have received. I discharged the ship from pay 14 Dec. I sold all the wines as soon as they were landed: 75 pipes at £20 per pipe and 64 pipes at £21 per pipe, a price which was never known in former years. The wines proved generally green; only 50 pipes in the ground tier proved gallant rich wines. The master told me 30 of them were from Orotava. Yet there are several men had far better wines, yet I must confess the *puestos* are good. Garachico wines prove in general this year small, hungry wines. Mr Cramp brought the best ship of Canaries that ever I saw in my life, laden by Mr [John] Turner, and likewise Mr Brooks laden by ditto. But Hussy's and Steward's proved but small, green. Likewise Mr Sheeres', laden by Mr Campion, proved excellent, whose were Alonso de Lugo's wines, as I am told. And Mr Smith's wines, laden by Mr [William] Clerke, proved rare wines, above 40s per pipe better than Barber's [on the *Blessing*], yet the others are as well sold as them. The Canary trade is so much cried up for this year that I am confident there will be above 20 new principals next year. So of necessity the Islands will be overlaid, and all men send the half of their effects for San Lucar and Seville. So that next year there will be so many credits [accumulated in peninsular Spain by Canary merchants] that you will scarce get any premium [for peninsular money in terms of Canarian money] except you make some agreement in time with someone or other.

Now you may please to take notice that I have freighted the ship *Matthew* of Dover, burthen 120 ts, whereof is master John Brampton, who may be ready within this 10 days at farthest. I have 300 hhds pilchards bought in Fowey and have given order for 50 or 100 hhds more, if to be got. The rest shall fill up with pipestaves, according to your order. God sending her well into the West, she will be laden in 3 days at most. Mr William Bulkley tells me hath 250 hhds in Plymouth, which says will send for Tenerife if could get a ship going thither, which I question; but I know yours will be there before his, God sending the ship in safety. I have them 15 per cent cheaper than his. I would have freighted Mr Murwill, but he asked me £150 per month which was £20 too much. Per advice French wines are still prohibited; 'tis much feared we shall have wars with them, though may be not suddenly. I shall go on buying this ship's lading with Newfoundland fish. As yet no price broken; I am in hopes will be reasonable. God sending the ship well and that she have a quick dispatch with her pilchards, it will be too soon to go directly from thence to Newfoundland because those that sell their fish will not oblige themselves to deliver it sooner than 15 or 20 Aug. So that if you can get 100 pipes of wines with some tonnage, you may send her here. So she come by 10 May, will be soon enough to go for Newfoundland. And, if need require to abbreviate the dispatch, she shall put them out in the Downs. If more, I am confident they will sell so far forth as they are good, and in my opinion it's the best course you can take. So that if you do anything about the wines, must be on receipt of this because I know there go several orders for buying of those wines which are left. Here are 2 or 3 ships to go from hence about a month or 5 weeks hence. Now in case you do not send this ship back again, then you may let her carry some wines for Newfoundland, and the proceeds of those wines may lie there for a ship's lading of fish the next year from thence.

11b. Now I shall give you my reason why the ship that I sent you doth not load New England fish. First, there are so many going thither that there will not be fish to load them. Secondly, I cannot get a man to take one pipe of wine in part payment. Thirdly, there is so much difference in the fish and cheating that some men sold last year in Bilbao at 80 *Rs* per kt and others had so much refuse that they sold for 40 *Rs* most part. And more, if a man buy 2 or 3,000 kts, if it be dearer there than it's sold here, then they will pretend they have had bad fishing year, when if another man come, shall buy it for 2 *Rs* a kt more. For you must conceive they sell their fish with this provision, that in case they catch so much. Now in Newfoundland, fish is more certain. If I agree with a man to deliver me a quantity, in case they do not catch it, then will endeavour to comply although they buy it of another. But our New England brethren will not do so. There came several ships last year from thence half laden although their full lading was bought here. So that if any of abovesaid reasons should prove true, as I doubt too many would, then the voyage is half overthrown.

Your bill [of exchange of] £175 in favour of Mr Barber [the *Blessing*] have paid. For the rest we have not yet made up account. You may take notice that I am to abate £8 upon 8 pipes of Barber's wines, 6 of them being ropey. The custom, freight, petty charge of Barber's wines, with the bill, hath cost me near £600, and as yet I have not received £1,100 of all. I must do as other men, that is, give three-crane law for payment, $\frac{1}{3}$ money, 3 and 3 months.[1] Otherwise, I could not advance such prices. Only one parcel sold for half money. Now I leave you to judge what I shall be out of purse when your ship is dispatched with the pilchards and staves. I must deal truly with you: I was fain to take up £300 for 6 months, which cost me £12 per interest, only to comply with your orders and to do your business advantageously.

By Mr Brampton [the *Matthew*] I shall be more larger, this going by an uncertain conveyance, under covert Mr Roger Kilvert. I hope the next ship will be yours. ...

[P.S.] Pray let me hear from you per all vias. I sent my letters to go by Mr Sidrake Blake via Nantes, but came 3 days too late, so are gone via

Bilbao. I have sent you a copy of this under covert Mr Kilvert per this ship, who hath promised me his son shall deliver it you safely.

1. One-third cash on delivery, the remainder in two payments at three-month intervals thereafter. Three Cranes Wharf was used especially by vintners for unloading wines (*The Port and Trade of Early Elizabethan London*, ed. B. Dietz (London Rec. Soc., viii, 1972), 161, 164).

12. to William Clerke   22 Jan. 1650

a. ... Your letter, 15 Oct., came to my hands but 4 days before Mr Barber [the *Blessing*] arrived in the Downs, but as soon as I received it, I presently got the policy made and upon no terms could get nothing insured. I proffered 10 per cent, but they would not [insure], being the ship was small and just then we had notice of Prince Rupert's being about our Channel; insomuch that I protest I never was at rest day nor night, seeing I could by no means effect your desire. I never had any business that troubled me so much; but, thanks be to God, it fell out for the best at last and saved you £80. But if it had fell out otherwise, then—well, I could not have remedied it. If I had received your advice in time, might have done it as well as Mr Paynter's, who gives me a general order to insure for him in every ship which I think fitting. I have insured on Mr Chalke [the *Mary*] £600 for his account and mine in equal halves, which is within a very small matter to the full that was aboard him.

I perceive by yours you have bought a parcel Varinas tobacco, which, except you have it reasonable, will lose by it, in regard great quantities have been brought from San Lucar of late, worth at present 6s per lb if right. It pays 2s 6d per lb custom and excise, being risen of late by order of Parliament.[1] For your other West India goods, I perceive you have ordered Mr George Clerke to send you a ship for it, whom God send in safety whenever she goes. I have freighted a ship for Mr Paynter's and your accounts in equal halves. She is to depart from Gravesend 28 instant by charter-party. For other particulars I refer you to a joint letter written you per this conveyance. Only if there are any good wines left, you may send her back with some and will be soon enough to go for Newfoundland after, always provided she have a quick passage outward and that you conceive she may return here fine April or first May at furthest.

1. On 14 Dec. 1649 Parliament levied an excise of 2s per lb on tobacco not of the English plantations (*C.J.*, vi, 332–3). The customs levy on Spanish tobacco was 6d per lb.

12b. I received your welcome lines, 13 Dec., per the *Love* which came to my hands yesterday by Mr Brampton. Shall give answer at full. In the interim I cannot omit to give you a thousand thanks for my red Canary which as yet is aboard. The wines you loaded in Smith proved rare. I could wish they had been for your own account. I am confident they will clear by them near 50 per cent, which is a thing never known before, neither do I think ever to see the like year for Canaries as long as I live. Jerez and Malaga wines prove base this year.

Per advice, the King of Spain hath sent in great haste for his ambassador from hence, who goes away next week. 'Tis very much feared we shall have wars with both Spain and France and likely the peace will be concluded betwixt France and Spain. I do counsel both you and my friend Mr Paynter both to so order your business as that when occasion offers that you may clear yourselves of the country. For I must tell you it is not safe to have your estates there as the times now govern; for when such a thing comes, it will be with[out] much warning. Of this I thought good to give you a hint, being a well-wisher to your affairs. I shall desire you to order me some monies per first [occasion], whereby I may have full effects for the codfish business, which intend to buy suddenly. ...

13. to Gowen Paynter and William Clerke   6 Feb. 1650
a. My last unto you was of 16 Jan. per a Fleming which Mr Roger Kilvert sent from hence, to which refer you for what then proffered. And since, I have received yours of 10 Jan. per Sidrake Blake and Mr William Webber. I have written you a brief letter per this ship [the *Matthew*, Capt. Brampton] of 30 Jan. Therein gave you notice how have shipped aboard her 12,000 of pipestaves for your accounts as per bill of lading; likewise sent you a true copy of the charter-party, to which refer you. Now you may please to take notice that I have ordered Mr William Arundell to load aboard this ship at Fowey 300 hhds of pilchards for your accounts in equal halves, which fish he writes me is excellent good and well saved, cost 7s 6d per m. There will be some petty charges on it at the shipping which I cannot give you account of at present. Mr William Bulkley hath 200 hhds at Plymouth which he now intends to ship on John Young. They cost him 8s 6d per m first penny, being bought long since. God send this ship a fair wind to get out of the Downs. I hope she will be there 20 days before Mr. Young, being he cannot be ready to go hence this 10 days.

Per advice good Canaries at present are in request, worth £21 per pipe and like to continue so, which is a great price and a trade too good, I doubt, to continue long. Therefore you may make use of the occasion. In case that the ship have a good passage over with her fish, it will be too soon to send her directly from thence to Newfoundland. She may very well return here again and go for Newfoundland, being the sacks from hence do commonly go out of the Downs 20 May. Now in case that you do not send the ship here as aforementioned, then you may send in her 100 or 150 pipes [of] wines for to land them in New England and so to come away for Newfoundland, which will not be much out of her way. And the proceeds of your wines, when sold, may be ordered to buy a ship's lading of New England fish for next year. I was days past in company with Sir David Kirke's brother [John] who is his correspondent here. I would have bought 2,000 kts of dry fish of him, to be delivered by Sir David [Governor of Newfoundland], provided that he would but take 40 or 50 pipes wines in account and the rest I would have paid him here per bill of exchange. But upon no terms I could not get him to take any wines, being the land is every year overlaid and, as I am informed, there goes from Madeira 100 pipes this year. As yet here is no price broken for Newfoundland fish, being somewhat soon. But I shall very suddenly buy Mr Brampton's lading and order the business so that we may have the first fish whereby to have the benefit of good market. I shall write the master from hence per several ships and send him orders for receiving the fish, of which you may be confident that I shall use the utmost of my endeavours for the furtherance of the design. You may do well to give the master a charge that he have a care in the choosing of his fish. Now in case that Mr Brampton should be long windbound in the West Country, or have a tedious passage over, then I would not wish you to send him back to me, doubting that his Newfoundland design may be overthrown by coming too late, all which I leave your consideration.

13b. Now I take notice you have contracted with Mr [William] Webber for a parcel of Galicia pilchards, and I like the business very well and do believe will prove beneficial for both. For Mr Webber, I am confident he will make at least 80 per cent profit off all his goods from hence to Galicia, so that although he get nothing by his pilchards yet he will make a good voyage. I sent a small parcel of goods there not long since for my own account, therefore have some small experience in the trade. And truly it was my full intent to have had a bark of 50 ts this year to load pilchards from thence and so for Tenerife for my own account. But seeing you have gone through with this, I shall forbear and send some from England at the vintage. According to your order I shall supply Mr Webber with the £400 and see that the business be put in execution at the time you write of and shall aid and assist him what in me lies whereby to further the design, assuring yourselves that there shall be nothing wanting in me to see all things punctually performed, which is as much as I can say or you desire.

I have promised Mr Brampton that in case he should lose a cable or anchor, mast, or sail, or any other necessaries, that you shall furnish him with money to provide new, if occasion, provided that it do not exceed above a month's pay, for the term of the whole voyage. Therefore, I shall desire you to give order unto your friend at Bilbao, or any other place where you shall send him, that he may be supplied, hoping that he will prove an honest, careful man and give you content, of which I should be glad to hear of.

Campeachy wood is risen of late, worth at present £17 to £18 per t; hides, 6½d per lb, on which will be great loss; fine grana, 32s per lb; Varinas tobacco at 5s per lb; campechena and sylvester a very drug; ginger worth £4 per cwt. Wines is the only commodity now in England. Pray advise me who is your correspondent in Bilbao and pray advise him to give me notice whenever it pleases God to send Mr Brampton safe there. I shall write you per our friend Mr Leonard Clerke who may be ready to be gone hence within this 10 days at farthest in Mr James Blake [the *Constant John*]. ...

14. to William Clerke   16 Feb. 1650
My last unto you was of 22 Jan. per a Fleming which Mr Roger Kilvert sent from hence, and now I have received yours per the *Love* [Capt. William Rouse] of 13 Dec. and 12 Jan. per Mr Thomas Hart. I do not strange at your not writing me the first of the vintage, being partly sensible of the multiplicity of your business.

I have written you in my former concerning the proof of wines this year. Those which you loaded for Mr George Clerke [William's cousin] in the *Love* proved the best of a small parcel that I have seen this year, insomuch that the vintners did quarrel who should have them. Mr Rawdon loaded a parcel of excellent wines in Sidrake Blake. Indeed you writ me that Orotava would prove the best wines this year, and so I do find it generally. From Garachico they prove hungry, green wines, and Rambla somewhat better but not comparable to Orotava. Yet in my opinion, one year with another I like Rambla the best. Wines at present are very scarce, not a good parcel unsold.

I perceive you intend this ship [the *Matthew*] from Newfoundland to Bilbao with her fish. If in case she have a quick passage over with her fish, you may do well to send her home with 100 or 150 pipes wines and some logwood, being risen of late 40s per t, worth at present £17 to £18 per t. But, however, if you do not send her and that she go directly from thence, her full lading of fish shall be bought according to your order. I shall supply Mr [William] Webber [who intends to carry pilchards from Galicia to Tenerife for Clerke and Paynter] with the £200 for your account and insured it per month, being not certain of his ports.

Mr Holle [at Nantes] writes me would fain have another design for the Canaries. I could wish that you had laden those wines in Smith for your account. I am confident that they will clear for the 300 pipes above £1,200, which is a hit that I never look to see the like again. Neither is it possible that the vintners can subsist to give such prices. I doubt many of them will go for Ram Alley this year. I am sorry Mr George Clerke doth not send you a ship with expedition according to your expectation. I must tell you he hath too much phlegm to be a Canary merchant. Although it doth not concern me, yet I cannot but give you a hint of it, being a well-wisher to your affairs. I have received your kind token [a pipe of red Canary wine] out of the ship *Love* and have given your cousin his part. For mine I am not able to express my thankfulness, not knowing how to make you requital, esteeming the favour as from the hands of so intimate a friend as I have found you. Having written you and Mr Paynter in my joint letters at large of all passages, whereunto desire reference, which maketh me the briefer now and especially because Mr Leonard Clerke stays for my letters.

[P.S.] I had almost forgotten to write you of this particular, which is that I conceive you writ me that you would send me home some West India commodities this summer whereby that I might have sufficient effects for your Newfoundland business. ...

15. to Gowen Paynter and William Clerke   16 Feb. 1650
... Mr Brampton [the *Matthew*], ... I hear, is yet in the Downs by contrary winds. I did think when I dispatched him from hence that he would have been [gone] long before these ships; but since it please God that falls out otherwise, there's no remedy but patience. It will be a means to hinder her return here, and likewise the pilchards will not come at first of Lent as I thought they would.

I am sorry to hear of your imprisonment, hoping you are cleared long ere this. It seems strange to me that the [Capt.] General [of the Canaries, Don Pedro Carrillo de Guzmán] should lay a charge against you for bringing in contraband goods when that he takes money for quick

13

dispatch and gives admittance, and now to contradict what formerly hath acted.[1] There have some acquainted our States with the wrongs that you suffer; but if you do not get out before they seek to clear you, for ought I know you may perish. They are informed by some busy masters of ships that you are all in general enemies to the present government, so that you are taken to be the greatest malignants that live beyond the seas. In these dangerous times it's good for men to be circumspect and cautious of what they say. We live in a sad [time], God help us. Prince Rupert is now in Lisbon with a fleet of 12 [war]ships and frigates. God grant he do not give the Islands a visit.

I propose to insure the major part of your interests in Mr Brampton although our coast here hath been very clear of rogues this 10 weeks. In case that you have occasion for any tonnage homewards, you may have it in Robert Newman [the *Tenerife Merchant*] who goes wholly to seek. He hath engaged himself to me that you shall have the first refusal of his ship in case that you have occasion for her. I would have freighted you a bigger ship than Brampton but could not have such a sailor in this river, which did invite me to take her. I would have had Newman, but he came home after I had freighted Brampton. Mr. [William] Webber hath a great desire to Barber's ship [the *Blessing*] for the Galicia design. If you will have any tonnage charged at vintage, pray give me timely advice, as likewise for what else you please to have done. I have disbursed £300 more for your accounts than at present I have received of Barber's wines but hope shortly to get in more monies. For the future, in case that you do send any business of consignance unto me, I shall desire you order so that I may always have large effects whereby to go through my business as well as other men, that I may not be constrained to undervalue my commodities to defray charges, which is a thing I hate of my heart. I would have bought Brampton's lading of fish in New England, but very few will sell except they have half money beforehand, which was never done but this year. There are so many ships going that I doubt half of them will not come with fish. Besides, it is a very uncertain trade because some years falls in great quantities and other years not 10,000 kts. ...

1. The Capt. General had imprisoned English merchants in Tenerife in an attempt to force them each to pay 1,800 *Rs* (c. £45) as a penalty for having imported contraband goods, French linens in particular, since 1640. On 15 April 1650 the Council of State entertained a petition from London merchants complaining of this and other grievances, and referred the matter to the judges of the Admiralty Court (*C.S.P.D.*, *1650*, 105, 109; B.L., Add. MS. 32,093). Cf. **9, 19a**.

16. to William Clerke   21 Feb. 1650
I have written you and Mr Paynter at large per Mr Brampton, your ship the *Matthew*, who I hope is at present taking in 300 hhds pilchards for your accounts. Likewise have written you at large per Mr Leonard Clerke, to which desire reference. These are only to give you notice that this day I had a little discourse with Mr George Clerke, who I find to be very backward in freighting your ship, insomuch that by what I can perceive will send none. And yesterday I received letters from Nantes wherein Mr Holle writes me that yours, 15 Jan., is come to his hands,

wherein you write him will send a ship thither. He gives me advice that there are no hides to be got in all Nantes and that linens are very reasonable and for any embargoes there is no doubt. This is chiefly his advice unto me. Now because your design may not be frustrated, Mr Newman hath engaged himself unto me that you and Mr Paynter shall have the refusal of his ship [the *Tenerife Merchant*] before any men. So that in case you have a mind that way, I know may have him on reasonable terms, being he goes wholly to seek. He had last voyage £125 per month. Of this I thought good to give you notice. ...
[P.S.] This goes by the Downs post aboard Mr Newman.

17.[1] to William Clerke   22 March 1650
... [H]ave received none from you, which makes me the briefer at present, having written you and Mr Paynter at large per several ships which have gone from hence.

Our principals here do lay load. I never knew such quantity of goods sent and now to go. I believe Mr [John] Turner hath £10,000 cargazon in this ship [the *Island Merchant*], Mr Steward, and Sidrake Blake will be ready to go 20 days hence, which ship will carry at least 400 packs of goods. Likewise Mr Fishman is making ready to carry a great cargazon to Mr [John] Webber and [Robert] Pearson. I was told yesterday for certain that Mr Garland and your cousin [George] Clerke hath freighted a ship of 150 ts which will be ready very suddenly. God send her well to you.

I hope by this time Mr Brampton [the *Matthew*] is with you, where I hope will find good vent for his pilchards, although they come somewhat late. The fault is not mine nor the master's. We had nothing but southwest winds here for 2 months together. I believe you will find the fish to be as good as any that hath gone there this many years for I gave Mr Arundell a very great charge about it.

All sorts of West India commodities very low at present: Palma sugar sorted [i.e. good whites] worth £7 5s per cwt; hides, 6½d [per lb] if very good; cochineal mesteque worth 30s to 32s per lb; campechena a drug; indigo at 4s per lb; Varinas tobacco worth 5s 6d to 6s [per lb] if right; logwood worth £17 per t (if no great quantities come home, a small parcel may sell). Good Canary wines worth £22 per pipe, at which rate I sold the major part of Mr Boulden's lading, the rest at £21 6s 8d per pipe without giving one pipe choice and to as able vintners as any in London, which is such price as 'tis impossible, in my opinion, that the vintners can hold to pay it. Yet I hope that I shall be paid to a farthing for all the wines I have sold this year, both for you and Mr Paynter, which is more than a great many can say.

Sir, I have a[t my house] with me a youth which is a kindred of mine and is newly [come out] of France where he learned h[is French, to read] and write it as well as his natural tongue. I have a great desire that he should be your apprentice, when not, that you will let him be with you for 2 years to learn his Spanish. The youth is about 17 years old and very fit for your turn or else I should not wish him to you. The former part of this letter is his writing, which is a good hand in my opinion. His parents have

15

bestowed good breeding on him although can give no money with him, which I know you may have with another. But if you take him I shall esteem the courtesy so much the more. And for his truth, I come bound for it if so be that you desire it. Did I know the least vice or [im]perfection in the youth, I protest I would not so much as notion the business to you, but I am persuaded you will like him very well. Of this shall desire 2 words answer, referring you to my joint letter which I have writ you per this conveyance. ...

1. The manuscript is damaged.

18. to Gowen Paynter and William Clerke   22 March 1650
... [L]ittle or nothing offers, in regard I have not heard from you of late days. I hope Mr Brampton [the *Matthew*] is safe with you ere this time in regard we have had easterly winds here this 12 days. May please to take notice that I have insured on him for your accounts £700 at $3\frac{1}{2}$ per cent, which is one per cent less than was given either upon James Blake or Crispe. By this you may see that the ship is taken notice of for some excellent sailor. I had not done so much but that I did consider it was reasonable. I conceive it will be too soon to send her from thence directly for Newfoundland. I should be glad to hear 2 words of her arrival and how you dispose of her. The price of Newfoundland fish here is broken at 24 and 23*Rs* per kt, so that now I am upon buying 2,500 kts, which, you may depend, shall effect, not doubting but per Mr Blake shall be able to give you a further account of the business.

I have disbursed £200 already to Mr [William] Webber for goods which I have bought for him. The rest will be ready very suddenly, only as yet hath got no ship, although hath been about several. Men do look upon him here, in regard he lost his ship and most what he had, as an undone man, so are mistrustful of his ability. But the design shall not be hindered for want of that. I told him that I would engage myself for the freight, which I shall do for your sakes. Mr Barber [the *Blessing*] and his owners are at difference, and Mr Webber hath a great mind to the ship. He doth much solicit me to take $\frac{1}{4}$ part for your accounts, and he and a friend will take $\frac{1}{4}$ more. The other $\frac{1}{2}$ the old owners will hold with him. I have half promised him, yet I must confess it is not a usual thing of me to do or act any such thing without your order. Yet on the other side, I do look upon the business as a vessel very fit for your occasions, and the $\frac{1}{4}$ put to sea will not stand above £130 at most. I could wish you had the other $\frac{1}{2}$ at ditto rate. I should willingly hold a part myself. I have a good opinion of Webber that he will prove honest and go through with the design. It behoves him, for I am confident he cannot find 2 such friends in England as you. He much depends on your favourable countenance. ...

19. to Gowen Paynter and William Clerke   1 May 1650
a. ... Here arrived a small Fleming which Mr Bonfoy loaded at Santa Cruz and likewise another at Amsterdam by which conveyance several men had letters. Your general letter of 6 March is come to hand by which I perceive Don Pedro Carrillo [de Guzmán, Capt. General of the Canaries]

does molest you and that you are prisoners only out upon bail. Some 20 days since we presented your general letter of grievances, with petition, unto our Council of State, who pretend they will do us all the right they can and assist so far as honour and justice will reach [See **15**]. This was the Lord President Bradshaw's answer unto it, they referring the business unto the Committee of Admiralty and Judge Advocate. Whereupon Mr William Bulkley, Mr Edward [? Edmund] Cowes, Mr George Webber and myself were examined upon several interrogatories [in the Admiralty Court, 20–24 April], being acquainted with the use of the dispatches in those Islands, to which we did declare. So that now the Committee are perusing our examinations, and accordingly they are to give in their result unto the Council of State, upon which I hope they will take our parts so far as to write the King of Spain to take some course with that tyrant Don Pedro. If Mr Blake stay but 10 days in the Downs, I shall write you more at large concerning this particular. But I must tell you that our Parliament's agent [Anthony Ascham], which they sent from hence some 10 weeks since, was landed at San Lucar, and the Duke [of Medina Celi, Governor of Cadiz] hath detained him under pretence that he shall not go to Madrid until answer of his letters from the King, which I do not like. In case they do not admit him, you will be in a very sad condition at the Canaries. Besides, there is a new proclamation come out from Madrid which is that you are to dispose of what contraband goods you have by you within 2 months after publication, if not, to be confiscated. And if you bring in any contraband goods after the 2 months, you are not only to lose your goods, but [be] proceeded against as a traitor, which, if this be executed, there can be no trading.

I hope long ere this you have your pilchards out of Brampton [the *Matthew*]. I should be glad to hear how you dispose of him, whether home or directly for Newfoundland from thence. May please to take notice I have bought his lading of Newfoundland fish, to say 800 kts, at $21\frac{1}{2}Rs$ per kt and 1,500 kts at the price a friend of mine hath bought, which I conceive will prove to be 22Rs per kt, but he that sells it says $22\frac{1}{2}Rs$. The next post we shall have advice about it, to resolve each other. I hope Brampton will have a quick dispatch in Newfoundland for I have to do with able men and the fish is bought on as reasonable terms as any man hath bought this year. I have already sent away orders for Newfoundland and written Brampton at large. So much for this design.

19b. Now I come to give you account about Mr [William] Webber's design. Mr Barber and his owners were at some difference about the ship [the *Blessing*], and I found Barber to be upon reasonable terms. Have bought of his ship $\frac{5}{16}$ part, and Mr Webber and a friend $\frac{3}{16}$, and the old owners hold the other $\frac{1}{2}$. So that Mr Webber is now master. We have bestowed above £40 in carpenter's work and bought new cables and other necessaries, so that I conceive the ship will stand, put to sea, about £500. I can have profit for our parts if I would sell her again, but I, finding her so commodious a vessel for our trade, have interested you $\frac{1}{8}$ part each and myself $\frac{1}{16}$ part, not doubting but you will approve of what I have done, and have made the bills of sale in your names for each man's part. The rest of the owners would sell on reasonable terms if you would buy, they being

17

men that do not understand themselves in shipping. I have bought all the goods up for Mr Webber, hoping that he shall be gone within this 6 days from hence and so for Rochelle to load salt and from thence to Pontevedra in Galicia, there to load his pilchards. He did propose to make 2 voyages to Rochelle, but I have barred him that he makes but one. If we had not light of this vessel, I know not where we should have furnished ourselves in all this river with the like, for Mr Webber of himself could never have freighted any. I hope he will prove honest. Hereafter I would not wish you to make any more contracts with him, not but this is very hopeful on your part and likewise on his. He makes at least 100 per cent profit of all the goods he carries with him from hence. I shall have a pretty interest with him for my own account. I hope he will be the very first ship with pilchards at Tenerife. I have taken as much pains about this business as though it did wholly concern myself. If he makes another voyage there after this, if you please, let it go in ¼ parts, yourselves and Webber and myself.

Per advice, Prince Rupert's fleet and our Parliament's fleet were both in Lisbon some 20 days since. It's now reported that the King of France hath sent some ships there to assist Prince Rupert, upon which our Parliament is now setting out another great fleet to engage with them if they take Rupert's part. What the event will be I know not, but all men of our nation remit away their estates out of France, doubting that we shall have an open war. All kind of Spanish wines will be a great commodity next year if the prohibition of French wines hold, as it is very probable. I conceive you will have 65 ts to load for yourselves in Mr Webber's ship. I doubt Bilbao will be overlaid this year with codfish, there being abundance of ships bound for that market as ever I knew of. ...

20. to William Clerke   8 May 1650

... [H]ave received none from you, being of late days we have had no ship from the Canaries, which makes us doubt very much that your troubles with the [Capt.] General [of the Canaries] do increase. As yet no news of Capt. Pyle [the *Swan*] who tarries much. Your bill of exchange for £30 payable to Mr Barber [former master of the *Blessing*] I paid, which I had almost forgot to give you advice of it, and have put it to your particular account, which I shall draw out and send you at the vintage. I have interested you ⅛ part of the *Blessing*, whereof now William Webber goes master. I hope you will approve of what I have done, although I confess it is not a usual thing of me thus to act without the order of my friends. But finding her reasonable and very convenient for that trade, made me enlarge. I wish that you and Mr Paynter would give me order to buy out the other owners. I will hold for myself proportionable because that we might say that have a ship at our own disposal, to send her whither you please, which is advantageous many times. Of this, 2 words by the first, and accordingly shall govern myself.

I understand by Mr John Holle's letter, which I received this instant, that he expects a ship from Topsham hourly in which he is to load a parcel of linens for Tenerife consigned to yourself and Leonard Clerke. Were they but any way sensible of the late proclamation which the King of

Spain hath put forth about French goods, I conceive they would have desisted. If it be prosecuted with that rigour as now in the Main of Spain, it will not be possible for you to receive her. I am now in expectation every day to receive some welcome lines from you. Till then shall have little subject to enlarge, referring you to my joint letter. For prices of West India goods, little or no difference since my last advice.

[P.S.] This very instant I saw a letter which came from San Lucar overland, dated a month since, wherein they writ that the Spaniards have seized upon 1,200 fardels of French [goods], some ashore and some aboard the galleons for the Indies, and no man durst own them. Which may serve per advice, wishing you as my real friend to be cautious in the[se] dangerous times. ...

21. to Gowen Paynter and William Clerke   8 May 1650

... Per advice I received yesterday a letter from Rouen wherein have notice that all our English ships are embargoed there, which is no good sign. Upon which I have ordered that Mr Webber [the *Blessing*] shall not go for Rochelle at all, whereby our ship and goods may be lost, which makes him say it will be £150 out of his way. I told him plainly that he should not go there except did give me security to free both our parts of ship and goods, which hath altogether broke him of that design. I hope shall be cleared from Gravesend this week at the farthest so that now he will have sufficient time to get his pilchards ready in Galicia.

I doubt your codfish that goes in Brampton [the *Matthew*] for Bilbao will come but to a sorry market. It's now too late. My reason is that this year few or none goes for the Straits as formerly because the French take many of our ships, so that there were never so many designs for Bilbao as now. It had been a better way for you to have ordered me to have shipped pack-goods from hence for San Lucar for your accounts, which would prove to be a more certain way for you to value yourselves on than upon codfish, being an uncertain commodity. Which course you may take for the future if you find not the other beneficial. I have a friend in San Lucar that will do your business to content if you please to make use of him. He is now expected every day and goes over again in August next.

Here is advice that now our State's agent in Madrid is very honourably received and that the King of Spain desires union with England as formerly, which may be a means that your business in Madrid may be the better composed. As yet no news of Mr Breton's arrival. I have formerly advised you the needful, which makes me thus brief at present.

[P.S.] God blessing Webber well, I hope will be there the first ship at vintage with his pilchards. You may do well to secure in time your *puestos* for I am confident there will be a great fleet of ships at vintage, here being great preparation making. ...

22. to William Clerke   3 Sept. 1650

a. My last unto you was of 19 July via Rotterdam, where I wrote you somewhat briefly. I have received several letters of late from you, namely per Capt. Pyle [the *Swan*] of 4 May and 11 ditto, likewise yours 23 May from Palma and 28 ditto per Mr Crispe, to which shall now answer at full.

I have received out of the ship *Swan* the 6 chests of indigo which want 91 lbs of the weight you write me. Likewise have received the chest of mesteque cochineal which I have sold at 34s per lb, ½ money and 3 months' time for the other ½. It weighed net 130 lb 12 ozs so that there wants likewise 6 lbs. I cannot challenge the master because the chests, I am confident, were never opened. Give its due, the cochineal was as good as hath come for England this 7 years. Likewise I have received out of the *Constant John* [Capt. James Blake] 12 chests of indigo and 4 of campechena which is, for what I have seen, indifferent good. The indigos in Pyle are good, but the last 12 chests are not right. The campechena I think shall dispose of very suddenly, having some about it at this present. But for the indigos, they are a very drug at present. Here have great quantities come lately from East India, about 300 skins quantity, 200 lbs each, which makes the market low at present, not worth above 4s 6d per lb, besides garbling which is above 2d per lb. Worse I hope it will not be for sales; rather I hope of better. I am resolved not to sell under 5s per lb, so that I must be fain to keep them a little time rather than to undervalue the commodity. Likewise I have received out of the aforesaid ship 460 kts of *leña noel*, so that it breaks 68 kts in weight. The bill of lading was signed with that caution.[1] The weight I know not so that I could not compel the master to make anything good. For his part I think there's nothing diminished. Neither could I find that he had so much wood for his account as Mr Leonard Clerke writ me, which makes me void of jealousy. It seems it came very green aboard, which must needs dry much. Mr Bulkley complains the like of his wood in Crispe. There is 800 kts more in a Fleming which is now at the Isle of Wight; it belongs to Pedro del Prind. So here is enough to serve England, France and Holland this 7 years. I have put it in a Cheap warehouse which cost me 5s per week, for I am doubtful I shall have it lie this many years. I wonder who did advise you to send such a quantity. I am sorry that it doth not come to that market which you expected, I mean for advance. I have written in Holland where they write me that 5 or 6 ts may chance to sell there at £10 per t, so that considering charges, little will remain of the principal. In France they spend little or none as they advise me. Those small quantities that the masters brought home for their accounts have much prejudiced us in the sale of ours. You may rest confident that in this or what else concerns you I will not let slip the least opportunity that may tend to your advantage. The 9 sugar loaves I have received, which shall make sale of.

1. The bill of lading shows 528 kts. Thus 68 kts were lost by breakage in transit.

22b. I am very sorry that your cousin George Clerke hath done you so much injury by frustrating your intended design. For what business you commit to my charge, I shall as near as God enables me endeavour to the utmost of my weak knowledge to give you content. Diligence there shall not be any wanting. The success must leave to God.

Seeing that you were pleased to give me a hint in your letter, 4 May, that I should carry an equal hand betwixt you and Mr Paynter, or to that purpose, I cannot but give you 2 lines answer thereunto, whereby you may rest satisfied. True it is I had rather that all your adventures were in company, and especially those which I send from hence; yet when it shall so fall out that it stands not with your convenience, for my part I shall not cleave to your right hand nor your left, leaving all partiality aside. And his advice that first comes shall be first served, having effects, which is as much as I can say or you to desire. Whatever India goods you send me for the future, pray let be such as is most in request here, whereby, if occasion offers, I may not be forced to undervalue my commodities, for I do not love to have the fame of a spoil-market. Yet my credit is not so low but that I can command £500 of friends when occasion offers. I perceive you intend to send your wines in company with Mr Paynter this year, for which I am glad, hoping that both he and you will strive to load rare liquors, to which purpose I have given Mr Paynter a hint in several of my letters. For what you write me concerning insurance, for the future I shall observe your order as near as the times will give me leave, it being a thing of more difficulty to perform than other businesses are.

I have given both Capt. Pyle [the *Swan*] and James Blake [the *Constant John*] the money for 2 pieces of plate, according to your order. Likewise I have paid your bill of exchange payable to Mr Bradick for £100 with £6 more which he paid *Sr* Antonio [Rodrigues] Vaiez, consi[gna]tus, premium of ditto £100; but in case that you do not allow of what is done, I have Mr Bradick's engagement to return me the money.[1] Whereas I formerly writ you the excise of Varinas tobacco was risen 12d per lb, may take notice that presently after the Parliament ordered that it should be taken off again.[2]

1. Before he left Tenerife for London, Bradick apparently gave Canarian money to Clerke for a bill of exchange drawn in sterling on Paige at London which Bradick then assigned for payment to Rodrigues Vaiez at London. Cf. **22d.**
2. 'An Act for continuing the receipts of the excise for one year until 29 Sept. 1651', 20 Aug. 1650. Cf. **12a.**

22c. Mr Leonard Clerke gave me advice from Palma of the arrival of Mr Presman [the *Robert and John*] and that you intended him for Lisbon with hides, which I hope otherwise in regard we have open wars with Portugal at present. To give you the full relation of the business, it would be too tedious. In case that the ship went for Newfoundland, it will be very late before she get there. I understand by Mr Robert Garland, who did not conceive that I was acquainted with you, that you are interested in Mr Presman $\frac{4}{6}$ parts. Some thereby answered that the ship would make but a bad business of it, to which aforesaid R[obert] Garland answered that he did not care for that you would have the greatest loss. These sudden wars with Portugal will make a thinner exchange of merchants before 6 months pass, and I think Mr Garland hath but all there. As a friend I give you timely advice have a care what bills [of exchange] you draw for his account except you have goods of his to satisfy them in case they come protested. I do admire that your cousin [George Clerke] would recommend you to such a contentious, wrangling man. He far exceeds Mr George Frere. Amongst all I cannot but give you notice of another because you may know your friends from your foes.

Mr Richard Lant doth rail on you in that manner as I never heard the like. He speaks openly that the Canaries never bred such a knave as you have been to him. He began to say the like of Mr Bradick but since he [Bradick] is come home you will not believe how he flatters with him, pretending great matters of friendship. But by what I understand Mr Bradick will clear and have no more in company with him.

I for the future take notice what you advise about the pilchard business. But withal you must consider that when the fish is bought and the wind fall out cross that a ship is 5 weeks windbound in the Downs, as Brampton [the *Matthew*] was before he could get the west, it is not to be imputed to me his late coming there. Weigh all things in the balance of equity and you will find my words to be true.

22d. The wines which you loaded for Mr Richard Baker's account in Newman [the *Tenerife Merchant*] consigned to Mr Markham, proved pretty tasty liquors. Mr Markham did conclude to ask about £23 per pipe for them, but hearing that I sold my wines in Newman upon the lee for £25 10s per pipe, did advance him to 20s per pipe more than he was resolved to ask for them. So that I think I was £100 in Mr Baker's way. Those wines which Goncalo Rodrigues Vaiez bought for 39 Ds in the cellar were sold for £23 and £24 per pipe. Here have of late several vintners broke and more will daily if wines continue these prices, as I think they will be little under. Here is advice the vintage at Malaga is far less than last year, by what men of knowledge do quest.

I have written you and Mr Paynter in my joint letter at large concerning all business in company. I do now expect bills of exchange from Newfoundland. Although your goods be not disposed of, yet all things shall be satisfied punctually. It doth much trouble me that my letters in Steward should be thus kept from me; *Sr* John [Turner, factor in Tenerife for Wilson and Bradgate] will never leave his old tricks. The best is they did not much import; if they did, it were all one to them. Such doings will never thrive long; the event thereof will be evil. I received your letter of credit in favour *Sr* Antonio [Rodrigues] Vaiez and have complied with your desire in showing courtesies in the Spanish style, with which he was very well satisfied. Is now gone over in Mr Blake [the *Constant John*] for Palma.

Per advice, West India hides good worth 6½d per lb; ginger worth £3 12s per cwt; Campeachy wood worth £18 per t; cochineal mesteque, 33s per lb; campechena, 6s 6d per lb; indigo very good 4s 6d per lb. I have sent you in this ship, the *Swan*, Capt. Pyle, 2 or 3 small trifles for your house which pray be pleased to accept. ...

[P.S.] one firkin of Suffolk butter, one keg of sturgeon, one box containing a dozen of neats' tongues.

23. to Gowen Paynter and William Clerke   3 Sept. 1650

a. I received yours, 28 May, per Mr Crispe, which advice came a little too late for me to send a ship for Danzig, being all men advised me that the Sound would be frozen up before she could come forth, which I was loath to put to hazard. Likewise I writ Mr John Holle and others in France who gave me advice that wheat was worth 140 *livres* per t, which makes out about 24 *fanegas*, so that by calculation it would come off at 24*Rs* per *fanega*, which is too dear. Likewise I writ into Holland, and there it was dearer than in France, besides I could not get any English ship that would go for Nantes because the French did then embargo all our ships.

Now seeing myself deprived of all those places, and your order extended so far as that I might send anywhere else I thought most fitting, upon consideration I presently freighted a ship of 140 ts called the *Elizabeth* whereof Christopher Shadforth is master, who went out of the Downs about a month since bound for Safi in Barbary or any other ports upon the coast (I am to give £4 15s per t), to go from thence with his lading of corn for Tenerife and from thence home with wines, which is reasonable in my opinion. For other particulars I refer you to the copy of the charter-party which I send you per ditto ship. I have shipped John Clarke to go pilot and have promised him £3 for a beaver hat. The cargazon I have consigned it unto Mr Richard Jewell, who I send upon the ship, a man very able to undergo the business. Here enclosed I send you a copy of my order given him and likewise a copy of the invoice of goods sent in ditto ship, which, for a small cargazon, is as well sorted as any that hath gone for those parts this 7 years, and I hope that with the advance there will be enough to load the ship with wheat. I have interested you $\frac{3}{8}$ parts each man, which I charge to your accounts and $\frac{2}{8}$ parts for my own account. I would have insured the full [cargo] outwards, but they ask me no less than 6 per cent, or 12 per cent for out and home, so that I am resolved to do nothing outwards on such rates, in regard she went out in company with 30 gallant ships, most bound for Malaga and the Straits, which will carry her out of all danger. I have done my endeavour here to accomplish your desires. The success we must leave to God; be it good or bad we must submit our wills to His.

Some 3 days since I received a letter from Mr Webber [the *Blessing*], dated at Pontevedra 16 Aug., who writ me that then had most part of his pilchards aboard and did hope to be gone by 20 ditto, according to his obligation. So that I trust in God is arrived with you by this time to a good occasion. By others which came from thence I understand he sold his goods for above 80 per cent profit, *vellon*, which is a good advance. Likewise his pilchards stood him but 1½*Rs* per m fresh, so that with curing, salt and all other charges, I believe they do not stand him in above 8*Rs* at most, *vellon*, so that he will make a good business of it and I hope you will do no less. But for the future I would not wish you to make any contract with him, but let the goods go from hence for your accounts, allowing him that does the business his commission, only let Mr Webber have a ⅛ part. Likewise I shall desire to have a share in the business for my account. Mr Webber writes me that if I had given him a credit for 11,000*Rs vellon* for Madrid according to your orders that then he had secured some pilchards for another voyage against Lent. To which I give answer that when Webber came home here it is well known that he was worth nothing, and I think we trust him with enough in delivering the goods with[out] any security for the performance. And besides that, we have the most part of the ship. Yet, if he had left his brother-in-law, as he told me he would, at Galicia, I would have remitted effects, but he advised me that he carried him with him for Tenerife. I pray give him a

23

quick dispatch that he may be home one of the first, which will come to a good market if bring rare liquors, and pray think of some employment whereby to send him out again.

23b. Per advice I have received a letter from Mr Brampton [the *Matthew*] of his safe arrival at Newfoundland, dated 21 July, who writes me that had disposed of all his wine at £13, £14 and £15 per pipe to take fish at 23 and 24*Rs* per kt and that then had taken in about 600 kts of fish and that the fish which I had bought here would be punctually delivered according to contract, and withal writes me that was in great hopes to be dispatched out of the land one of the first. Mr Davies of Bilbao is here at present, who is now going there overland, who hath promised me that Brampton shall have a quick dispatch and likewise will endeavour much for speedy sale of the fish, for I have told him I conceive you will have occasion to value yourselves on them for the proceeds thereof suddenly. I doubt the market there and all other ports in Spain will be overlaid with codfish in Spain this year in regard all the ships that were to go for Lisbon, Oporto and other places in Portugal are now designed for Spain in regard we have now wars with King John.

I wonder I have received no letters from you by Mr Avery nor Mr Cruchman via Topsham. I hope ere this time you are satisfied that it was no neglect of mine in not writing you per Peter Steward, but rather a knavery of theirs [i.e. Wilson, Bradgate and Turner. Cf. **22d**] to keep away my letters. Indeed I do not much admire at it in regard it is no novelty of Mr John Turner to do so.

I gave Mr Jewell order not to stay upon the Barbary Coast above a month although he came [to Tenerife] a small part empty, otherwise I should have sent a greater cargazon in the ship but that I was very doubtful that it might be a hindrance to the ship's sudden dispatch. Most of our grand traders here do admire that I have freighted so many ships for you and do not a little envy at me to see that I do outsell them in prices of wines, which hath made them rail at their factors [in Tenerife] to the purpose. I have now gotten the chiefest vintners in London to my customers, many of the old Rowland's [i.e. Rowland Wilson's] which if I have good wines, I know they will not buy a pipe of him. A good fame here is worth 20s in a pipe, which I have got this year. Therefore, I shall desire you to endeavour whereby I may keep it. The business only consists in good liquors. I need not mention this to neither of you, yet I cannot but give you a hint in regard it imports my credit and your profit. Repair not in 2 or 3Ds per pipe or in a little extraordinary payment. The market here will repay you with an advantage. For bad wines there will follow many inconveniences, first a torment to me and second I must be fain to sell them to such men as perhaps will never be able to pay half.

Now in case that you conceive the year to prove very bad, then better let out your tonnage or else forbear sending Brampton [the *Matthew*] home, all which I leave to your serious considerations. In the meantime I shall, according to your orders both now and hereafter, take notice of what you write concerning insurance for your accounts. Although I do not observe it in the Barbary man [i.e. the *Elizabeth*], blame me not, for I have given you my reasons, with which I hope you will rest satisfied however the business falls out. I shall now endeavour to insure your adventures homewards, which will cost somewhat dear, being our coast at present is very full of French men-of-war and likewise of Ostend men-of-war. And further I must tell you that many insurers of late have broken so that now it is a difficult thing to get in good men, but I doubt not but I shall do as well as others. I had almost forgot to give you notice of my agreement with Mr Jewell [supercargo on the *Elizabeth*]: he is to have 3 per cent for sale of the goods at Barbary and 3 per cent for employing the stock in corn. If you like this design, let him come home in the ship and then we will treat further. ...

[P.S.] After I had gone through with our ship for Barbary, then Mr Holle of Nantes wrote me that he would send a ship to you with corn and linens, the cargazon to be about £3,000, in which you should bear half. To which I gave answer I could not, being had engaged in the other design.

24. to William Clerke   10 Sept. 1650
   ... This instant here is arrived ships that lay off Lisbon which bring very sad tidings: all the English merchants are prisoners and their estates sequestrated and no hopes of composing the differences between us, so that here will be many merchants undone. I am very sorry for your brother Mr George Clerke who, I understand, was resident in Lisbon. Here are now this week 2 merchants broken, accounted formerly very sufficient men, but these unhappy differences with Portugal is the chief occasion of their absenting. Beware what bills you draw for R[obert] G[arland]'s account, for truly it is the opinion of most men that he cannot hold out, which you may please to keep to yourself, and the sooner you shake off, the better. I understand both he and Mr George Clerke [William Clerke's cousin] have charged you with a pretty quantity of tonnage in one Mr Henecker's ship, which I conceive is without your orders. ...

25. to William Clerke   20 Sept. 1650
a. Yesterday by great chance I received yours, 15 Aug., per a Fleming which put the letters ashore at the Isle of Wight, and being brought upon the Exchange to deliver, it was not my fortune to be there, so that my letters were catched up by some well-wishers to you and me. Hereafter I shall be able to give a better account, being now am upon searching out the truth.
   I perceive by yours of the scarce vintage you are like to have. How men will come off I know not. I am confident that you will say yourself that never [have] so many ships [come to Tenerife] as this year. I hope that you and Mr Paynter will comply with what tonnage I have charged on you in wines and West India goods. I have a policy made upon Brampton [the *Matthew*] from Tenerife home and have got this day underwritten £1,500 at 4 per cent, being for Mr Paynter's and your accounts in equal halves. Likewise with what formerly, I have £1,000 insured on Mr Webber [the *Blessing*] homewards for your accounts. I shall endeavour tomorrow to get £400 or £500 more done upon ditto ship and upon Mr Brampton near £1,000 more so that you will run no great adventures. As for the Barbary

25

ship [the *Elizabeth*, Capt. Shadforth], I shall forbear to have any insurance done on her homewards before I hear what you load on her and for whose accounts. Pray forbear sending any *leña noel* for I know not when I shall sell that which came in Mr [James] Blake [the *Constant John*]. Logwood worth £18 per t, and if no quantity come in, will hold its price; hides, 6½d per lb; ginger, £3 15s per cwt; cochineal mesteque, 32s per lb; campechena worth 6s 8d per lb; indigo, a drug, worth but 4s 6d per lb. Pray endeavour to send what wines you possibly can for your account for India goods hath no good vent at present. The vintage at Jerez and Malaga both will be very scarce this year as per late advice from thence, so that of necessity wines must be far dearer here than last year if that they prove but sound and clean. I make no question but those which you load will be of the choicest *puestos*. What designs you intend to have put in agitation for next year, pray give me timely advice.

25b. I hope ere this time our ship [the *Elizabeth*] is laden with corn at Barbary, of which I should be glad to hear 2 lines and of the proceedings of the voyage, as also what market it comes to at Tenerife. I shall endeavour what I can to buy the rest of the *Blessing* when a good opportunity offers. However, we having but $\frac{9}{16}$ parts, may send her where we please though the rest do not give their consents; the major part carries the votes. So that if you resolve to have her return back for the Islands after her arrival here, it shall be effected according to your orders. I am very glad you dispatched your Nantes linens in so good a time without any charges, which makes me admire that you durst adventure on so desperate a business. I hope your new [Capt.] General [Alonso Dávila y Guzmán who had arrived in June 1650] will be more accommodating than Don Pedro Carrillo [de Guzmán].

I perceive by yours that then you were upon dispatching Mr Henry Hawley for Barbados upon a small vessel which you bought there and have laden her with wines for your account. God bless her well to the desired port. May please to take notice that the Barbadians have about 3 months since declared for King Charles II and will not be subordinate to any officer that our State shall send over. So that here is now 8 ships making ready, which our States set out, to ply about that island to keep all provisions from them, whereby to reduce them to obedience, which I conceive they will do in a very short time. So that until then there will be no safe trading for you to that island, they being now in a tumultuous way, everyone his own master. I am informed that your wines will come to a gallant market. I intend tomorrow to write Mr Hawley via Amsterdam whereby he may understand how business goes here. All those which declare for the Parliament in the island are banished and their estates sequestrated, which may serve per advice.

By yours I understand that you have procured a licence for 300 camels under the King of Spain's own hand, which in my opinion is a great privilege.[1] You must have a good ship to carry them. Mr Garvis Russell is now building a frigate [the *Katherine*] just of the same length and breadth that Sidrake Blake's is, which will be a fit vessel and man for such design. Mr Paynter and myself do hold a small part with him, being I know him to be an honest, diligent man. He is very desirous that you should be one of his owners but told me that would not be so bold as to write you, having no great acquaintance, so hath enjoined me to write you about it.

What letters Mr Hawley sends under my covert for you shall be sent forward with care per first opportunity. I shall do my part from hence in writing him the needful; and if he send me those blacks you write of, I shall send them over to you per first with the dispatch you desire. If Mr Hawley do want any monies, I shall supply him to the quantity you write me if need require, on which you may depend. Nothing shall be wanting in me for furthering your designs, neither money nor diligence.

You write me of some encloseds which you desire me to deliver with care, being they import you. I opening your letter find not a letter for any man, which makes me conceive that you left them out. You desire to be resolved concerning France and us. They give commissions to take English ships, and our States give the like to take theirs. And yet they make no embargoes of late upon the English merchants' estates which are there resident. How long it will hold so I know not, but in my opinion a man's estate is not safe there.

The enclosed is from Mr Bradick, unto whom I have given your message. But he is so taken up in wooing a gentlewoman that he scarce minds anything else. ...

1. Paige writes nothing more about importing camels, which were used as beasts of burden in Tenerife. But he tried to procure a licence allowing the importation of 300 black slaves into Tenerife (**42, 44**). And he attempted to hire Russell's ship for a slaving voyage to Guinea (**40c**).

26. to William Clerke   15 Nov. 1650
a. I have received yours, 20 Sept., via Amsterdam per Mr Thomas Yardley; the contents perused. I have written you per this conveyance a joint letter at large, to which partly refer you. By great chance this morning I had notice of this conveyance via Falmouth. My time being short, cannot give answer in full to your letter according to your desire, the post going away this night, which I hope will be sufficient to excuse me. As yet I hear no news of Mr Hawley's arrival at Barbados. There is a ship now in Plymouth newly arrived from thence. I have written down about it to make inquiry.

I have sold 3 chests of your campechena at 7s 6d per lb, a price that none hath been sold at this 7 years. I have to abate discount for the money. The other chest is promised at ditto rate. The *leña noel* is all in cellar; neither do I know when shall sell a t of it. None makes inquiry after it. Therefore, pray send no more. I am doubtful you will have a dead loss on this. Your indigos are all unsold save 4 chests which I sold last week at 5s 2d per lb garbled. They are a very drug, being great quantities in the City at present, especially the East India Company's. I shall do my utmost endeavour to dispose of the rest as soon as may be.

I must crave your pardon in not being so good as my word to send you your accounts, which I shall now go about very suddenly. I have of late been hindered somewhat of my business in regard of my removal to a house which I have taken. I am glad you have put your money business in so good a posture that you were to have it in with 20 days, which in my opinion, as the times now govern there, is a mighty business, insomuch that you may do what you will, having such a considerable sum.

It seems by Steward's report you were doubtful where the ship which he left upon the Barbary Coast were ours [the *Elizabeth*] or no. I am glad that you are now resolved of the doubt and that she comes to so good an occasion at both places. Indeed I made haste after I received your advice. Seeing I could not get it no other ways, I freighted the ship and bought up the cargazon and cleared her from Gravesend all in 10 days time. I hope the staying of our fleet will prove advantageous to you.

26b. I cannot give you a satisfactory answer concerning the orchil which you write of. I have writ into Holland about it but have no answer about it. I perceive by yours that the next spring there will be good quantities of West India goods with you, which goods both here and at Holland are sold at low rates at present. Per advice ginger worth £3 10s per cwt; hides at 6½d per lb; Campeachy wood at £18 per t (it is now a free commodity here provided you pay £3 10s per t custom); campechena, if any come from Spain, it will not be worth above 6s 8d to 7s per lb; indigo, no hopes of exceeding 4s 6d per lb; sylvester a worse drug; cochineal mesteque worth 32s per lb if very good; Varinas tobacco worth 5s 6d per lb if right.

I have written you in the joint letter how we stand affected with France. Spain and we are very good friends and like to continue in regard we plague the Portuguese which, you know, is a rebel as they account him.

Your letter to Mr George Clerke [William's cousin] and Mr [Stephen] Slaney I have delivered with the other for Exeter. I do admire I have no letters from Bilbao of Brampton's [the *Matthew*'s] arrival there, yet I do not any way doubt of his well-being because I have advice that he went out of Newfoundland in company with 6 ships more. I have paid his bills for 1,800 kts of fish which he received there per my order.

I am very sorry to be the messenger of such ill tidings unto you, yet I cannot but acquaint you of it, whereby you may order your business accordingly. The ship *Robert and John*, Mr Presman, is taken by a Jersey man-of-war coming from Newfoundland to Bilbao with his lading of fish and is now brought into Jersey. This day came home one of his men which brought the news. Now for your comfort I went this afternoon to the insurance office and searched the register book where I found one policy upon ditto ship insured by George Clerke for his and your accounts £900; another which he made for £200 more which was for *bomaria* [bottomry] money; likewise another, a policy which Mr Garland put in, wherein he insured his full interest, so that I hope will be no great loss to you. This I thought good to acquaint you because peradventure you may keep her lading there in expectation of the ship's coming. I am now in expectation of the *Blessing* and *Elizabeth*. God send them well. ...

27. to Gowen Paynter and William Clerke   15 Nov. 1650
a. I have received yours, 14 Oct., per Mr Steward, perceiving thereby that Mr Shadforth [the *Elizabeth*] and Mr Webber [the *Blessing*] were both arrived with you, for which I am hearty glad, giving the Lord praise for it. I do now expect them daily, God send them well to arrive. The times are very dangerous. Prince Rupert is come out of Lisbon with 24 sail and hath

taken 2 or 3 ships from Malaga. He lies off the southern cape. God grant he send none about your Islands. Insurance is very high upon the news, but I had done most of mine before the tidings came. I have insured for your accounts on the *Matthew* from the Canaries to London £2,500 at 4 per cent, and on the *Blessing* I have insured £1,500 for your accounts in equal halves at 4 per cent. Likewise I have insured on the *Elizabeth* £2,150 in the proportion as I freighted her. When Mr Warren was upon the Barbary Coast and taken by the French,[1] he writ me of his mischance and the danger that Peter Steward [the *Island Merchant*] escaped, upon which I was very doubtful of Mr Shadforth. So that I presently caused £800 to be insured on him for our accounts from hence to Barbary and so to the Canaries, for which I gave 6 per cent and glad it was done so, which, as it falls out, is so much money cast away, but I hope our voyage will bear it. I am very glad that my project hath list [i.e. pleased] so well, hoping that our corn will sell very well.

Mr Steward's wines prove but reasonable, small, green wines. They have neither body nor richness, but they are clean and sound, which is a good property. The Malaga fleet is arrived here, which [wines] prove excellent, cost there 700*Rs* per butt put aboard, a price that was never known. The vintners have of late met at their hall and have combined not to exceed £20 or £21 per pipe or butt of wine this year, upon which Mr Wilson hath not sold a pipe of wine of Steward's lading. Malagas, there are a few sold at £24 per butt; Jerez prove very well this year but not the quarter part made as in former years. Likewise Malaga fails of above half the quantity as it gave other years. So that of necessity wines will be a good commodity if they prove excellent. But I must tell you the vintners must of needs break to give these prices, yet they draw Canary at 9d per pint. Here is now an act of Parliament come forth that whereas we formerly paid 33s 8d per pipe custom, we are now to pay 42s 8d per pipe, which will be no small matter out of our ways.[2] They pretend it is for keeping and maintaining of convoys for our ships, which they say we shall have hereafter to go out with our merchantmen to your ports. I hope you bought up all your wines before our grand fleet arrived there, by which you will save above £1,000 in the prices, considering the quantities you both are to load.

1. In 1651 Thomas Warren testified in the Admiralty Court that the *William and Henry*, on which he had served as factor, had earlier been taken by a French man-of-war off Mogador (H.C.A. 13/64, 28 April 1651).

2. 'An Act for settled convoys', 31 Oct. 1650 (Firth and Rait, ii, 444).

27b. The times are so dangerous at present and like to be worse daily, that for the future I would not wish you to adventure your estates in small ships because there will be no insurance done upon them at any rates. I admire that I have no news of Mr Brampton's [the *Matthew*'s] arrival at Bilbao, which I impute to the master's neglect and Mr Davies [Paige's correspondent at Bilbao]. At present we have no trade with France, neither have we proclaimed wars with them; but I believe it will not hold long before we have. They take all English that ever they met withal, and we do the like by them, so that the poor merchant suffers on both sides.

I here send you 2 acts of Parliament. The one is that we have open wars with Portugal and the other is that the Barbadians are proclaimed rebels to our State for revolting and not being subordinate to the present government.[1] Here is now going a fleet of 10 ships to subdue them to obedience if they can. Here is at present above 20 sail of French prizes brought in, the major part of them laden with codfish. Likewise here is 6 Brazilmen brought in which have 4,500 chests of sugar, besides 2 more left at Cadiz which are sold there. So that we have now almost all nations to be our enemies, God in mercy look upon us and help us. The Prince of Orange is dead as per advice from Holland last post. What business you will have done by me for the future, pray give me timely advice per all conveyances because things cannot be done with that facility as in former times.

I have nothing more to enlarge at present until I hear from you. I shall be put hard to it to pay customs and freight of my wines this year. I must of necessity make use of the usurer's bags, the charges will be so much. I have put a friend to pump the owners of [the *Blessing*], Mr Webber, but they're now somewhat unwilling to sell. They say they will not pick a price till she come home, God sending her well. I shall use such a way as that I doubt not but to buy her reasonable; otherwise I shall vex them, being I have power to send the ship where I please whether they will or no, hav[ing] the major part.

I had last week letters from San Lucar wherein they write me that the King of Spain hath put out a proclamation that all pieces of eight of Peru stamp shall pass but for 5*Rs* per piece, in regard that sort of coin is found to be generally false.[2] Although you are seldom troubled with overmuch cash, yet I would advise you to clear yourself of that coin, for I am confident the proclamation will be suddenly with you, which may serve per advice. Mr [John] Turner's principal, Mr Martin Bradgate, is grown distracted of late.[3] ...

1. 'An Act for making ships and merchandizes taken . . . from the King of Portugal or any of his subjects to be prize', 8 Nov. 1650 (Firth and Rait, ii, 449); 'An Act for prohibiting trade with the Barbadoes, Virginia, Bermuda and Antego', 3 Oct. 1650 (Ibid., 425).
2. Spanish officials had discovered that *reales* recently minted in Peru were of defective fineness. By royal proclamation of 1 Oct. 1650, owners of such coins were allowed two months to have them cut in half or refined and recoined or to exchange them for Castilian or Mexican *reales* at the ratio of 8 to 5 (E. J. Hamilton, *American Treasure and the Price Revolution in Spain* (Cambridge, Mass., 1934), 68–9).
3. In May 1652, a London merchant reported that Martin Bradgate had recently died after 'having somewhat long lain by his weakness and disturbance in his head' (C. 110/151, Richard Best to John Turner, 11 May 1652).

28. to William Clerke   6 Dec. 1650

... I have written you at large in my joint letter, to which desire reference. These chiefly serve to give you notice 3 days since the enclosed came to my hands, which was welcome news to me to hear of his [Henry Hawley's] safe arrival [at Barbados]. He writ me very briefly, referring me to the next conveyance. So I can say little, only writ me that if possible he would send me those Negroes which you wrote me of, wherein I shall observe your order when they come. I perceive Mr Hawley intended speedily to dispatch from Barbados, being sensible of the dangers which may approach upon the islanders, in which he does very wisely in my opinion. Here is come an agent from the islanders [George Marten, emissary of Francis, Lord Willoughby] to treat with our State, which as yet hath no audience. But it is hoped by many that there will be an accommodation; God grant it. ...

29. to Gowen Paynter and William Clerke   12 Dec. 1650

This very instant I received letters from the Isle of Wight, wherein have advice from Mr Webber [the *Blessing*] as also from Mr Shadforth [the *Elizabeth*] of their safe arrival; God be praised for it and make us thankful. Canary wines are sold at £24 per pipe, I mean those which prove good according to the year. I have received no letters from you per the ships as yet. Therefore have nothing to an[swer] until they come to hand, being writ you last post via Amsterdam per Mr. Yardley as also per one Mr Thomas Wright. This goes overland to Bilbao, which is a tedious, uncertain conveyance, yet I thought good to adventure these few lines. [P.S.] The dead tonnage this year and small returns will make many of our Canary merchants go to Ram Alley. A list of ships arrived: Mr Steward, Sydrakeson the Fleming, Mr Hoptkins, Mr Bradick, Mr Hayes, Mr Sheere, Mr Casby, Mr Young, Mr Rouse, Mr Bankes, Mr Newman, Mr Shadforth and Mr Webber.

30. to Gowen Paynter and William Clerke   15 Feb. 1651

a. I have received yours, 14 Oct., per Mr Steward to which have partly given answer via Amsterdam per Mr Thomas Yardley, who I hope is safe arrived with you ere this time, where I have given you notice of the safe arrival here of the ship *Elizabeth* and likewise the *Blessing*. May please to take notice that I have sold all the wines that came in ditto ships, save 6 pipes which are not merchantable, at £25 per pipe, ⅓ money, the rest at 3 and 3 months [see **11b** note]; only I am to abate £14 upon one great parcel which I sold some winecoopers.

The sale of said wines did give me much anxiety unto whom I did let them go, the times being crazy at present especially for vintners, as some will find to their cost before this year goes about. For those which I have sold unto, I do not anyway doubt of their performance, which is no small heart's ease to me. My ambition this year was not so much for prizes as good able men. But to tell you the truth, the wines were not so good as I did expect, insomuch that many of my old customers bought of old Rowland Wilson who hath had two ships of very rare liquors. Rouse's ship's lading were all sold at £27 per pipe and Mr Audley's ship's lading was sold at £29 per pipe ready money. Indeed they were the best wines that ever I tasted. As I am informed, they were Don Alonso de Lugo's, Bartolomé de Ponte's, Juan de Mesa's, and Diego de Benítez'. I do admire that Mr [John] Turner's wines should so exceed yours and all other men's in proof above £5 per pipe. The company [i.e. Henry St John, Rowland Wilson and Martin Bradgate] is now sending Peter Steward [the *Island Merchant*] for San Lucar with a cargazon of £14,000. From thence he carries pieces of eight for Tenerife as I am told. I believe their drift is to

31

engross all the choice *puestos* in the Island (the word came from one of the company's mouths here), yet I question not but others may have a small share with them. I do admire you did not make better use of the opportunity which you had in having 2 ships there so timely and not buying their lading before the fleet's arrival. I am confident you might have saved in price above £1,500 what you gave afterwards, but now it's too late to recall what hath been omitted.

I perceive you have sent Mr Brampton [the *Matthew*] for the Barbary Coast. I have paid £300 for men's wages and am now suddenly to pay the other £300 to the owners. I have motioned to some of them for 4 months' time longer upon the ship if need require, which I am partly promised by some, so hope shall send you an order about it per next conveyance. I have paid the master's bills of exchange here for 1,850 kts fish which he received in Newfoundland by my order.

I cannot but give you a hint of the general proof of wines this year. Garachico proved the worst; Rambla had better bodies though green; Carrera and Realejos both green and small bodies. Orotava malmseys prove the only wines both this year and the last. Though there have come home but few, yet there are above 1,500 pipes unsold. The ablest vintners will not meddle with ordinary wines if they can have good wines for love or money. Jerez wines prove pretty good, and for Malagas, they prove extraordinary rich, worth more money than Canary at present. I am confident that if you do not beat down the Islanders in price that vintners cannot hold to give such prices another year. I have not had the fortune this year to have one good parcel of wines, insomuch that I have partly lost my fame with the grand vintners, whereas last year none so much in their books as I was. But I hope next year you will endeavour to vindicate my credit again by loading some rare liquors. Though but few, yet will be more acceptable than a great quantity ordinary.

30b. If you can with convenience, I would wish you to keep Brampton out till next vintage rather than to send him home with India goods, they being much out of request at present and here are great quantities expected home daily from San Lucar, being the *Nueva España* fleet and the galleons are both arrived very rich, worth 25,000,000 [*Rs*]. The most part of the pieces of eight are Peru coin, which breeds great difference [see **27b**]. I did insure £2,500 on Brampton homewards this vintage; but seeing he came not, I have taken it off again for $\frac{1}{2}$ per cent. Wheat is very dear both here, France and Holland, and likewise in the Eastland, Danzig, so I conceive no great quantity will be shipped for your parts. God sending Brampton well back to you with his lading, I question not but you will make a gallant business of it. I am told you intend at his return back from the [Barbary] Coast to send him for Ireland with some *vidueño* wines, which you may do well to forbear that design because wines are no commodity there at present, being overlaid with Jerez and refuse wines from hence.

Of late, by very great chance, I have discovered a knavery that was shown us by Shadforth [the *Elizabeth*] when he was loading at Rambla. It seems they staved a pipe of wine of ours which the master never made you acquainted withal, but he and his men very orderly mended up the pipe and went and overdrew at least 15 pipes to fill up the other. To give you the relation how I came first to discover it will be too tedious, but he being gone for Newcastle, I was fain to enter an action against 2 of his men and had them in the counter 3 days till at last they discovered the truth to me, so that I shall make Shadforth pay dearly for it ere we are ended. It seems Shadforth made a protest against you for not giving him his full lading. To avoid vexation we put it to arbitration, who awarded me to pay him £18 for 5 ts. He swore point blank that he could have carried 15 ts more, which carried the business against me, but I shall cry quits with him ere long.

I have received from Mr Jewell [supercargo on the *Elizabeth*] an account of our Barbary voyage which is far short of what I expected. He writes me that you are mightily well contented with it. For my part I am not. I have questioned John Clarke [pilot of the *Elizabeth*] how several things were sold (who, I conceive, knows very well), who informs me of much more than Mr Jewell makes us good, which he will depose upon oath if occasion. As for example, the guns he makes good at 4Ds and Clarke swears that they were sold at 4½Ds, which is £50 upon that one parcel. Now I am loath to question a man but that it is unsufferable. What makes me to have a jealousy is that he carries out [for his own account] but 25 guns from hence, which I spared him, and nothing else; now the proceeds of them and his commission could never load so much corn as to come to 27 pipes wine which he loaded in Shadforth. Pray give me 2 words advice per first how many *fanegas* wheat he brought for his account. As I am informed the ⅙ part was for his account.

Mr Warren hath bought a ship of 200 ts and intends for the Barbary Coast about June or July. This ship was entered for San Sebastian in a politic way, so that I knew not of her going till yesterday. By the next I shall be more larger, which I conceive will be a month hence by our State's fleet which are bound for Barbados, being in all 10 sail of gallant ships which intend to stop at Santa Cruz [de Tenerife] to refresh and take in some wine for beverage. ...

31. to William Clerke   17 Feb. 1651
a. I have received yours, 18 and 30 Dec., per Capt. William Pyle [the *Swan*] and Mr Audley. My last unto you was via Holland per Mr Thomas Yardley, where I wrote you the needful. I have written you and Mr Paynter at large per this conveyance of your joint business, to which desire reference, under which covert I sent you a letter which I received from Mr Henry Hawley. He writes me that he sold his wines very well and hopes to make a good business, for which I am very glad. He writes me that he sold the small vessel which he went in [from Tenerife to Barbados] and that after sale of her is now demanded of some which have power to stop her at Barbados, so is like to have some trouble about the business. He writes me to stop the proceeds of 10 pipes wines which you should have consigned me in account, ditto vessel, which I conceive you did not load by reason of the scarce year. I have written Mr Hawley to get himself out of the island before our State's fleet comes there. He advises shall have no occasion to value himself on me for your account, which agrees

with your desires. I doubt he cannot send those blackamoors which you desire to have.

I perceive by yours the oversight in not buying up your wines before the fleet came in was chiefly committed by Mr Paynter's covetousness, which I am sorry for it, not knowing when you may have the like opportunity again. In case that Brampton [the *Matthew*] come from the Barbary Coast with his lading wheat, you may keep up the price, for I durst say there will none go from Holland nor France any. The Eastland is frozen up.

The bills of lading for the wine in Shadforth [the *Elizabeth*] and Webber [the *Blessing*] came in the same conformity and for ditto accounts as they went out for. Whereas you desire to know the particular proof of each ship's wines, the truth is Shadforth's were the better bodied wines, but they were bad enough both, being very green, not so good as Mr Wilson's wines by £5 per pipe. Likewise Mr St John's proved pretty wines and also those which you loaded for Mr [Stephen] Slaney's account in the *Champion* proved better wines than those which I had by £3 per pipe. ...

31b. Good hides worth at 6d per lb; ginger, £3 10s per cwt; Campeachy wood worth, clear of charges here, £15 per t; cochineal mesteque worth 32s per lb; campechena at 6s 6d per lb; sylvester not worth sending; indigo garbled, 4s to 4s 4d per lb; Varinas tobacco is risen within this 10 days, worth at present 6s 6d per lb if right. In the 2 fleets that are come to San Lucar there are not 200 chests and that worth nothing, being half rotten, sold at 10*Rs* per lb. I have written into Holland about the orchil, who write me that 300 kts will cloy that country, there being no vent for it. What I shall advise you is to secure some good *puestos* against next year, which I conceive will turn better to account by far than any other goods that you can send.

I have now advice from Lisbon of the Brazil fleet's arrival there with 35,000 chests of sugar; so that of necessity they will be cheap all over Christendom, that quantity being enough for all nations. The [English] merchants [in Portugal] are all out of prison upon bail. I have advice that hides are worth there from 3,000 to 3,500 *réis* which is money enough. There's great hopes that our States and their ambassador here [Guimãres] will conclude a peace. As soon as it's effected I shall advise you and, if you please, I will bear a share with you on a design that way. I have yet one chest of campechena left and the indigos, save a few which I formerly writ you of that I sold. The times are very dangerous, which makes all commodities at a stand; nothing doth off so well as good tipple. The *leña noel* is all unsold.

I have paid your bill of exchange for £45 in favour of Mr Leonard Clerke as soon as ever I received your letter per Mr Audley. The very next day I remitted Mr Richard Baker of Madrid a bill of exchange for 12,000*Rs plata doble* to be paid by himself after 30 days' sight, which bill I conceive may be in Madrid within this 20 days being 15 days since that I sent it per post overland, first and second bill. In my opinion I have it upon very good terms, considering the value of pieces of eight here: I gave 8 per cent. Now I must confess I could have remitted my money for Antwerp at double usance, and from thence to Madrid at double usance, and have saved 4 per cent. But then it would have been 5 months before the money would have grown due, which peradventure might have proved [a] prejudice to your affairs. So I thought rather to remit it directly from hence and not to run the risks of several men's bills. I think there have not broken so many merchants this 7 years as within this 6 months past, and yet I doubt many more will follow. Amongst them are 2 Canary traders, by name Mr Henry Lee, brother to Robert Lee at Mr Campion's; likewise Mr Norton the packer, partner to Mr William Clapham, is broke for £12,000. Several other men I could name, but it will be too tedious. I conceive in the order which you gave me about remitting the money to Mr Baker you did mistake; your letter mentions but £3 sterling, but I conceive your meaning was £300. You being a friend and I having confidence that you will allow of what I have done, made me not to waive the business so much as I should have done were it another's. Therefore, pray per first give a confirmation to what I have acted.

31c. I shall excuse you to Lawrence Browning in the best manner I can when he comes home, the poor man being a prisoner in Ireland, was betrayed ashore, he putting in there coming from the Canaries. God sending me life and health this summer, I will both draw out your account and all men's else. I am sorry that you should be so long without yours, but for the future I shall be punctualler in that particular. It's an old proverb and very true: short accounts makes long friends.

I wish that you may continue your resolutions of what you writ me about, that is to act no man's business but your own, which I conceive enough to employ any reasonable man. If so be that you had laden those wines which you have shipped for Mr [Stephen] Slaney's account and others for your own account these last 2 years, I believe you might have had £3,000 more in your purse than you have, which the commission comes not to £300. I have given Mr Paynter a hint about the same, which I hope he will take into consideration and not plunge himself into engagements for a poor 3 per cent. And besides that, there is another inconveniency: in regard that you load quantities for your own accounts, if so be that yours prove anything better than your principal's, then you are presently exclaimed on. So that considering all things rightly, you had better give 3 per cent to be rid of business, than to have it in these times.

Here is mighty great preparation making for next year for the Canaries, especially by way of Spain, chiefly to carry pieces of eight from thence. Likewise here will go from hence quantities of goods in James Blake [the *Constant John*], which is now entered in the Custom House for the Canaries. What encouragement they have I know not. I perceive you have taken to freight our small bark, the *Susan* [Capt. Giles Paynter], at such a rate as I doubt will hardly find victuals and pay men's wages. I take notice you have bought 80 pipes wines in Garachico for several years, which, if the price be accommodating, I hold it well done in regard you say they will be ready with the first to be shipped, which will be no small advantage to you in their sales. I should be very glad to hear of the *Susan's* arrival at Bilbao, in regard you have so great an interest. If your order comes, I shall make some assurance on her.

I am informed by a friend that Mr Bradick and Mr Richard Lant have broken their partnership. I have long looked for it, therefore do not much admire at it. He [Lant] being a man of a malicious spirit, there are no words bad enough for you. I never knew a man bear such a perfect hatred to one as he does to you, but it's an old saying that cursed cows commonly have short horns. I think you need not much care for what he can do to you, yet threatens that if ever you come home he will order you. Formerly he did pretend to be my very great friend, but now I am out of his books.

Sir, as a loving friend I cannot but acquaint you of my late change from a bachelor to an honest man: I have married Mr [Gowen] Paynter's daughter [Katherine]. Wishing your presence to honour us, but nevertheless seeing could not enjoy the happiness, have emboldened to present you a pair of gloves, as accustomary, desiring you to wear them for my sake. When God sends you well home, I shall be ready to do the like for you. ...

32. to Gowen Paynter and William Clerke   6 March 1651

I have written you at large per this ship both particularly and jointly, to which desire reference. The occasion of my writing to you at present is chiefly to give you notice that I have received yours copy [of] 19 Jan. and 30 ditto, via Bristol, which came to my hands this instant. The original of 19 Jan., which I conceive came by Mr Oliver, is miscarried, he being taken by 3 Jersey men-of-war and carried into Scilly, so that I know not what goods to send for Mr William Clerke's account, being the memory is lost. But I hope by Capt. Cramp shall have it, otherwise I desire may have order per first what to do.

According to your earnest desire I have motioned the business to Mr Brampton's [the *Matthew*'s] owners here for 4 months' time longer above the 20 months which I formerly hired her, who have granted my request, Mr Richard Hill and Mr Murwill by name. If this ship stay but 4 days longer I shall send you their order to that purpose, they having writ down to Dover to the rest of their owners to sign it. Of this you may be confident, to which purpose Mr Richard Hill hath written the master per this conveyance, as he tells me, of which you may acquaint Mr Brampton.

I shall endeavour to get Mr Clerke's assurance done on the *Susan* [Capt. Giles Paynter] from Tenerife to Bilbao and back, which I doubt will be at 10 per cent. I have letters, 18 Feb., from Bilbao. Then she was not arrived; God send her well at last. Here is a ship now going for Bilbao per which via shall write you a few lines, and likewise tomorrow I intend to send a letter via Nantes by one Mr Salter which is there in Cruchman's ship, bound for Tenerife laden with linens and pipestaves consigned to Mr Stephens and Body. Here is now ready at Gravesend Peter Steward [the *Island Merchant*] and our ship [the *Mary*], Mr Chalke, both bound for San Lucar, from thence to the [Canary] Islands. As I conceive, here's great preparation making for next vintage via Spain notwithstanding I have shown your letter to several whereby they may see the misery that is befalling them Islands if so be that rain do not fall speedily. Pray when Brampton arrives, let me know what success you have had in the voyage, where he brings corn [from the Barbary Coast] or no. Here is this day advice from Seville that the sickness begins at Gibraltar again, so that is much feared it will break out again in those parts this summer. ...

33. to William Clerke   15 March 1651

... I have received yours, 19 Jan., copy, via Bristol. The original is miscarried, which seems came by Mr Oliver. In ditto letter you mentioned something of a memory for some goods which you desire I should send you. Had you sent the memory with the copy letter, I should have made them ready to send with the first, but now I am blindfolded, not knowing your will. But I hope by Capt. Cramp you will enlarge, whereby I may be able to comply with your desires.

I have now made a policy upon the *Susan*, hoping to get it done for 9 per cent. If Mr Davies and Ackland [Paige's correspondents at Bilbao] had order to give me advice, perhaps it might save you money, for I am persuaded she is arrived, as I learn by a shipmaster that came from thence. But I, having no certainty, durst not forbear making your insurance upon such a slender report.

Per advice, Varinas tobacco is risen much of late, worth at present 7s per lb if right, and I am confident it will rather rise than fall. In case that you can have hides cheap, as I believe you will, I conceive it will turn to account, if freight cheap, to send some here to land at Dover and so to ship them for Lisbon, if you send none from thence thither. I make no question but we shall have a peace with Portugal very speedily. I have endeavoured of late much to sell off your *leña noel* which dries very much up, insomuch that it is worse for the stillers. The longer it's kept the less it is worth for their use, and warehouse room is very chargeable, so that if I can get £12 or £13 per t I am resolved not to keep it. There are but 3 men in town that buy the commodity. Mr Bulkley sells at £10 and £11 per t and tells them he hath great quantities in the Canaries. And for your indigos, they daily fall, are scarce worth 4s 6d per lb garbled, so that now I wish had taken our first market. All commodities at present are at a fall. Trade is much decayed and in these uncertain times we know not whom to trust, being weekly we hear of some or other break. I am informed that your hides [on the *Susan*] for Bilbao will come to a good occasion. ...

[P.S.] If you write Mr Hawley, the bearer hereof, Mr [Abraham] Langford [who is going in the fleet for Barbados] I know will endeavour to deliver it him, if possible to be done.

34. to Gowen Paynter and William Clerke   15 March 1651

... [L]ittle or nothing hath offered worth your notice, only at this present our States and the Portuguese ambassador are upon the matter agreed, which if the business take effect, I shall write you via Bilbao. I have advice from Lisbon hides are worth from 3,000 to 3,500 *réis* per hide, which is a great price. If so be you have no employment for Brampton [the *Matthew*] at his return from Barbary, it would be a good design to send him for Lisbon with hides and 20 ts logwood. A small vessel's lading of West India goods would vent pretty well in Nantes at present, as Mr Holle writes me. Linens were never cheaper this 7 years than they are now in France. All sorts of West India goods here are drugs, no vent at all for them. Varinas tobacco is risen much within this month, worth at present 7s per lb if good, and I am confident will rather rise than fall. Ginger garbled worth £3 15s per cwt. For all other commodities, not worth sending.

Here enclosed I send you a brief letter from Mr Brampton's chief owner, Mr Richard Hill, who gives him order for 3 or 4 months' time more, if so be that you please to keep him out, I having agreed with the owners for said time to pay after the rate of our charter-party, £85 per mensem.

Here is Mr James Blake [the *Constant John*] now making ready to be gone for the Canaries within this month, who will go as full of pack-goods as ever he can stow for several men. What encouragement other men have I know not. I am sure you give none to send goods. ...

35. to William Clerke   25 March 1651
... [H]ere is arrived Capt. Cramp per whom had advice you have let out Mr Brampton [the *Matthew*] to come home, which in my opinion have done very well. Better do so than keep her out upon monthly pay upon uncertain employments. I am sorry the Barbary voyage [of the *Matthew* for wheat] proves so unsuccessful. May please to take notice that I have made insurance for your account upon the *Susan* for Bilbao and back for 8 per cent, which I think is pretty reasonable considering her burden and force. There's insured £700; I hope tomorrow to get the other £100 underwritten.

Per advice Varinas tobacco rises daily, worth at present 7s 6d per lb if right. The enclosed came to my hands yesterday. Mr Hawley [who is sailing from Barbados in the *Medea* with sugars] writes me that he will be speedily in Amsterdam if pleases God. Mr Blake may be ready to go hence for Tenerife a month after the date hereof, in which ship [the *Constant John*] I would have sent you your goods if could have a memory, which I hope will come per Mr Brampton. In the interim I shall provide the ozenbrigs and hounscots which your letter specifies. This I send down to Plymouth per post. ...

36. to William Clerke   4 April 1651
... I have written you and Mr Paynter at large per this conveyance under covert Mr Ackland and company [of Bilbao]. I have this instant advice of the *Susan*'s arrival at Bilbao. The insurance was done out and home for £800. As yet no news [from] Mr Henry Hawley. ...

37. to Gowen Paynter and William Clerke   8 April 1651
... Mr Brampton [the *Matthew*] is now unladen and going to be girdled in the dock. I shall endeavour to freight him per t and send him you at vintage for our accounts, empty, except I receive your order to the contrary for corn. I am confident there will go such quantities that it will be very cheap with you, being every man hath order for that commodity. I do now daily expect answer of my letters from Middelburg where I have given express order to buy up 80 or 90 ts wheat, which I am confident will be effected. [William] Webber is making ready his ship [the *Blessing*] with all expedition that possibly can be. I doubt not but shall dispatch him hence within this week, God sending him well to Middelburg. He will be laden in 3 days so that you may depend upon his coming, God sending him in safety. The corn shall go for our accounts, but, if you please, I

desire to have no interest in the Newfoundland fish [Clerke and Paynter intend to send the *Blessing* on to Newfoundland] because I have made a kind of promise never to deal in that rotten commodity. I shall buy 1,400 kts which, I conceive, will load her. If you excuse me of the fish, I shall take it as a courtesy, of which I desire your answer per first.

Cramp's wines, laden by Mr [John] Turner, prove but ordinary; likewise those which Mr [John] Webber loaded in Brampton are but little better. At the first of the year they would have yielded £25 per pipe, but now I am confident they will not yield £21 per pipe, wines being fallen within this 2 months £5 per pipe, notwithstanding there have no quantities come home this year from Malaga, Jerez [or] the Canaries of what hath come in former times, which you will admire at. All the reason I can give is that we have here very sad times and little money going. Wines being drawn at 10d a pint, men do give over drinking it, and the vintners do very much complain of their draughts. They pay their money very slowly. I do begin to find it so, at least. Except you send very rare liquors next year, they will not turn to account as you do expect. You may be assured the vintners cannot give the prices this year to come as they did the last. All those men which have their wines upon their hands unsold will not get by £5 per pipe for them as much as they were offered at first of year, which is no small loss. I am glad all yours are disposed of. I hope I shall be well paid for them though I believe long after the dates appointed for payment.

I never knew men break so fast as now, insomuch that makes all trade at a stand. One man durst not trust another. Per advice from Amsterdam, Mr Isaac Ellis is broken for near £15,000, they having his person in prison, upon which here broke 2 merchants of this city; men that were engaged for him deeply are now utterly undone.

The fleet which was bound to reduce Barbados have now given over their design, as I understand, which is what I have to say at present. This goes per a small Southampton man which is now at Plymouth, as my cousin John Paige advises me. ...

38. to Gowen Paynter and William Clerke   10 April 1651
... I have written you at large per this via already, to which desire reference. Mr James Blake [the *Constant John*] may be ready to go hence for Tenerife within this 10 days, per whom shall advise you the needful. Mr Webber [the *Blessing*] may be gone hence within this 5 days. His lading of wheat lies in readiness for him at Middelburg where I make no question but he will have a quick dispatch. The Portuguese ambassador and our States are near agreed; there's not above £20,000 between them in their demands so that I think it would be better for to send Webber for Lisbon with hides than to send him for Newfoundland. Hides are worth from 3,000 to 3,500 *réis* per hide, which may serve per advice. ...

39. to Gowen Paynter and William Clerke   6 May 1651
a. ... I have received yours, 8 March, per Mr Brampton [the *Matthew*] who hath promised I shall have his ship for the vintage if no good freight proffer before. I have made over the freight homewards to him, which is

received in to a small matter, besides which I shall owe near upon £200. When I had news of his first arrival, I was doubtful had brought me some West India goods, which would have come to a miserable market. He was far more welcome to me with nothing than though I had had his full lading, by which you would have lost 30 per cent besides the freight. I will not excuse Duarte Enríquez for £1,000 loss upon the parcel. Hides worth at present 6d per lb; ginger garbled, £3 10s per cwt; logwood clear of charges here, £14 per t; cochineal mesteque, 28s per lb; indigo garbled, 4s 4d per lb; campechena, 6s 6d per lb; Varinas tobacco if right worth 7s per lb; that which Duarte Enríquez loaded in Brampton will not yield here at most above 5s per lb, being not excellent. Sugars are very cheap at present; good whites worth £6 per cwt.

And amongst all nothing a greater drug than Canary wines, here being at present above 1,500 pipes unsold in town, which are as good as those which were sold at first of the year for £25 per pipe, and now I am confident they would sell them for £20 per pipe with all their hearts, which is no small loss to them which have not sold. I am glad I took my first market as it now falls out. Indeed wines are such a wasting commodity that I do not delight to keep them upon my hands as some men do, yet I never was a spoil-market to undervalue the commodity. These times do much impoverish the commonalty insomuch that these men which formerly did drink wine have now scarce money to buy small beer or ale. The vintners do very much complain of their draughts, and it's not without a cause. Those men which formerly did draw 80 pipes per annum will now scarce draw 40 pipes, so that they will have many remaining against new wines come home. So that we must not expect the prices of these 2 last years. If so be the Islanders should stand upon their terms this next vintage as they did last, if you take my advice, load not home a pipe for your own accounts. I do foresee so much that we shall have a glut next year, and the vintners do begin to tell us that we have had the time of getting this 2 or 3 years, but next year we must leave it and they must take it. If ever the [Vintners'] Company wants to have the upper hand, to say a good quantity of wines in town, then they will blow upon our wines and have them upon their own terms, for here is a generation of new traders that will sell upon any terms to make monies to pay for their goods, which they commonly take up at 6 months' time. Except you can procure the wines to be afforded here for £19 or £20 per pipe, there will be no good done by the trade. Nevertheless, men do run on to provide for the vintage [as] though there were great encouragement here, as per this ship [the *Constant John*] you will see, who goes as full as she can stow. And here is Crispe [the *Prosperity*] that goes the like, who may be gone hence within this 3 weeks.

I am sorry your voyage [the *Matthew*'s] for Barbary proved unsuccessful; no remedy but patience. Mr Warren is now gone for the [Barbary] Coast with a ship [of] 200 ts and carrieth about £2,000 cargazon. Likewise Mr Wilson is setting out of another ship of 300 ts which carries a great cargazon, upon whom goes William Cowse. I am very confident they will come to a sorry market. I shall not interest you upon that design this year, which may serve per advice.

39b. Whereas you desire me to return Brampton [the *Matthew*] with his lading of corn at vintage, I have considered that then every man will be sending, being their ships go empty, so that it is probable there will be a glut. Upon which I have given order to my correspondent Mr Baldwin Matthews at Middelburg to buy me up 80 ts of the very best wheat he can get, which order of mine is effected by ditto and hath been ready bought this 5 weeks. You may please to take notice that our ship *Blessing* [Capt. William Webber] is now at Gravesend ready to go for Middelburg with the first wind to take in ditto corn, where I am confident she will be dispatched in 4 days, so that I hope he will come into the Downs soon enough to have the company of Mr Blake. The winds proved contrary this month, otherwise Mr Webber might have been well in his way for Tenerife. Besides, just as he was ready he received an unhappy mischance: the ship grounded upon an anchor in the Thames and sunk, which proved chargeable to the owners, as he will inform you.

Now whereas you advise to have ditto ship go for Newfoundland and Bilbao, if you so please may send her there, I shall send the master credits to buy up his lading. For my part I shall desire to have no interest in codfish designs because I have made a promise never to deal in such rotten commodities as long as I live. In case that Portugal continue wars with us, then all the fish goes for Spain and Biscay, which of necessity must be a very drug. Now in case that we do conclude a peace with Portugal, as we shall know within this week at farthest, then you may send her for Lisbon with hides which are worth 3,500 *réis* per hide, which is the gallantest design you can send her. Of this I hope to give you a further account ere this ship [the *Constant John*] be gone out of the Downs. But if not, I would not wish you to send her for Newfoundland. However, I will send credits that shall be in readiness against his coming there.

If so be that I do send Mr Brampton at vintage, I shall not send any corn in her, except your further order, because I send Webber unexpected by you, which I hope will come to a far better market than at vintage. However it falls out, you may not blame me for, God knows my heart, my endeavours are for your most advantage. Our corn cost in Holland £40 per last, Flemish money, which, by my calculation, will come at £12 sterling per t, which is about 22*Rs* per *fanega*. I am informed that there is a Fleming that goes from hence with corn, which ditto ship brought in, which they paid 54s per quarter for it, which is about 20 per cent dearer than ours, so that if they do good by theirs, we must do far better by ours. I wish that your advice had come for corn per the Bristol man as it did by Brampton. You should have had 3,000 *fanegas* there by this time.

In the former part of my letter I have given you a hint of what is likely to fall out next year concerning our wine trade. Yet I would not have you altogether disheartened. I make no question but you can do as well as great Mr [John] Turner, and I hope, if my wines prove accordingly, to do as well as old Rowland [Wilson]. But I shall entreat you to be very curious in your selection, which is the main principle, for ordinary wines are never in request though the year be never so scarce here. Now in case that I should not be able to resolve you per this conveyance concerning the peace with Portugal, then you may conclude that there is nothing effected. Now if that should not take effect, then your only way is to load some hides, etc. and send her [the *Blessing*] directly for Nantes where I am confident we shall have a good return as hitherto we have no embargoes. Therefore you need not much doubt. I refer you to Mr Holle's advice, who writes me [from Nantes], and send via Bilbao. If you send her for Newfoundland, I will not excuse for 40 per cent loss upon your fish. The corn in Webber goes for our accounts in equal thirds. I shall make insurance upon him for the major part. ...

40. to William Clerke   8 May 1651
a. I have received yours, 5 March, per Mr Brampton [the *Matthew*]. My last unto you was via Bilbao, which I hope came in due time to go per the *Susan*. The insurance upon ditto ship is made according to your order, home and out. I wonder you did not give Mr Ackland [Paige's correspondent at Bilbao] order to advise me of her arrival. If had been punctual might have saved insurance thither, for the ship was arrived 18 days before the insurance was fully made. Your insurance on the *Medea* [on which Henry Hawley was sailing from Barbados to Amsterdam with sugars] I have done at $4\frac{1}{2}$ per cent, God bless her well to arrive. In my opinion she begins to tarry.

In my last I advised you of Mr Isaac Ellis, his failing for a very great sum of money, so that I have sent your packet for Mr Hawley unto my friend and correspondent Mr Tobias de Hem in Amsterdam, who hath written me that will assist Mr Hawley in anything that shall be requisite, which I am confident he will really perform, he being a very punctual man by what I have found. Before your contradicting order came, I had bought up 30 pieces of excellent good says, which, if I cannot dispose of them suddenly, shall send them you in Mr Edward Crispe's ship [the *Prosperity*]. As yet I have had no answer from Mr Baker [at Madrid] about the £300 which I remitted him, at which I do wonder, but I am informed is daily expected here overland.

Per advice this day here came letters from Bilbao wherein they advise that Mr Pawley of Madrid is failed once more for great sums of money. Here is such breaking abroad and at home every week and I protest I am fearful to trust any man. I am confident his failing in Madrid will break 2 able merchants in this city, one of which I was like to take his bill for 12,000*Rs* to be paid Mr Baker for your account, but I bless God it's otherwise ordered. Yet, if it had so happened out, I could not have remedied it. Thus you may see the danger of these uncertain times that where a man thinketh himself most secure commonly is in most danger. I am glad you did send home Brampton and not to keep him abroad on monthly pay upon uncertain designs. Ships by month eat deep without very good employment.

Concerning your lignum rhodium [in a London warehouse], I do admire who should persuade you to have it sent for Rouen, I having letters from thence weekly where they advise me that 5 ts will cloy the place, and it is not worth above £18 Flemish per t, which is not £10 sterling. Besides, there will arise charges. I am resolved to put it off here for £10 or £11 per t rather than put you to more charges or risks, which may serve per advice. When I send your account you shall also receive the weight of your indigos. How to send you the net weight I cannot tell because they are most unsold; it is the greatest drug that is this day in London. Trade much decays, insomuch that dyers do not use half the quantities as formerly. By estimation here is enough of that commodity in town for to serve it this 5 or 6 years. There's scarce a ship that comes from San Lucar but brings 100 or 200 chests, besides great quantities from East India. You may very well conceive it's no content to me to have them lie in cellar. If you are any way enforced to take goods of the [West] Indians, let it be good hides, which is the staplest commodity of all India goods; and if we have peace with Portugal I am confident they will rise there. Besides, they are a commodity that will yield money, and I know that this year you will have them at the [Canary] Islands upon very reasonable terms.

I have given order for the 2 cables to be made. Likewise shall provide the bays and strong waters to be sent in first ship at vintage, on which you may depend shall be punctually effected, all according to your directions. I am upon making a truck for the strong waters for lignum rhodium, but you may be assured that I will have as good as though I paid ready money.

40b. Your calculation of effects might have been excused though I had not effects in my hands, yet your order should have been put in execution to the full. You estimate to have the half of 373 pipes, and, whereas you strange at the short weight of the *leña noel*, it was weighed by the Custom House beam, and Mr Blake [master of the *Constant John*] had always there a man to take the weight. How the weight will be at the delivery again I know not. Likewise for the weight of the indigo in Capt. Pyle [the *Swan*], as yet is all in cellar. Now for the chest of cochineal, I saw it weighed both at the Custom House and when I sold it, and upon my conscience there was not an ounce more than what I advised you. Sir, it's no novelty, the wanting weight upon such kind of goods. I do find generally all men complain, yet that is no reason to excuse me, neither shall it be a rule for me to walk by. Had I trusted another to see the weight, then I should have had a jealousy it was mistaken, but in such kind of valuable commodities I always see the weight myself. I am confident that your weighing by a steelyard is no exact weight.

My correspondent in Rouen is an Englishman, Mr Humphrey Wilkings, a man whose face I know not, only have now and then some letters directed to him to send overland. I shall, according to your desire, procure you a Dutchman to do your business if occasion should proffer, which I shall give you a further account of per first. But if you take my advice, have nothing to do that way. If you send a ship for France, let her go to Mr John Holle [at Nantes], which is a far better market than Rouen, and if you have occasions for roans, giving him timely advice, he will provide them. I would not wish you to send the ship for Amsterdam because India goods are there a very drug, there being great quantities.

Now in case that you send the ship [the *Blessing*, on her return from Newfoundland,] at neither of these places, but send her home with wines, then I pray let them be choice or none. I hope you can have them there upon as good terms as any man, and I make no question but I shall sell them here for as much as another, so that without doubt you will do as much good by the trade as any man. Though in my joint letter I have given you little encouragement, the prohibition of French wines still continues and I see no likelihood taking it off, which will somewhat advantage us in the sales of our wines.

You may please to take notice that in this ship, the *Constant John*, James Blake master, I have loaded for your account 200 guns and 6 barrels of very fine powder, as per invoice and bill of lading appears. I would have put 4 barrels powder more aboard, but the master told me he could not take in one more, his powder room being full, which may serve per advice. You may do well to send away the *Susan* [Capt. Giles Paynter] with as much expedition as may be that she may get there [to the Barbary Coast] before William Cowes who will be gone hence within this month. Mr Browning hath been with me several times. I have excused you in the best manner I could. He tells me that he will not build till next vintage after this, so that you will see him there about October. When you write me hereafter via Holland, pray direct my letters to Mr Tobias de Hem, and at Middelburg to Mr Baldwin Matthews. For what concerns the joint affairs, I have written you and Mr Paynter at large, to which desire reference. I hope you will persuade Mr Paynter, so far as that Webber [the *Blessing*] may not go for Newfoundland, Lisbon is the only voyage. Now in case that fail, then you may send him with a small cargazon for Nantes to Mr Holle or to any other place where you shall think fit.

40c. Now concerning your Guinea design, it is a business of much difficulty and requires a great deal of extraordinary care, notwithstanding I shall account all my pains therein too little to serve so good a friend as yourself, and rest assured that there shall be nothing wanting in me. I have discoursed with Mr Jewell about it, whom I find much unversed in those parts, likewise knows not what is proper for those parts, which I shall take that to my care if he do proceed. But I must tell you, we must have a very able merchant to go along with him that is well acquainted with the coast, otherwise the design will come to nothing. Besides, men are subject to miscarry in those voyages, being unhealthful, as you did hint to me in your own letter. Now in case that I should procure another able man to go with Mr Jewell, you must think if he be a man of any worth or parts that he will not go as an underling but be in joint commission with Mr Jewell, which I find Mr Jewell somewhat unwilling, though I see little reason because he cannot do the business of himself alone. Now in case that we can get a man upon other terms, then I shall be very glad, but if not, then we must go the other way, which, if Mr Jewell shall refuse to condescend unto, for my part I will have no interest in the design, of which I shall be more larger in my next when we have had a little more conference.

I have any time this month been looking out for a ship and cannot meet with any master that will go that way except those which have ordinary sailors. We must have a frigate that will sail well, or else the blacks may chance to be starved before they arrive at their port. I proffered Mr [Garvis] Russell for his new frigate [the *Katherine*] which is just the burthen of Sidrake Blake, £160 per month for 8 months certain and 20 months if occasion, which is an unreasonable freight, £20 more than she deserves, and yet cannot get her. They ask £170 per month, which I will never give. I doubt we shall be forced to freight a ship and victual and man ourselves, which will be chargeable. There is not one in 20 masters that will go this way, though you would give them double freight, because it is a sickly voyage. By the next I shall be able to give you a further account of the business. Mr Jewell tells me that he cannot hold above ⅛ part at most, so that there remaineth ⅞ parts. I wish you had referred the business a little more to me and less to some else peradventure it might have been ordered a little better for our benefit.

The bearer hereof, our friend Mr William Bradick, will deliver you another letter. It will seem strange to see him in those Islands again. He hath passed through a great many troubles here of late days, and I think he would hardly have come off clear if I had not stood by him when all his pretended friends failed him, especially Mr Richard Lant. To give you the true relation of all passages, it would be too tedious, so I refer you to his own relation. ...

41. to Gowen Paynter and William Clerke   29 May 1651
... I have advice that Webber [the *Blessing*] was laden some 8 days since with wheat, who I hope may be with you as soon as this comes to your hands. The treaty between the Portuguese ambassador [Guimāres] and our States is broken off insomuch that they have voted him to depart the Commonwealth within this 3 days. My uncle George Chappell carries him away, so that now we may expect no peace with Portugal. Here enclosed I send you a letter which if you send Webber for Newfoundland may carry with him. No man here will scarce adventure upon fish insomuch that the West Countrymen must be forced to carry it to a market themselves, which will be bad enough in regard the Portuguese trade is shut up which used to vent above 60,000 kts, all which must now go to Spain. Wherefore, upon no terms let him not proceed that voyage; rather keep him at the Islands till vintage.

I am now upon freighting Brampton [the *Matthew*] whom I intend to send with the first fleet at vintage. Men do now begin to freight ships for the vintage already. I do long to hear from you to know how the year is like to prove. This goes via Topsham by an uncertain conveyance, otherwise should be larger. ...
[P.S.] As yet no news of Mr Hawley's arrival [at Amsterdam].

42. to William Clerke   2 June 1651
... I have written you larger in the joint letter, to which desire reference for what concerns the general business. I have freighted Brampton [the *Matthew*] for the vintage for our accounts in thirds. As yet I have no certain news of Mr Hawley's [the *Medea*'s] arrival [at Amsterdam], but there is a ship arrived in Zeeland that came in company with the ship *Medea* who supposes that he is gone by the back of Scotland to avoid our Parliament ships. God send good news. I hope to write you of his arrival per next.

Now concerning our Guinea design, may please to take notice that through much difficulty and great pains I have freighted a ship for that design by name the *Swan* whereof Capt. Pyle is commander. The condition, shall give you an estimate hereunder. I was about several ships, but no masters would go upon any terms, so that I was fain to close up with Capt. Pyle, though not upon so good terms as I would wish. I shall now go [about] providing the cargazon and give Mr Jewell [supercargo on the *Swan*] a speedy disp[atch], hoping to have him ready by 20 July at farthest. I shall advise you in my next the share which I intend to have in ditto design.

I wonder that I have not heard from Mr Baker concerning the bill [of] £300 remitted him [at Madrid] for your account. He is daily expected here via Bilbao, God send him well. I wish he had sent the licences [see **43n**] to go with Mr Jewell. ...

[P.S.] The heads of Pyle's charter-party, viz. the ship at £150 per month, 8 months certain, 20 longest; to pay 6 months' pay after 8 months' service, the rest at his arrival here; to carry 32 men, 20 guns; to pay port charges as customary; to go so far as the Line [the Equator]. ...

43. to Gowen Paynter and William Clerke   2 June 1651

... Mr Webber [the *Blessing*, on her way from Middelburg] touched at Dover, and not finding any letters of mine, was informed not to proceed for Tenerife with his corn, although had no such order from me. So sent me up an express that would stay at the Isle of Wight till my further order, which, for ought I know, may lose a good passage by that presumption, as I may term it, which makes me now send an express on purpose to get him gone, being a fair wind. Here enclosed I send you a letter of credit in case he go to Newfoundland, which by no means let him go for former reasons given you. Besides, I doubt it will be too late.

May please to take notice that I have yesterday freighted Mr Brampton [the *Matthew*] to go for the Canaries for our accounts in equal thirds at vintage. I am to give £4 per t. There are above 15 ships already freighted for vintage, which is a thing never known, so rare. Men run on as though there were very great encouragement. What wines you load at the vintage except they be rare you had better send none, for I am confident they will not be so much in request this year as last except very good. Mr Rowland Wilson hath now received letters from Mr John Turner of 15 April via Bilbao from Tenerife, which is a great satisfaction towards his proceedings. No man else hath a line. I admire you did not write per that via a letter; now were worth 10 another time.

This day I have received letters from San Lucar of 7 May where they write me of Mr Chalk's [the *Mary*'s] and Steward's arrival there, who are both bound for the [Canary] Islands. Likewise they advise that Sidrake Blake and a great Fleming is there arrived from your Islands, wherein is come the old [Capt.] General [of the Canaries, Don Pedro Carrillo de Guzmán], for which am very glad that you are rid of that torment. The Portuguese ambassador [Guimãres] is now at Calais, who stays there to take shipping. My uncle George Chappell is now going to take him in and to carry him away for Lisbon. The treaty is quite frustrated and no hopes of peace with them, which may serve per advice.

In case you do not send Webber for Nantes, I conceive you had better keep him there till vintage. Had not the business of proceedings fallen out cross, he might have been with you long ere this, but we cannot be against God's decreed will. Wind and weather hath proved cross and the owners a little perverse, which at present I cannot give you the full relation, being somewhat tedious. Webber is not so discreet a man as I take him to be. God send him well this voyage, we shall go near to change a master, which you may keep to yourself. He writes me that he was informed in Dover that much corn hath gone from Cadiz for Tenerife, which I hear no such thing, neither have any such advice. If had, cannot now remedy it. The quantity which he hath aboard is not much, but I conceive you can very well dispose of it to your parishioners were there a glut, as I hope there will not be. This staying of his in the Isle of Wight will hinder above 200 leagues' sail. He might very well be there within 2 days after James Blake [the *Constant John*], which may now prove to be longer.

Mr [John] Turner advises Mr Wilson that Jenkins was coming home from the Islands at the date of his letter; as yet is not arrived, so that I doubt cannot be well. I have not heard from you since Brampton came home. ...

[P.S.] Mr Webber's ship goes per month. I am to give £62 per month for 8 months certain and 20 months if need require, which may serve per advice. Tomorrow we are to have a letter from the Council of State unto the King of Spain about our general business, upon which I hope Mr Breton will be able to do something against Don Pedro's coming.[1]

1. As early as 15 March 1651, the Council of State had entertained a petition from merchants complaining of problems at the Canaries, but it was not until 27 June that Parliament ordered the Council to report the grievances to Madrid (*C.S.P.D.*, *1651*, 107, 268, 272). The complaints were probably similar to those raised against Carrillo de Guzmán, the former Capt. General, for his prosecution of English merchants who imported contraband goods. Cf. **9**, **15**, **19a**. At the same time, Paige was expecting either Robert Breton or Richard Baker, partners in trade with contacts at Madrid, to procure a licence allowing Clerke to import 300 black slaves, 'merchandise' which was considered as contraband at Tenerife. Apparently Paige hoped that this could be accomplished before Carrillo de Guzmán reached Madrid and justified his earlier actions against the English. Cf. **25b**, **42**, **44**.

44. to William Clerke   6 July 1651

My last unto you was 2 June per Mr William Webber [the *Blessing*], where I wrote you briefly giving you to understand that I have freighted Capt. Pyle [the *Swan*] to go your Guinea design, though with much difficulty and trouble. Since which, have freighted a small frigate of 30 ts [the *Turned-out*] to go with him, being absolutely necessary for the rivers. I am to give £9 per month and I to victual and man, which in my opinion is very reasonable, she being brand new, never made a voyage, and must of necessity sail singularly well. Likewise I have bought up near £1,000 worth [of] goods already proper for that place, which now I wish I had the money again in my purse.

Mr Baker is come from Madrid and brought no commission [see **43n**], upon which I showed him your advice to me. He denies that ever he writ positively he could procure it, but says that if he could possibly he would, which excuse does not agree with your advice. I shall be more larger in my next concerning this particular. In the meantime, you are very much mistaken of Mr Baker if you take him to be your friend. I believe you will find a great deal of self-ended treachery in this business. My opinion is that Mr Baker aims at the same business and so endeavours to frustrate you. I acquainted him how I had per your order freighted a ship [of] 300 ts for the design and had bought up £1,000 in goods, who replied in a slight manner that I must sell the goods again and release the ship. I replied it could not be done under £500 loss, to which he answered if were £5,000 he could not help it. So much for your pretended friend Mr Baker.

Now I have laboured what I can but cannot obtain a commission from our States [so that the *Swan* might go to Portuguese Africa with a letter of marque] against the Portuguese upon no pretence whatsoever, being they expect to have another ambassador from King John, so that are now calling in all private men-of-war commissions. So that now we have begun, we must go through as well as may. Your only way is to compound with the [Capt.] General [of the Canaries] in time. I am almost in the mind to have Mr Jewell stop one day with you to take your good advice.

Blessed be God, Mr Hawley [the *Medea*] is safe arrived at Amsterdam with his sugars, which came to a reasonable market, worth $7\frac{1}{2}$ stivers per lb, and small charges. In regard there hath gone great quantities of corn to the [Canary] Islands from hence and Holland, makes him at a stand whether shall freight a ship or no, and the more because we could not hear from you, neither by Jenkins, Warren, nor this Southampton man, at which I admire.

I have received your credit, 24 April, via San Lucar and accepted the £400 bill of exchange which Mr Abraham Lee [of San Lucar] drew upon me at 20 days' sight, which bill came 12 days before any credit or letter of advice, a thing not usual. Upon which it was like to go back protested had not your letter of credit come in the nick of time. All which might have been imputed to Mr Lee's strange way of drawing bills without letters of advice. Besides, you should have done well to have given me timely notice whereby I might have been provided. I must be fain to borrow every penny for present, being the vintners pay extremely slowly, as I have formerly advised you. I am confident I shall not be paid for the wines by Christmas next. Therefore, I pray hereafter give me notice when you intend to value yourself on me. For other business I refer you to the joint letter. ...

45. to William Clerke   26 Aug. 1651
I have written you and Mr Paynter at large in my joint letter, to which crave reference, being somewhat straitened of time at present. Per Mr Russell shall write you at large, who will be gone within this 3 days, in which ship [the *Katherine*] you may expect your goods. These chiefly serve to give you notice, seeing you so earnestly desire it, that this day Capt. Pyle's ship [the *Swan*] is gone for Gravesend with our small pinnace [the *Turned-out*] to proceed on our Guinea voyage, though with as much trouble and difficulty, I think, as tongue can express. If I might have £500

I would not undertake the like business again. In fine, thanks be to God, I have almost overcome.

Now I want nothing but money. I cannot get in my money from vintners insomuch I am at a strait. Your bill [of exchange] of £400 payable to Mr Henry Lee of San Lucar I have paid, but was fain to borrow every penny of the money. And now to help all, you have drawn several other bills upon me, at which I much admire. You do not consider the slow payments of the vintners and the disbursements I have been out for you, especially this Guinea design, so that I shall not be able to satisfy all your bills.

In my last I gave you notice of Mr Hawley's arrival at Amsterdam, who writ me last post would remit his money for Madrid, for that corn was very dear in Holland would freight no ship. What reason is for it he knows best. I writ him that you did expect him [in Tenerife] according to your former order.

When Webber's bills [of exchange to pay for the *Blessing*'s fish at Newfoundland] come, I shall be put to it. I never was so short of money as this year since I came to England. ...

46. to William Clerke   6 Sept. 1651
I have received yours, 24 and 27 July, via Topsham and per Mr William Bradick. For what concerns your and Mr Paynter's joint affairs I have written you at large, to which desire reference. To comply with your very earnest desire, may please to take notice that I have dispatched away from hence Mr Richard Jewell upon Capt. Pyle's ship [the *Swan*] and likewise a small frigate of 30 ts [the *Turned-out*] with a complete cargazon, both for the river Gambia, the Gold Coast and the Bight [of Benin], all which stands us above £1,700. The particulars of which you may expect per Mr George Kilvert per whom shall write you at large. Ever since I knew what business was I never undertook the like. Indeed I was not sensible of it before had undergone it. I protest if I might have the ¼ part of the cargazon I would not be bound to do the like. I do not write it in a boasting way to applaud myself, but Mr Jewell was an eyewitness to all. For 10 weeks' time I had no quietness. After Pyle had sealed [the] charter-party, he like a knave discovered the design and would not proceed the voyage, notwithstanding I had bought £1,000 worth [of] goods. The one-half thereof was aboard so I was fain to sue him in the Admiralty Court, where, it please God, I overcame him. The copy of all shall send you per Mr Kilvert. Here is no commission to be procured from our States nor the States of Holland [allowing the *Swan* to go as a private man-of-war] against the Portuguese, upon no terms. Therefore you must endeavour to compose your business with the [Capt.] General [of the Canaries] there.

My cousin Mr John Paige of Plymouth advises me that he loaded on Brampton [the *Matthew*] 319 bushels wheat for your, Mr Paynter's and my accounts in equal thirds, to whose advice I refer you. I loaded aboard the *Katherine* frigate [Capt. Garvis Russell] 10 pieces Colchester bays for your account and 2 new cables, the invoice of which you shall have per next.

The trouble in dispatching the *Swan* hath made me neglect my writing you and other friends per the first ships at vintage, so that you must have patience until the second fleet arrives, which I hope will not be long after. Only what I shall desire is that you load none but choice wines for your account, though they cost something in price and payment more. The price here will make amends, if good. I have observed ever since I received wines from you that you have every year loaded better wines for other men's accounts than for your own, especially to Mr [Stephen] Slaney, for which I think you have no great thanks. I would have you to take the parson's proverb, that is, to christen your own child first. Since others have had the cream other years, pray reserve that for yourself and let them have some milk, 'comprehending much in a few words' [Ecclesiasticus 32:8].

If you can buy a parcel West India hides reasonable, I conceive they will turn better to account than dear wines, worth at present 7½d per lb; and if our peace be concluded with Portugal, I am confident they will be somewhat dearer, which may serve per advice. ...

47. to William Clerke   10 Sept. 1651
a. ... My last unto you was of 6 instant via Plymouth per Mr Taylor, where I wrote you a few hasty lines. I purposed to have written you per Mr Russell [the *Katherine*], but being then upon dispatching Mr Jewell [supercargo on the *Swan*], I was resolved to follow it and leave all other business.

I shall give you a brief narration of some passages concerning our proceedings, for to give you the whole will be too tedious. As soon as ever I had agreed with Capt. Pyle [the *Swan*], within 6 days I got him to seal our charter-party, for I was jealous of recantation. Upon which I went providing the cargo and got him to take in £600 in goods because would make a beginning and by that time I had near provided all things to go aboard. Comes Pyle to me and says that all his men that were shipped had forsaken him, saying they would not go no Negro voyages, and for his part would not go if would give him £1,000, telling me the voyage was unlawful [because of the Guinea Company's monopoly of that trade] and that he valued not the sealing of the charter-party a button and that I might even take my goods ashore, discovering our design to every man. Thus he went on in a malicious way, endeavouring to destroy our design which had cost me so much pain. But since I understood he was put purposely to spoil our voyage by many of the Guinea Company, notwithstanding I had such high opposition, I thought I had reason and equity on my side. I immediately got out an admonition out of the Admiralty Court to bring Pyle's person to appear before the judges and to show cause why he did not proceed according to agreement in charter-party. The business was 2 days debated before them by our counsels. Pyle brought several witnesses to prove his pretence, which was the unlawfulness of the ports, but my witnesses were more material in the business, upon which Capt. Pyle was notified by the judges' sentence [24 July 1651] to proceed with the ship else to forfeit the penalty of his charter-party which is £2,000 sterling.

After this was ended Pyle comes to me and says would make ready his ship but desired me to excuse his person going the voyage, being his wife would not permit him to go such an unhealthy voyage. Upon which I considered that to force him would not do well; and, weighing all things, I condescended that he might stay at home provided always that I might have no master but with our joint agreement, which accordingly he granted. And so we got his chief mate formerly to go master, whose name is Henry Pulman, a man that I have known this 7 years and truly I conceive him every way to be as fit a man as Capt. Pyle himself. After all this, then they complained they could not get men for money to go such a voyage. Likewise I freighted a small frigate of 30 ts [the *Turned-out*] to go along with the great ship, which is absolutely necessary for the rivers upon the coast; which vessel we are to victual and man.

47b. Here I send you a true copy of *Swan*'s and frigate's charter-parties and likewise of my proceedings against him in the Admiralty Court. More I send you an invoice of our cargo and what the frigate stood set to sea and per store for the voyage. I have disbursed some small trifles since the account, likewise purpose to have £1,000 insured upon the general account for 8 months certain and so many more as we shall think fit until intimation of a cessation. When I received your advice at first to go upon this design, I was not sensible of what I undertook. I have ever made assured of myself for these 10 weeks. I bless God that all business that ever I undertook in my life did never give me such vexations as this. I do not speak it to applaud myself, but Mr Jewell is and hath been an eyewitness to all the transactions. If you would give me a quarter part of the whole cargo, I protest really I would not act the like business again; but I thank God I have now overcome it through much difficulty and vexation of spirit, and the ship and pinnace are both gone out of the Downs the 8th instant with a fair wind. The Lord send them a good passage and safe to return.

We have notice here that Negroes at the river Gambia are very scarce and dear. Our cargazon was most sorted for that river. But since I provided a parcel of brass bars and other commodities proper for the Bight [of Benin], so that if the first fail the other might take, I hope the proceeds of our cargazon will buy 300 blacks and load a £1,000 besides in beeswax, elephants' teeth and hides, all which commodities may have at the river Gambia. The making of our voyage will really be the quick dispatch of our ship upon the coast, which I have pressed to Mr Jewell many times and find him to be sensible thereof. He carries a young man [Thomas Dixon] along with him that hath the Portuguese tongue and is a pretty understanding man, by what seemed to me. He lived some years in Lisbon in your brother's house. I did endeavour to get another second but could not meet with any to my mind. I trust in God Mr Jewell may be with you in the month of February next at farthest.

You are interested $\frac{1}{2}$ part in this design, and Mr Jewell $\frac{3}{16}$ part, and myself $\frac{5}{16}$ part as per bill of lading and invoice appears. I write my father-in-law to take $\frac{1}{8}$ of my part, which I conceive he will accept of, when not I will hold it as now I do. You see how much our cargo amounts unto besides insurance, likewise freight at 8 months' end, all which will stand us £3,000 which we shall be out on this design, which is a great deal of money. So that you must act your part in 2 things: the first is you must make way with the [Capt.] General [of the Canaries] in time whereby the ship may be received when it please God she arrives. For my part I have endeavoured to get a commission both here and at Holland [allowing the *Swan* to go as a private man-of-war] against the Portuguese, but none will be granted here nor there for love nor money, which may serve per advice. What the times hereafter may produce I know not. Nothing shall be wanting in me to procure it. Secondly, you must from the receipt go on providing some lading for the ship *Swan* whereby she may come directly home from thence, though she comes half empty, for £5 per diem arises high notwithstanding she is the cheapest ship that ever went freighted for Guinea. Pyle scarce knew what he did when he let her. I have formerly written you the slight answer Mr Baker gave me about the business of the commission and how much mistaken you are in taking him for your friend, but [by] your last I see you perceive his intentions. You know I cannot send the Spanish ambassador's letter except had a commission granted. [See **43n**.]

47c. I am glad the guns and powder came so opportunely to go per the *Susan* [Capt. Giles Paynter]. I am informed that corn is scarce upon the Barbary Coast, insomuch I doubt the ships will get none. Those wines which you bought last year which you intend to load upon the *Susan* are very cheap as this year falls out. I wish they [i.e. the Canarian winegrowers] may not play the knave and mix them with *vidueños*. Both in those and all others which you load for your own proper account, I beseech you have a special care in the selection. It imports your own profit and my credit here. Pray do not this year, as you did last, load the worst wines for your own account and other men the best. I would have you to follow the parson's rule, to christen your own child first. It is very honest policy. Mr [Stephen] Slaney hath not spared in charging tonnage on you this vintage. In my opinion he was very sensible of the badness of the vintage before he took freight upon Taylor, therefore cannot plead ignorance, which peradventure he may to you. And whatever business or designs you intend for the future, pray let them be kept private from some which you have in your house, for other men know your intentions before my letters come to hand. These things are not convenient in our affairs. It proves many times disadvantageous and prejudicial to my negotiations here because envious men will thwart me in my proceedings. I have forborne a long time to write you concerning this particular, but I cannot hold longer. Therefore, pray endeavour to prevent it for the future.

I have written Mr Paynter very earnestly about the loading of rare liquors. Now in case the wine should not prove excellent with you, then you may buy some hides and fill up part of your tonnage. And among all, pray load good cask and see that they be well rabbeted, for soon is 4 or 5 per cent lost, which comes to a good sum of money.

I delivered Mr Jewell a packet of letters for you to be sent per Mr Russell [the *Katherine*], which seems came too late, so he writ me would leave them aboard the Admiral in the Downs to go per the first ship for the Canaries. In which packet were 2 letters from Mr Hawley which I hope will come safely to your hands.

47d. Whosoever did acquaint you about observing season of the year for wheat in Holland, to say that in Sept.-Oct. were the best months for buying by 20 per cent, tell him from me he is in an error. Corn is now dearer 20 per cent than it was when Webber [the *Blessing*] loaded; therefore you may judge whether that observation be right or no.

You may please to take notice that I loaded aboard the *Katherine* frigate 2 new cables and one truss of bays for your account. The ship's sudden departure left my bills of lading unfirmed. I do not use to omit such things, but to tell you the truth I left all business to do to dispatch away Mr Jewell [and the *Swan* for Guinea], which I think to you may be a sufficient excuse.

As concerning my kinsman you write for [to come as an apprentice], I did 12 months since write you about him, but seeing you never gave answer to that particular, I did before your advice came to hand promise him to my father-in-law and accordingly did send him to him over upon Mr Russell. I wish with my heart you had advised me of your want a little sooner. However, I am now endeavouring to get you a youth that shall be for your turn, which I make no question but shall procure one suddenly; it may be to go away in Jenkins if possible. You may depend I will send you over one; therefore make so good a shift as you can in the interim.

By your last I see you have drawn several bills of exchange on me unexpected and contrary to your advice of 10 March, at which I wonder. That bill of £400 payable to Mr [Abraham] Lee [of San Lucar], I borrowed the money and paid it. Likewise have accepted your bill of £100 to James Blake [master of the *Constant John*] to pay at 50 days' sight; and that payable to Mr Casby's order is paid. That [of £84 for freight] to Mr [Giles] Paynter [master of the *Susan*] shall pay, but the bill of £150 payable to Mr Breton not come to hand. I doubt shall hardly be able to pay it, yet I am loath you should have it go back. But one thing you should consider, what I wrote you by James Blake, how miserable the times were and how slowly my wine debts come in. Besides, I have disbursed near £400 upon the *Swan*'s cargo for your account and other ways. As you well know, if I had the cash of my own stock in hand, I valued it not to supply it. But I have a great part out of my hands, insomuch that I am much straitened for money at present, which is a very discontented life. And were you not a real friend of mine, I should not do what I have done for treble commission, for I value a quiet life more than much gain. Therefore, for the future, pray order your business in such a manner that I may always have money in cash to go through my business with courage. I know not what I shall do for money to pay Webber's bills of exchange [for the *Blessing*'s fish at Newfoundland] and likewise customs and freights of wines at Christmas. All these things must be considered.

I know you will strange very much I have not sent you your account, which I cannot absolutely finish because I have been overbusied of late days. ...

48. to William Clerke   28 Sept. 1651

... May please to take notice that I have disposed of 6 chests of your indigos unto Mr Thomas Canham at 4s 8d per lb, to pay at 6 months' time.

And after the bargain was made, I found him inclining to recant, saying that Antonio Fernandez [Carvajal] sold at 4s 2d per lb, which was very true, insomuch that I was fain to take half with him rather than to have them turned down upon my hands. We sent them for Lisbon where they were sold very well, as it happened, 750 *réis* per lb. There remains yet 8 chests in cellar and one chest campechena grain. As for your lignum rhodium, I cannot dispose of one t for money nor upon truck, insomuch that I doubt warehouse room will eat out the principal. Besides, it dries very much. I would willingly dispose of it upon any reasonable terms. Those chests indigo which remain unsold are the best of all the parcels. I proffered them at 4s 2d per lb garbled but cannot get above 4s per lb and at time [i.e. to be paid for later]. So that now I am resolved to keep them until I hear from you again because for future when you send me any goods, pray give me such order as that I may send them to any place where I shall think most convenient for your most advantage, if you can repose so much confidence in me. If you think it convenient, I will send them for Lisbon for your account. Of this, pray 2 words per first opportunity.

Your brother, Mr George Clerke, is daily expected from Lisbon here, who, I understand, intends to make a speedy return thither again. God sending him well to arrive, I shall kiss his hands in giving him a visit, and if he return before I receive your answer, I will presume so far as to send your indigo per him, though I do not usually do such things.

Your bill of exchange, £150, payable to Mr Breton I have accepted with all the rest you have drawn on me according to your last advice per James Blake [the *Constant John*]. I was loath any should come back again though I wrong myself, but how I shall get in monies to pay them I know not. You cannot imagine the miserable times for trading which are here at present. I never knew such an alteration in so short time.

I trust in God Mr Jewell [supercargo on the *Swan*] is at his port by this time. Here is at this present 2 of the Guinea Company's ships now in Downs bound for the same ports, so that I hope our ship will have the start of them for sale of our goods. There is no hopes of procuring any commission against the Portuguese [legitimizing a slaving voyage to Portuguese Guinea], so you must use your diligence there to make way with the [Capt.] General [of the Canaries] against our ship's arrival th[at] there may be no stop. And withal you must lay up a good round parcel West India goods whereby the ship may be upon employment, for we are at great charges. I have made insurance for £1,000 upon ditto ship for the general account for 8 months certain and more if need require at 20s per month per each £100, which, I conceive, is as cheap as ever was done that way. Likewise I have insured £1,200 upon the *Susan* homewards [from Tenerife to London] for your account at 4 per cent. I hope by this time Mr Hawley is gone from Amsterdam with his wheat for Tenerife. He had trouble there, which he will inform you at large.

In your last le[tter] you desired me to get you [a] pretty youth to live with you [in] apprenticeship, which accordingly I have used diligence to get one, but the time is so short that they cannot make ready to go over per Mr Jenkins. But by the first ship that goes after him, you may depend upon it, I shall perform your desire in sending you a youth for your turn. I am now about 2 which are very good scribes and of good parents which will give £1,000 bond for their truth. I make no question but I shall agree for one of them. ...

[P.S.] Here enclosed I send you an invoice of what goods I loaded aboard the *Katherine* frigate and *Peter Bonadventure*.

49. to Gowen Paynter and William Clerke   28 Nov. 1651

These chiefly serve to give you notice that this day I received a letter from John Brampton, master of the *Matthew*, who is safely arrived in the Downs with 40 pipes of wine and 50 ts of Campeachy wood, as he advises me. He would not send up my letters for fear of miscarrying, therefore I have the less to answer. I wish you had not laden a stick of wood, for I think it so great a drug as lignum rhodium and there is £4 per t custom upon it. Except I transport it, I conceive I shall not sell it here for above £10 per t aboard ship. Considering breakage and charges, there will be 30 per cent out of the principal loss.

I am informed wines are both bad and dear and that you have made a general agreement the [English] nation throughout [to limit your purchases of Canary wine]. I wish there may be no Judas amongst them. If they prove well I shall look upon it as a miracle. I do not like that Mr [John] Turner keeps his ships behind; formerly he used to dispatch them with the first. I do not like his tarrying. If in case he should break your agreement, I question whether you or any man could recover a penny forfeiture because Mr Rowland Wilson [Turner's partner in London] hath my lord [Bulstrode] Whitelocke, one of the Keepers of our liberties of the Great Seal, to his friend (who married his [late] son's wife), a man very potent both in Parliament and Council of State.

I writ you a few hasty lines via Bristol per one Mr Marshall who is bound for the Canaries, and this goes via Amsterdam per uncertain conveyance. There are 4 Flemings arrived from Tenerife which came in 6 days since. I wonder you would not afford me 2 lines to intimate what you intend to load upon Brampton because I insured so much more than we have upon her, so that we shall pay £60 premium for nothing. If you had given me advice, then I could have intimated unto the insurers and have taken them off what I pleased, whereas now I cannot. The like upon Giles Paynter, the *Susan*, who I understand came out with Brampton but by very foul weather parted 100 leagues off Land's End and as yet no news of him nor Robert Newman. Taylor and Huberly are arrived in the Downs. Notwithstanding there come so few Canaries, yet I question where they will sell at last year's prices. I know not how I shall have monies to pay freight and custom.

I understand Webber [the *Blessing*] was arrived to a good market with his fish; likewise Mr Russell [the *Katherine*] writes me Mr Jewell [supercargo on the *Swan*] came part of the way with him. If I have no more effects, I know not how I shall be able to pay the first 6 months of the *Swan*'s freight which is £900 in all, which, I pray, consider my engagements. God sending the ship well to arrive with you from Guinea, pray send her upon no designs because she is too great charge and too big. In the interim my earnest desire is that you would go on providing her cargazon of West India goods in time. Hides worth 7d per lb; ginger garbled, £4 per cwt; best cochineal, 30s per lb; campechena, 6s 6d; sylvester, 4s; indigo, 4s 8d. I hope the new act of prohibiting Flemings [the Navigation Act, 5 Oct. 1651] will make West Indian goods rise here. As yet we have no news of any ambassador from Portugal. ...

50. to Gowen Paynter and William Clerke   8 Dec. 1651
... I have received yours per Mr Brampton [the *Matthew*] as also per Mr Giles Paynter [the *Susan*]. I should answer your letters particularly as I received them, but time prevents me that I cannot. I have landed the wines out of Brampton and likewise out of the *Susan*. I did expect greater quantities in both ships, but I find by your contract [among English merchants in the Canaries] that you have laden your proportions allotted you, so that I cannot expect you to fare better than other men, it being a general calamity as I may term it. But seeing the quantities were so small, I did conceive that you would have been the more curiouser in your selection whereby to have sent special good liquors. But instead of doing so, I conceive you have recovered up your old debts or at least bought some low-price wines. If not so, you have much undervalued your judgements or palates. If this be your proportion of firsts, I could wish that I had not had the tenth. Such a parcel of trash I never saw in my possession, and which parcel proves best I cannot discern, they being poor green flashy stuff. I know not what to do with them. There's at least 8 pipes unsound in both parcels. No customer of mine will look upon them, they have such an ill report. The vintners have named me 'the Canary Scavenger', a name very proper for such a dirty commodity. I question though I should have good wines another [year] where vintners will buy them because I am now so much disgraced. If I had not written you sufficiently of the inconveniency of bad wines, it would never have vexed me, but from Jan. to Sept. in all my letters I never omitted to give you a hint. Peradventure you will answer unto what I have said that you cannot load good wines when there are no such to be bought. If I should require such impossibility, I should think it an unreasonable thing; but when generally other men's wines shall rise good and those which you load to be trash, not so good by £8 per pipe, surely you must give me leave to write my mind freely and not to soothe you upon such apparent losses as this will prove to you and myself.

Those wines in Capt. Huberly laden for Don Balthazar de [Vergara] Grimón's account prove generally fine wines. Mr Newman's wines laden by Mr Bulkley prove likewise pretty wines. And those which Mr Bowridge loaded in Mr Taylor, Don Luis Benitez' wines as I am informed, prove best of all. Mr Lant told me this day that he refused £26 per pipe for the parcel, and I believe they will yield 20s more at least. Whereas ours, I will sell them with all my heart for £18 per pipe. I cannot say that there's one good pipe in the whole parcel. Other men have above half part fine wines that will serve to drink without help of Malaga [admixed]. Were I sure that wines would yield the price at the Islands as last year, I would return you over some of these, otherwise I must be fain

56

to sell them to young vintners or to those which drive a country trade, which commonly pay one half and run away with the rest. Such is the torment of bad wines. All the men that know you do admire at your mistake and with much reason they may. Peradventure you may conceive that I am in some great passion; though I were, yet I am sure it does not overcome my reason. Neither do I undervalue your wines a farthing because you shall be sure I shall show them to some which shall certify you the truth.

The *Susan* and the rest of the fleet had very bad weather homewards and parted company; all came in single by themselves. Giles Paynter cut his mainmast by the board, staved his boat, threw one of his guns overboard. The ship was underwater 2 hours insomuch that the sea unstowed his wines and staved several pipes, which he and his men have deposed upon oath before the judges of the Admiralty Court. And the Trinity [House] masters have cleared them from damage so that now I must come upon the insurers as average. I believe the 43 pipes will not make out 32 pipes full.

Whenever it pleases God to send the ship *Swan* and frigate [the *Turned-out*] to arrive with you, pray think not of sending them anywhere but for England because they are too chargeable to be kept upon monthly pay. In the interim pray go providing her cargo of goods against her coming, which I hope may be in Feb. I know there are as good wines left in the Island as any that came in these ships. ...

[P.S.] As for the Campeachy wood, it's yet aboard Mr Brampton, it being a commodity that I always objected against, it being a very drug. Varinas tobacco, if right, worth 6s per lb; indigo begins to rise, worth 5s per lb, which may serve per advice.

51.[1] to Gowen Paynter and William Clerke   8 Jan. 1652
a. My last unto you was via France of 15 Dec. under covert [Mr] Roger Kilvert, where I writ you at large. And since, have sent a co[py] ditto ship under covert of Sr Antonio Fernandez Carvajal who [promised] that it shall be faithfully delivered, God sending the ship to arr[ive]. I am informed she is a Fleming and goes laden with wheat.

[In my last I] advised you how Mr [William] Bulkley's wines in Newman proved, [and now] all are sold at £27 per pipe. Likewise Mr Lant's ... sold at £29 per pipe. And since, here are arrived 11 or 12 sail. ... Likewise those wines which Mr Marmaduke Rawdon loaded ... [prove] very good, being sold at £30 per pipe. ... Several others are [proved] not so good as those aforementioned, but I know no man's prove [so bad as] mine, insomuch that no man will taste them. ... The most [that has] been bid was £18 per pipe and leave some unsound. By this [you will know] what it is to be plagued with bad wines ... when as other men shall sell at £11 or £12 per pipe more than I. ...

As yet here is no [news of the] arrival of Crispe, Broad, Jenkins, Rounton, and Neale. All the rest arrived. Mr Forster and Mr [Thomas] Bonfoy's Fleming are in the Downs [but are] not permitted to come here to unload their wines by reason [of the] act of Parliament [i.e. the Navigation Act]. Here are at present 3 ambassadors from H[olland] ...

over which as yet have acted little. Both they and our States are [firm in] their demands; it's much feared they will not agree. Besides, [our State] has granted several letters of marque against the Hollander. ... Several ships are now gone out and have brought in Flemish prizes, which is no good sign. It's reported that there are 6 sail of war going out of Flushing to take English. ...

[We have] had many easterly winds, by which means no news from [Portugal]. The last letters say that the King had upon the matter consent[ed to lift] the embargo upon Englishmen's estates, monies excepted. [If] we could have an absolute confirmation thereof, then a man [could] trade with some security.

1. The manuscript is damaged.

51b. By the next ship I shall send all those [papers Mr] Clerke desires about the *Swan*'s dispatch, as also, question not, ... a letter from the Spanish ambassador to the [Capt.] General [of the Canaries]. I would have sent [the papers per this] via, but it is somewhat uncertain and of great bulk to send out, [and as] yet I cannot learn of any ship bound for your place from hence.

[We] have been with your papers at the Committee of Trade. ... We set forth in our petition to them to have a prohibition of Canary wines for ... after the last of Feb., provided they bring not above their fifths [i.e. the principal English factors in the Canaries export no more than their shares of a predetermined number of pipes] and ... other necessary things for a regulation of trade, which I cannot advise at present.

[In] my former [have] given you the prices of West India goods. Campechena is [fallen] to 6s per lb and likewise sylvester to 3s 4d per lb, and cochineal to 26s per lb; [logwoo]d not worth £11 [per t] aboard ship. Of all the commodities have some good quantities [come] last vintage ships, and more expected. Hides at 7d per lb. Sugars a good commodity.

Pray send me a memory of what goods is most proper to be brought [from Genoa, see **53b**] to the [Canary] Islands because I am entreated by some Straits merchants to [go in] with them for a ship from thence, which I conceive will turn well [to account in] regard oils are worth ... *vellon* per rove in Seville. ...

[P.S. Have he]ard that Diego Benitez' and several [other] *puestos* are unsold in the Island. Pray, [if you] send [wines] home in the *Swan*, let them [be] all good, or else send none. Good wines [are worth] from £28 to £30 per pipe any time of [yea]r, which may serve per advice.

52. to William Clerke   15 Feb. 1652
a. I have received yours of 15 and 26 Nov., 17 Dec. and 21 Jan., part of which I have answered in some joint letters written you and Mr Paynter. I shall not need to write you any more about the *Susan*'s wines, being you have received my advice thereof, both what quantities and the quality of them, which is inferior to every man's wines. I know no man hath such a parcel of balderdash. Surely you could not but know it before they were shipped. I admire you should so little regard your own interest. You know I did all last year write you the inconveniency of bad wines, but it seems

my advice is little regarded, so I shall hereafter not trouble you so often with my lines except they be to more purpose. I am confident it troubles me more to see your wines lie than it does you that own them. Good wines are a precious commodity at present and will be all this summer, worth £30, but bad wines as great a drug. I cannot get one able vintner to bid me anything for them, and to sell them to those that will never pay me, I had better keep them in my cellar. You are not fully sensible what it is to be plagued with that commodity. If do not sell them within this month, I must be fain to rack them and keep them till Michaelmas.

As for the average on the *Susan*, I doubt I must be forced to sue the insurers before they will come off, which I shall put in execution. Next, as for your Campeachy wood, I have not sold a stick nor know not when I shall. Had you advised me that there were quantities of that commodity to come home in several ships, as there did to 600 ts, I would have taken £12 per t aboard ship at first arrival, which now shall not get £10. You thought to have saved dead freight by sending it and now will come to lose double freight. Except you follow advice hereafter, you had better forbear trade. You know in my letters at vintage I excepted against that commodity, desiring you to send none. And as for the barrel of cochineal, I have sold it at 27s 6d per lb. It holds out full weight and more, which is a novelty to me. I pray, hereafter what India commodities you buy let them be opened and shifted, though you be at cost to new pack them. I mean cochineal, campechena and sylvester, and indigo, etc., for there's deceit in those commodities and come many false packed. If you buy any indigo and find it hard-backed, meddle not with it.

I wonder you kept the *Susan* so long for a few wines, especially being upon monthly pay. Mr Rodden hath received all those wines you loaded him in Mr Neale, which prove well considering the year, and hath sold them already at £28 10s per pipe to able men. I understand part of them were Diego Benitez', all which does but add grief to me to see that you should prefer strangers before yourself. Not that I envy at their happiness, but methinks common reason tells a man to prefer himself in first place. But this is not the first you have ever done it since I did your business. What reason you have for it I cannot imagine. Mr Rounton is now come in the river. How his wines prove cannot tell. Mr [Stephen] Slaney tells me they are Don Melchior's of Garachico, so I do conclude they are far better than those you sent me.

52b. I cannot get a farthing taken off per the insurers upon no terms. This ship I understand goes for the Isle of May to load salt and touch at Santa Cruz [de Tenerife] to take in 40 pipes of wine, which I never knew of before she was at Gravesend, otherwise should have sent you over a servant in her, which shall go per next, which may be 6 weeks hence. We are almost resolved to set Mr Russell [the *Katherine*] that way if can get but 120 ts certain. He accepts of your proffer so that you have $\frac{1}{16}$ part of his ship with the profit of last voyage, as you writ me. I here send you a letter from your brother George Clerke who tells me is not absolutely resolved whether shall return for Lisbon or no. What he writes about it I know not.

I take notice of the proclamation about the linens, which you do well to dispose of in time that you may not trust to the mercy of those cruel, unjust people [Cf. **19a**], for I know their malice is great against the [English] nation in general by reason you have left their wines upon their hands, which is the most commendable act that you did since you were men. It's not rendered so by me alone but by all the merchants upon the Exchange that know what trade is.

As for the provisions for your house, I shall buy them with expedition and such as you shall not dislike when God sends them safe to your hands. Your watch I have received, which shall be done according to your desire and sent you in next ship without fail.

Mr Warren and Mr Lee, owners of the *Susan*, do think they are wronged because you do not send home the account you writ of. In the meantime I have stopped £20 [of the freight payment]. Pray hasten it over per first. They likewise demand a pipe of wine which was due per charter-party, of which I am ignorant of, so desire your order about it. We have lost half our principal per said vessel. I have sold my part to Mr Warren.

If so be that the *galeones* and *Nueva España* fleet be detained from coming to Spain this year, there will be many men broken by it, which will cause very bad times for trade. Mr [John] Shaw's ship [the *Civil Society*] is brought into a port about 30 leagues from Nantes [by 5 French men-of-war], as Mr Holle advises me, she being very richly laden, worth £30,000.

By yours in Nov. and Dec. last I perceive that God sending Mr Jewell [supercargo on the *Swan*] well to arrive from Guinea is like to prove a very hopeful design, which indeed you ever writ since the first putting it in execution. Only in your last unto me of 21 Jan. you do seem to be much discouraged in the business. Besides, you have in all your letters this vintage written me that you expect good quantities of West India goods and in yours by Mr Rounton advise that you have not a *real*'s worth to load upon Webber [the *Blessing*], a great alteration in so short a time, which makes me beside myself, having taken so much pains in that design. Besides, I should not had a *real*'s interest in it but merely upon your encouraging advice. Methinks it's strange that so many West Indiamen should arrive and you buy nothing, having one ship in port and another expected and both per-month pay, a devouring moth, as I may best term it. I am sure no man hath had better advice than you. Whenever it please God to send Mr Jewell well to arrive, if the ship do stay for West Indiamen's arrival, the monthly pay will eat out stock and block. It was ever my earnest desire unto you to get in readiness a good part of the ship's lading before her arrival, for I had rather you should stay for the ship than she to stay for you. By yours I understand that there's another ship bound with Negroes for Tenerife besides ours, which I have inquired after and find to be true. She went to the Bight [of Benin], so that if Mr Jewell dispatch his business at the river Gambia, of necessity must get the start, which if do, I hope you will lose no time in disposing of the commodities.

52c. As concerning the bill of exchange which you remitted me upon Mr Richard King and Mr Christopher Boone, I have according to your direction presented it, who denied acceptance thereunto. So I have made a protest in forma. They pretend a £100 error in the account, which as yet I have not seen. For the rest, they proffer to pay, but I have refused it. I demanded the joint letter from Mr George Clerke, written you from Mr King and Boone from Seville, who hath delivered it me. The account, [Clerke] tells me hath it not, nor the copy, it being delivered Mr Richard King, as he tells me. They have promised to show me their objections in your account next week. Until then I cannot write you my opinion. However I conceive you had better lose somewhat of your right than contest or go to law. For such or any other differences which may hereafter concern you, it's necessary that you send me a general letter of attorney, otherwise what I act in your behalf is not valuable to your adversaries.

I have written you and Mr Paynter what concerns your joint affairs, which makes me the briefer in this particular letter and especially because I have so short warning, the ship being gone from Gravesend, as I am informed. By any means procure what goods possible you can for the *Swan* against her coming there and think not of sending her anywhere but directly home. If you can get 100 or 120 pipes of rare choice wines, there may very well a £1,000 be gotten by them surely I know. If need, you may pick out so many in the whole Island. Repair not in order of payment; for price you cannot exceed the agreement [among the English merchants]. Here is great want of good wines as ever was known, and I think as many bad as hath been this 20 years, insomuch that vintners do not draw a quarter part of what they have done. ... Pray let me hear from you per all vias, which is the life of trade. ...

53.[1] to Gowen Paynter and William Clerke   16 Feb. 1652
a. ... As concerning the wines which I received this year for your accounts, I have written you of their proof. As yet I have not sold one pipe nor God knows when I shall. I wish with all my heart that I had not had a pipe so I were £200 indebted upon that score. [You] are not sensible of the vexation. I writ in the former copy that Diego Benitez' wines were unsold, but since, I understand by one Mr Edward Rodden that he had them loaded by Mr [William] Clerke in one Mr Neale's [ship], which wines were sold at £28 10s per pipe, his parcel being 120 pipes. He told me of it in way of a jeer that he should have better wines than I, which he might well do if all things be weighed rightly.

I wonder that you do keep Webber [the *Blessing*] all this time and yet not settle where to send him. Such is the inconveniency of ships [hired] by month; many times make men go on upon desperate designs whereas otherwise they would not. It had been better you had sent home the ship empty as soon as she came from Newfoundland. You will find it hereafter to your costs.

I received your general agreement [i.e. among the English merchants in the Canaries to limit their purchases of wine] [per] Brampton [the *Matthew*], which was much desired by all the traders, being came home a week before Mr Wilson's [copy]. I must deal really with you; it is the best act that ever you did since you were men, and you are highly commended for it by all the merchants that walk the Exchange. It's very well resented by all men that are concerned in the trade, for had you given the Spaniard's price and laden your full tonnage, of necessity it would have ruined most of the principals' estates, for the wines would not have yielded £10 per pipe, they being so green that men do not drink one quarter part of what did formerly, Malagas proving very bad and Jerez worse, so that here is great quantities of bad wines in the city unsold, more than will vent this many [years]. We do follow the business about your contract whereby to have a confirmation of what therein contains, as also to have a [regulation] in the trade. The first thing is that we here may choose 2 of you every year as commissioners to break the price of wines after 20 Dec., and that no man may buy until that time nor above the price of what the 2 commissioners shall break at, and several other good rules which I make no question but the Parliament will grant.

1. The manuscript is damaged.

53b. By Jenkins I sent you the [Navigation] Act of Parliament which prohibits Hollanders to bring in any kind of Spanish or other foreign commodity, which I doubt never came to your hands because you give no receipt of [it] in your letters, so that I here send you another, it being a necessary thing to every merchant to have one.

I pray send me per first a memory what goods is proper to be brought from Genoa to the Canaries. I am desired it by some Straits merchants.

Here are at present 3 ambassadors from the States of Holland which come to treat with our States, both being upon very high terms and great difference. The ambassadors demand of our States 3 several articles, viz. that they may go on in their treaty where our ambassador, Lord St John, ended when was in Holland days past; secondly, that we call in all our letters of marque given against them for £50,000 damages done our nation; thirdly, and chiefly, they desire that our State would repeal the [Navigation] Act, which here send you. Our States' answers to abovesaid propositions is to the first, whereas the Lord St John left the treaty in Holland, it was not their pleasure to condescend to them propositions of his, so that now they will begin on new articles. Second, whereas [the Hollanders desire] those letters of marque recalled, their answer is that before they granted them they had sufficient proof made by oath that the people of this nation had sustained great losses and that they could not have justice nor [satis]faction in Holland, so that they can do no less but protect their own nation and put them in some way to get satisfaction. So they will not recall their letters of marque. Thirdly, for the repealing of the Act, it's so much against the grain of true Englishmen that I am confident it will stand in force, they being denied that likewise. So that you see all is contradicted, so there's little probability of any agreement.

I received letters yesterday from Amsterdam and Middelburg where they write me that Sir George Ayscue, who is General of our States' fleet for Barbados, hath taken 24 sail of Hollanders that were there trading with islanders contrary to the Parliament's act. So that these things makes our breach the more. If we have wars with the Hollanders, as 'tis generally thought, must give over our trade. Of this I shall per every conveyance give you notice what passeth. Likewise our States have granted letters of marque against the Spaniard for £20,000 to one Mr Maurice Thomson for losses sustained by them,[1] which I do not well like of, doubting the Spaniards will embargo [the goods of English merchants] ashore. This commission is granted a month since, of which I am very certain.

1. Thomson was joined by his brother William, Gregory Clement and Daniel Skinner in seeking letters of reprisal (*C.S.P.D.*, *1651–2*, 101).

53c. Here are 2 ships now arrived from Lisbon which bring very good news: the King of Portugal hath lifted the embargo which was upon all Englishmen's estates and hath delivered each man his goods, only some monies excepted, which is conceived will be speedily delivered, and hath chosen the Conde [Camar]eiro to come as ambassador to our States, who is daily expected.[1] So that I am confident we shall a peace conclude. Here are several ships going away for Lisbon upon this news. Indeed the King of Portugal cannot subsist except have peace with us. In case you have not disposed of [Mr] Webber [the *Blessing*] before this come to hand, may do well to send him to aforesaid place with hides and to load salt and come home, or else to return where you please.

Were the *Swan* lesser, would be a good design for her, but her lading would cloy that place with hides for many years, so that I would not think of sending her upon any design but directly home with her proportion of wines which will be 100 pipes or more, which, if you will take some care and pains to pick here and there so many pipes of choice liquors, though you give ready money, may very well get £1,000 by abovesaid quantity, for here is at present great want of good wines as ever there was since I came to England, worth £28 to £30 per pipe. Though wines were generally green, yet I am confident you may procure abovesaid parcel good in the Island. And for West India goods, seeing there arrived 3 ships from Havana, I wonder you did not buy some of it as well as other men, seeing that you expected so great a ship as the *Swan*. Hides are the only commodity in request, worth 7d per lb; Palma sugar a good commodity, worth £8 per cwt; ginger, £3 15s per cwt; Varinas tobacco, if right, 6s 6d per lb a small quantity; cochineal, 27s per lb; campechena a drug, worth 5s per lb; sylvester, 2s 10d per lb; indigo Guatemala, 4s 6d per lb. Send no Campeachy wood.

There's nothing gives me so much care as the ship *Swan* and the [*Turned-out*] frigate. When I consider what a vast charge we are at, it makes me tremble [to] think of it. There's nothing will make a rich man poor sooner than ships [hired] per month. It's a continual moth, as I may term it. God send me clear of this, I shall be cautious how I come in for my [part]. However, since we are in, now must endeavour to wade on [as well as] we can. I have done my utmost to promote that design. Do yours when God sends well the ship to arrive with you, and the success we must leave to God's providence. I shall desire that you write me per all vias. ...

1. The Conde de Penaguião arrived in England on 19 Aug. 1652. He was the Great Chamberlain of Portugal and signed his letters *Conde Camareiro* (E. Prestage, *The Diplomatic Relations of Portugal . . . from 1640 to 1688* (Watford, 1925), 128, n. 1).

54.[1] to Gowen Paynter and William Clerke   20 Feb. 1652
    I have written you both severally and jointly per this conveyance at

large, to which desire reference. These chiefly serve [per covert] to the enclosed [Navigation] Act of Parliament which I formerly sent [per] Anthony Jenkins, and you do not as much as give [me receipt] of, which makes me jealous it never came to your hands. So I thought too good to send you another [copy, being] very necessary for a merchant to have one of them by [him]. ...

About 20 days h[ence] here will be a ship ready which stops at Tenerife to take in [wines] for Barbados, per whom shall write you. ... [On the] *Swan* you may please to take notice that I gave Mr Jewell ... order let no man except the master bring a black, which he pro[mised] none should. And Mr Jewell for his part carried not £5 particular adventure, so that what the ship brings must be for the general account. Here is arrived Mr Bean. ...

1. The manuscript is damaged.

55. to William Clerke   5 March 1652

a. ... As yet cannot dispose of one pipe of your wines, nor of Mr Paynter's, nor my own. Had I but 50 pipes of good wines, it would be a means to carry off the rest, which I hope you will perform in the *Swan*, which if you should not, I doubt will lie long on my hands. If I could get £19 per pipe round for the parcel without any choice, I would take it, though you accounted me hereafter a spoil-market.

The last night I met with the insurers about the average in the *Susan*, when, after a great deal of dispute, have made an agreement with the major part of them, hoping that the rest will subscribe to it, which if do shall advise you. I was fain to put them in suit in the [Insurance] Court before could bring them to any reason. Our agreement is thus: they are to allow me 10 per cent upon the whole policy of £1,200, which is £120 so much more than I should have received if had gone to trial. I know not how you will approve of my actions herein, but this much I must tell you, that if it had been my own business, I protest, I could not have advanced more than I did.

I have likewise sold your Campeachy wood at £11 10s per ton, one-half money and [the balance in] 4 months, they to pay customs. I am only to pay lighterage and porters and crane, which is a small matter. Which bargain was very much against my grain, but, weighing all things in the balance of equity, I found there was 700 ts of ditto commodity in town, which is more than will vent this 3 years though not a stick come in. And sure I am that those which sell hereafter will come lower for several have offered their wood since I sold, at my price, but the salters refuse their proffers, which makes me think that I am happy to be rid of such a drug. I pray for future be cautious how you meddle with such commodities as you have no advice for. Mr [Stephen] Slaney hath sold his wood that came in Mr Taylor in truck of fustians, at what price I know not. Here is come 2 parcels of lignum rhodium in Sidrake Blake and Bean that I doubt now where shall sell yours at £5 per ton. I protest I know not what to do with it. No man will bid a penny for it, and I am at great charge per warehouse room which will eat out all. In Holland nor France it's worth nothing.

Such commodities with logwood and bad wines as I have had will make a man have gray hairs before his time. This year's business hath proved cross. I hope next will be better, otherwise I had rather sit still.

55b. As concerning those papers touching the *Swan's* dispatch [i.e. to facilitate the entry of the Negroes at Tenerife], which you desired me to send, they are not so soon procured as you conceived when writ for them. If you really consider, it's of dangerous consequence, which for my part I would not be seen in the business if might have £500 for doing it. However, so far I did to comply with your requests, though I did not act personally, yet I put them which did. Though with much difficulty, all things were performed at last: the bill of health and the [Spanish] ambassador's letter and the commission, which was sent you in the ship *Peter and John*, Abraham Filitter master, by his gunner, Thomas Harris, who I make no question but will safely deliver it you with his own hands. It hath cost me £12 and yet not all satisfied. I pray God give a blessing to that design; it hath cost me more money than ever I brought to account, besides no small trouble. When the letter was demanded of the ambassador [Cardenas], he presently fell into the account and said that was merely to colour contraband goods, or Negroes, but, being to a special friend of his, did not much repair. I was fain to give his secretary £5 besides some other small fees. In my opinion, all things go very authentic, which I am confident will be a mainstead to the ship's admittance without any demur. ...

56. to Gowen Paynter and William Clerke   6 March 1652
a. ... I hope ere this come to hand that the *Swan* will be arrived with you, which, if so happen, pray endeavour to load as many wines as possible will serve upon her and likewise some good sorts of West India goods. And if so be you cannot load the ship, then what [tonnage] remains, pray let it out as soon as she arrives because here is one Mr [John] Price, a ship of 160 ts, bound for Tenerife and goes to seek a freight. I have endeavoured what I can to discourage them whereby not to proceed, being doubtful the Spaniards will freight him, but to no purpose as it falls out.

Hides are the most staple and vendiblest commodity of all West India goods, worth 7d per lb; Havana sugars, white at £7 per cwt, ditto muscovados at £4 5s per cwt; Palma sugar sorted [i.e., good whites] at £8 per cwt; cochineal, if good, 27s per lb; ginger worth £3 15s per cwt; Varinas tobacco, a small quantity if right, 7s per lb; campechena, 5s per lb; sylvester, 2s 10d per lb; logwood, £10 per t aboard ship. Send none of the 3 last commodities for they are very drugs; the city is overlaid. Good Guatemala indigo, that is not hard-backed, worth 4s 6d per lb.

I do wonder that you keep Webber [the *Blessing*] there upon monthly pay, especially she being leaky and withal a very bad sailor, as I am informed. The ship did go very well before he had her; I believe [Webber] could never find out the right trim. If you have not disposed of her before this come to hand, send her for Lisbon with hides and 10 ts of logwood and let her come home from thence. You need not fear of embargo [in Portugal]; we have now free trade there. If you do not like that design, then may send her to Nantes with hides, which are worth 11 *livres* per piece, and Campeachy wood is worth 10 *livres* per kt. There will vent 50 ts. This advice I received yesterday from Mr Holle. There's free trade for English ships at present, there being now several, to my knowledge [gone to France]. If you doubt, may let the ship stop at Plymouth to take my advice.

56b. Webber, when was in the Calms, sent home certificate and several bills of exchange upon me to pay his wife, seamen's wives, and owners, all which I have not accepted, nor will not before hear from you, being I conceive [you] would pay him his freight there. However, Webber shows himself to be a froward blade, indeed a fool, to draw bills of exchange upon me when was in the Calms, and so be pleased to acquaint him of it.

I pray advise me in time what your resolutions are against next vintage. The vintners' cellars were never worse furnished with good wines than now. Therefore, if they prove right next year, be assured here will be great sales; but if, on the contrary, prove bad, then meddle not with any, better let the tonnage come home empty. For I have sad experience of this year's fruits to my knowledge. I never took more pains than last year, first in the disposing of your wines and to see that they were good paymasters, and secondly in disposing of their proceeds according to your orders in every particular, as the Guinea voyage and others. And whereas I thought to reap great content and some benefit by my endeavours, truly I am plagued into vexatious troublesome business, part of which I do impute unto the bad times, but somewhat may be laid upon the little regard you had of your own interests. For my part, I must deal ingenuously with you, I take no comfort in doing men's business when I see such apparent losses as this year produces. I am in hopes the next will be better or otherwise you had better leave trading, for I do more esteem my friends' benefit that way than all the commissions you can imagine of.

I received letters yesterday from Amsterdam and Middelburg where they write me that the States of Holland have embargoed their own and our shipping over all the land till 1 April next, all which are symptoms of a war in my apprehension and several others'. As yet the ambassadors have done nothing with our States, they being afar off in their demands from each other. Great preparations are making for the setting out a fleet of ships both by us here and likewise per them in Holland, yet our States have called in all letters of marque against the Flemings 20 days since. I have nothing else to enlarge at present, but I would wish you to send home all your shipping abroad and not to keep them out in such dangerous times. ...

57. to [William Clerke]   13 March 1652
... Pray let me hear from you per all vias, especially if you send home the *Swan* because I may make further insurance if occasion offers. This ship, Mr Shaw, which is arrived from Caracas, hath brought 30,000 lbs weight of tobacco, which, I conceive, will lower the price. But as for hides, they will hold up still, as formerly written you. As yet not sold a pipe of wine. ...
[P.S.] Mr [Stephen] Slaney's wines do not prove well, as I am informed.

58. to Gowen Paynter and William Clerke   13 March 1652

a. ... Only by mere accident I understood of this ship's departure for Tenerife, which nowadays men do all their business so private as that it's a hard matter to know where a ship is bound because they enter them for wrong ports. I understand this ship goes consigned to Mr John Campion, which carries the most part French linens, at which I admire [because of the recent Spanish proclamations against French goods], but I am sure it's so because I have a copy of the entries at Custom House upon her. Whither she is bound from thence I know not, but I conceive for Lisbon because they are Portugal merchants that freight her.

We daily expect an ambassador for King John [of Portugal]. In the interim he hath cleared all Englishmen's estates and admits as free trade as formerly hath done. This very instant here is one come out of Mr John [Shaw's] ship who is arrived in the Downs from Caracas or thereabouts. She brings about £30,000 cargo [sic, see **57**], most part is tobacco and 4,000 hides, which is nothing to lower the price a farthing of what have formerly written you concerning that commodity.

Likewise here is news that Barbados is yielded up unto Sir George Ayscue, commander-in-chief of the Parliament's fleet against it, and our ships have taken 26 sail of Hollanders at ditto island trading, which is against the Parliament's [Navigation] Act I sent you, so they will be condemned as prize. It's said that they are worth £100,000 ships and goods, most of them being fully laden, all which does increase the Hollanders' rage against us. Here is the greatest preparation making for a fleet to set to sea that ever was known, above 120 sail of men-of-war. The great ship *Royal Sovereign*, alias *Commonweal of England*, is fitting to go out in May. I am verily persuaded that we shall jar with the Hollanders, which if do must of necessity [give] over trade, for not one ship in 10 can escape them. Likewise [there are] great preparations making in Holland for a fleet.

I have now received a letter, 25 Feb., from San Lucar where they write me that the *galeones* are expected about April. They complain there very much not a piece of eight to be seen since the rise of *cuartos*, which undoes all trade in those parts.[1]

1. On 11 Nov. 1651 the Spanish government ordered that *vellon* coins be restamped to raise their denominations. Such crying up and excessive minting of *vellon* increasingly drove silver coins, like pieces of eight, out of circulation in Spain (E. J. Hamilton, *War and Prices in Spain, 1651–1800* (Cambridge, Mass., 1947), 9–14).

58b. Here is Mr Davis, a ship of 220 ts, which is freighted for the Canaries to return home with wines, which will be ready in 15 days to be gone. It is not known who are the principals here, the business being carried so private, only put in a broken fellow's name, one Horsnell, and friend of Mr Forster's; but the ship goes consigned to Mr John Campion. Therefore you may do well to look after her when she arrives. Here is likewise another ship, one Mr [John] Price, of 160 ts, which goes to look freight, and another small vessel bound out of Topsham, all which ships arriving, I doubt will raise the prices of wines and likewise of West India goods.

Pray hasten home the *Swan* as soon as she arrives. It's not good to keep her out these uncertain and dangerous times. In case that you will not send her directly home from thence, I desire that from the time she arrives from Guinea there you will take my part and discharge me from the monthly pay, and then you must needs send me home £1,000 or £1,200 to pay the ship's freight for 6 months and [the *Turned-out*] frigate's, I mean in good pieces of eight. Otherwise I cannot pay it. But I hope you will not any way see me suffer that way but consider my engagements. This I thought good to give you a hint in case the ship come not home. If you take my counsel, I would order Webber [the *Blessing*] to come home though empty. Here no man will scarce adventure till they see the event of the Hollander's treaty with our States. For prices of West India goods I refer you to my former. As yet not sold a pipe of wine. I expect daily to hear from you by the Bristol ship. ...

59. to William Clerke   27 March 1652
a. I have received yours of 3 present with the bill of exchange of Duarte Enríquez [Alvarez] for £150 upon Antonio Fernandez [Carvajal] which I presented yesterday, being as soon as it came to my hands. Antonio Fernandez will not accept it, pretending that Duarte Enríquez gave him order to pay unto his correspondent in Amsterdam all what he had in his hands, so he hath written to aforesaid correspondent in Holland where shall pay it or protest it, whose answer we expect in 14 days. But I am of the opinion it will go protested.

I have met Mr [Richard] King and Mr [Christopher] Boone and proffered to abate them £20 upon the whole, but would not be accepted. You writ them as though you had given me a very large order, and when I come to peruse your letters, I find my hands bound. But if you were not my good friend, I would not meddle in the business without your ample order or letter of attorney. You have been out of your money this 4 years, and for ought I know it will be 4 more except you allow them somewhat. For you to sue for it by law, may spend as much as the debt come to, for ought I know, and at last refer it to merchants [i.e. to arbitration], which is daily done here. Therefore, pray let me know your resolution per first with a letter of attorney. Indeed I cannot well be without one in regard I act your business and especially things of this nature.

You writ me will have a care to dispatch the *Swan* completely from thence at her arrival. I should be glad it may fall out so, but by your former I find that not a *real* worth of goods bought in readiness, and how you can comply with what you writ me I know not. I wonder you could not as well buy the Havana man's goods as Mr [John] Turner or Mr [John] Webber in regard you expect such a ship daily. When you writ me first to go upon the design, I thought you would have made better preparation than you now have. If the ship come to stay for West Indiamen, we shall be eaten out by freight. The business gives me a great deal of care. At the expiration of 8 months I must pay £1,000 and upwards. Except you send me home some monies, I cannot do it.
59b. Here is certain advice from San Lucar that they expect the *galeones* in all April, which does not agree with what you writ me about them.

Good Varinas tobacco is in esteem at present, worth 7s per lb; ginger garbled, £4 per cwt; hides, 7d per lb; cochineal, 27s per lb; sugars begin to fall. Buy no Campeachy wood nor campechena grain nor sylvester, being drugs. Indigo that is not hard-backed worth 4s 6d per lb; it's now bought in San Lucar at 6*Rs plata* per lb, as per advice from thence. There are gone and will go many ships for Tenerife this year which will make West India goods excessive dear. Therefore you must not pause long upon it, but if do anything let it be at first.

Yesterday I received a letter from Mr [William] Webber [the *Blessing*] from Falmouth of 22 present, where he writes me could not fetch his port Nantes by reason of contrary winds, and seeing his ship was like to sink in seas, was forced to put in for Falmouth where he is in a sad condition. He writes will make ready to be gone with expedition, but I am half-minded to alter your design and even send to order him to come for London, for it's a mere madness for you to adventure your estates in such a dangerous hull which is every month like to sink in sea with one leak or other. Such ships and such designs, with your tedious dispatch there, will soon make a rich man poor. I do not love to flatter my friends when I see so apparent losses. I have written Mr Paynter to the very same purpose about this ship and likewise about the *Swan*.

If you can but procure 100 pipes wine between you and my father-in-law to send home in the *Swan*, if that they be good, will yield £28 per pipe. Though they be but *abocado* [mild], as you term it there, they will sell well here. Never was such a scarcity of good wines in London as now, which may serve per advice. ...

60. to William Clerke   10 May 1652
a. ... I have received yours, 26 March, per Mr Peter Steward. As for the bill of exchange for £150 upon Antonio Fernandez Carvajal, he did afterwards accept and hath now paid it me, so that I expect Mr Abraham Lee's order how to dispose of it, as also of the £150 which you have passed on me payable to him. I could wish that you had forborne till that I had recovered the monies which are due to me, being I am at present somewhat short of cash. However, since you have drawn it, shall be punctually paid. But for the future pray be sparing, for with bills of exchange there's no delaying; if a man pay them not at the day, you know his credit is clouded.

Since my last unto you I have with much ado sold your wines which came in the *Susan*, all except 4 pipes which are not worth £5 per pipe. The others I have sold at £22 10s per pipe to pay ⅓ money, the rest at 3 and 3 months [see **11b** note]. Those men which bought them were my old customers, and they merely bought them out of respect they bore to me and not for want of them. After they were bought I protest they offered me 10s per pipe out of their purses to clear them of the bargain. I am glad that I am rid of that plague. I hope shall never be troubled with the like again. Likewise I have sold your *leña noel* in truck of strong waters at £9 6s 8d per t; the parcel makes out 23 ts, odd cwt. I have put off the strong waters at 12d per case loss and made money off my truck. I saw that warehouse room would have eaten up the principal made me sell it, and since, that which came in Bean's [ship] is sold for £8 per t. That which came in Sidrake Blake is yet unsold. I believe here is enough of that commodity to serve all Christendom this 7 years.

60b. After several meetings and many hot disputes, I have made an end with Mr Richard King and Christopher Boone in your behalf. Mr [Stephen] Slaney and your brother [George] were partly eyewitnesses to what passed between us, who did counsel me by any means to conclude though upon worse terms than I concluded. How you will approve of it I know not, but therein I have done for you as though it were for my own self. But if you ever put me upon any such business hereafter, I desire to have your letter of attorney, or at least a larger commission than I now had about this business. Otherwise you must excuse me for I shall not meddle in it, for I acknowledge I have gone beyond the bounds of your order, which is not merchant-like and a thing that I hate as much as any man living. In my opinion you were much overseen [i.e. mistaken] in the advice you gave to Mr King and Mr Boone, for you writ them as though you had given me as large [an] order about the ending that business as then could write, saying that whatsoever I did so therein you would gladly approve of as to the ending of that controversy between you. When they showed me your letter, I admired at it, looking to my own letter; there you tied my hands, not to abate a farthing, which advice not concurring with each other. Mr King etc. came to me desiring to meet them to end the business. I answered according to the tenor of yours to me, [i.e.] with paying the money as per bill of exchange, the business was ended without any further meeting. They answered, 'If Mr Clerke did not intend to have our business argued and settled rightly, to what purpose did he put in his letter that what you did with us he would approve of?' By that very expression there was some differences in dispute.

60c. In fine, to be brief, we met several times and at last concluded it viz. They came to owe you 17,245*Rs* which I would willingly have them paid it here, but they would not, so have given me bills of exchange for Seville to be paid in Seville and Mexico coin, which money I shall draw from hence when here the bills are accepted. The 933*Rs* which Mr Thomas Boone owes you they will not allow because Mr Thomas Boone will not allow it his kinsman [Christopher Boone] in account. So to speak justly, I see no reason for that particular on your side. I shall shortly speak with aforesaid Thomas Boone about it. Likewise they abate you 330*Rs* per tobacco you took, as they showed me, under your own hand, and I can see nothing made good in your account for it. Likewise you charge 313½*Rs* paid Mr Redwood per average, which he will make oath never received a penny. However, if you make appear that you paid it and allowed the tobacco, then they are obliged unto me to return the money again. There's likewise an error per commission in the account, as you may see, made good. Here enclosed I send you an abstract of the adjusted [account] and likewise a copy of their obligation to me. And likewise I have given them an obligation of 4,415*Rs* which you charge them in their account as paid to Lazaro Rivera on account of tobacco which you received of him for their accounts by order of Don Antonio de Castillo, which they say are not satisfied in that particular, being they paid the full of the tobacco unto

Don Antonio de Castillo. So that rather than they should stop so much money of yours in their hands, I thought fit to give them my obligation. So according to its tenor, be sure you send home an affidavit how you have paid it that so they may be satisfied. Otherwise I must repay the money here again. And withal I desire your approbation of the business that I may not bring myself into a praemunire for my good will and pains but, I hope, better things. However you may take it, truly I conceive I have done you a piece of very good service in ending the business, for men are mortal and Mr [Christopher] Boone is now going for Seville; and whereas you conceive to have gotten satisfaction by law, really you and them might have spent £300 and not brought it to a trial. Both Mr King and Mr Boone, after we had agreed, told me that it was £1,000 out of their way that this unhappy business broke out between you, but they desired me to write you that friendly correspondence might be renewed as formerly and that you would forget and forgive, which I engaged you should do and be ready to do them any friendly office that lay in your power.

60d. As concerning the *Susan* [Capt. Giles Paynter], from 1 July to the time she was discharged there's 5½ months' freight due, which I charge to your account. I cleared her out of your pay 19 Dec. last. I have made you good the balance of Giles Paynter's account, but he complains and says does not owe you so much. But I shall not take cognizance of what he says in that particular. As for the 235*Rs* which Mr Christopher Boone is your debtor upon his particular account, pray take notice that is not included in the former as I told him when I received it. I asked him the money; he told me that he and you would order that between you.

I am sorry that I must advise that which I never did any man before. I sold one Mr Cornelius Burras 3 chests of your indigo and have received all the money to £40, which is like to prove a bad debt, he being broke. It's the first that ever I met withal. I pray God it may be the last. The times are so dangerous that let a man be never so wary he may be caught.

For matter of your joint affairs, I refer you to my letter written you and my father-in-law. Yesterday I writ you a few hasty lines per Mr Thomas Bowridge, where I sent you a letter from Mr Boone which I opened merely to see what he writ you about the business which we ended. But I found he writ the truth so I hope you will excuse my boldness. I likewise sent you a letter from your brother Mr George Clerke who is my very good friend and now acquaintance through your good self. We have now sent Mr Chalk's new frigate [the *Mary*] for Lisbon and Faro with goods to the value of £3,000, whereof your brother [George Clerke] and cousin George Clerke have one-half, myself and a friend the other half. God send good success; it's a hopeful voyage. I am now upon agreement with the coachman [who is building a coach for a Canarian, Don Carlos], which cannot go over till the first vintage ship. Had he [Don Carlos] left some things to my ordering, I should have contrived it better than he hath in his order.

I have sent you in this ship [the *Judeth*, Capt. John Price] your watch; was all unscrewed and cleaned; is in a box directed to my father-in-law. Likewise I have shipped aboard this ship one quartercask and one runlet, containing 24 gallons or thereabouts, being filled with the best beef that ever I bought in my life, marked as per margin. It was at first in 2 quartercasks, but when I came to pickle it found some pieces faulty, so left them out and got a smaller cask for it. Likewise I had shipped aboard your 500 lbs candles and upwards aboard ditto ship, but those and 12 or 15 boxes more were all seized upon aboard the ship and are brought ashore again, being a commodity that cannot be shipped out, which business hath not a little troubled me. I shall endeavour the clearing of them, but it will cost above half as much as they are worth, clearing. The master can inform you, to avoid suspicions I entered them as Russia candles and paid custom, but there are rogues that swear that are English. The bad success of this made [me] forbear shipping your butter for fear the like misfortune should befall that, but I could not get any in pots. Of this you shall hear more per next.

I have writ Mr Abraham Lee that for the £150 which you drew upon me I shall satisfy him in San Lucar; likewise Antonio Fernandez [Carvajal's] bill, if he pleases.

As concerning your servant, I have now agreed for one [Thomas Leigh]. He plies his writing and shall go over in Mr William Bradick's ship, which may be ready within 10 days. Then shall enlarge concerning that particular. ...

61. to Gowen Paynter and William Clerke   12 May 1652
a. I have received yours of 2 and 26 March, the one via Nantes and the other per Peter Steward. In my last I gave you notice how that Mr Webber in the *Blessing* was forced into Falmouth having a very leaky ship, as he wrote me. I did then write you that I would stop his voyage for Nantes; but weighing all things rightly, I did conceive you might account it a great piece of presumption in me to contradict your designs; upon which I altered my opinion, and the ship is now safe at Morbihan, there taking in her lading of wheat, etc., as Mr Holle writes me. I verily believe she is now dispatched. Ditto Mr Holle hath drawn upon me a bill of exchange for £150 according to your credit and says that the next post might draw £150 more upon me for your accounts, being with what he disburses for the master to fit his ship and what upon the cargo, he shall be out far more money in disbursal for you, which I verily believe he will. Yet you have given me no more order than for £150. However, I must not protest his bills. Wheat is excessive dear there, worth 170 *livres* per t, which will amount in her lading, and you send but a very poor cargazon upon her, in my opinion. Methinks you might have sent £1,000 pieces [of eight] more in Peru money, seeing you have them so cheap at the Islands, I am told 6Rs per piece indifferent good money. [See **30b**.]

I wonder that you have not sent me home what money you have disbursed upon the *Blessing* whereby I might have discounted it upon the first freight. Webber hath made such a confusion about that. I cannot be quiet for the owners, they demand money. I have paid the men's wages and monies to his wife but shall pay no more until have account from him.

I formerly writ you that if hides were to be bought to send the ship for Lisbon, but now I would wish you to forbear because most of Steward's hides [brought from Tenerife to London] are shipped that way, about

2,000 of them. I bought 500 of them at 7d per lb. I wonder that Mr John Webber [in Tenerife] should surpass all men there as he does. He hath laden home his full proportion of good wines according to the year, and above £1,200 in pieces of eight, and £5,000 in the best sorts of West India goods. All this he hath done this vintage and in Steward [the *Island Merchant*].

61b. I wonder that you should stand and look on as you have when other men do these things. If that it were not for the ship *Swan* from Guinea, for my part I cared not whether you bought a *real*'s worth of goods or no, but you, knowing of such a great ship's coming unto you, and not to buy anything in readiness, it seems strange to me. When I went upon the design at first, I thought there would have been better preparations against the ship's coming than I now find to be, but I do foresee that we shall make a lame reckoning of it. The very freight will eat out our cargazon. God sending the ship well to arrive, I pray think not of sending her anywhere but home though she come empty. I care not, seeing falls out so cross, only I desire you that you will but send home so many pieces of eight as will pay the ship's and pinnace's [*Turned-out*'s] freight, which you must do if do not send goods, for I have no monies to pay it of yours. And if in case that you do not send home the ship before vintage, then you must send me home some goods, pieces of eight or bills of exchange to pay the first 8 months of the ship and pinnace.

I received a letter from Mr [Robert] Lang under covert Mr John Turner via Bordeaux where the great Fleming is arrived with her *leña noel*. If Mr Holle [at Nantes] have not sold yours, will hinder the sale much of it. By ditto letter I understand Mr Abraham Filitter [the *Peter and John*] was arrived at Santa Cruz [de Tenerife], in which ship I remitted Mr William Clerke all those papers concerning the *Swan*'s dispatch, which I hope are safely delivered. There went the commission, a letter to the [Capt.] General [of the Canaries] and bill of health, all very authentic, and I am confident will save us £1,200 in the dispatch. They cost me money and great deal of care and fain to make good friends. If this Negro voyage prove not right, I shall be laughed at by many upon the Exchange, for there's much notice taken of it and the more because of Pyle's lawsuit with me. The freight gives me the greatest care, which I hope you will consider my engagement here.

God sending Mr Webber to arrive safe with you, and if corn be a good commodity, may send him to Nantes again with logwood which is worth 11 *livres* per cwt. If not, then for Galicia for pilchards, or else you may send him home.

61c. In your particular letters I have given you advice of the sale of your wines, I mean all those that were good as sound. Though I sold them all at one price, yet I would not have you to think that I have done any of you wrong. They were put in several cellars, and I protest I know not 12d difference in them. I never knew so many bad wines in London as now, of sherries, Malagas and Canaries. I believe there's above 4,000 pipes and butts this day unsold, and God knows when they will be disposed of. Some men have their wines of this 2 years unsold, as Mr [Roger] Kilvert and Mr Bonfoy, which will prove unsufferable losses to them. By Mr

Lang's letter I see there's no hopes of having home any wines in the *Swan*, there being none fit to be laden, besides they ask above your contract. [See **53a.**] Good Canaries are now worth above £30 per pipe, but it's said by some Parliament men that they will put a price that the vintners shall not sell for above 7d per pint; so after that rate they cannot give us above £18 per pipe. Of this shall be more larger in my next.

The Hollanders' ambassador and our States are yet upon treating. I hope they will agree. Our States have this day 100 men-of-war at sea and the Hollander have not half so many. Besides, here is now abuilding above 20 frigates from 30 to 60 guns. Never had England such a navy as now. The Hollander does begin to stoop; they proffer £700,000 to the State in satisfaction to the injuries they did us 30 years since at Amboina in East India besides several of things. You may be assured the [Navigation] Act I sent you will not be revoked but still stand in force. If once this treaty were concluded, then our States would begin to treat with the Spanish ambassador upon new articles which will be more advantageous to us than the former, by far, I hope, beyond the Hollander's articles. To this purpose Mr Roger Kilvert is now drawing up a canto of all our wrongs and abuses to present before they come to treat.

61d. I am very sorry to hear that no rain hath fallen with you. I doubt you will have scarcer vintage than last year, yet here men do not take notice of it but run on headlong. As you may see, this ship [the *Judeth*], Mr Price, goes full of goods. Besides, men have great estates there already, by reason of last year's small return [of wines], they will charge home with tonnage this vintage, though you and others write never so much against it. Necessity will compel a great many to do it, for I'll assure you here are some certain men which are very low, and their whole dependence is upon a good return next vintage, which, if that should fail, I doubt some will be fain [to] go to Ram Alley for their habitation. Good wines will be a great commodity next year. Therefore be sure to secure your wines in time, for you will find very much looking after them as ever there was since you knew the Island, which may serve per advice.

The Straits memory which you sent me came 2 months too late. There is no oil about Genoa nor Majorca to be bought for money, it being most part shipped for this place where it's a great commodity at present, sold for £48 per t whereas formerly usually sold for £32 per t. I shall keep it by me peradventure it may be put in execution within this 12 months. Whenever it be, you shall reap the benefit of its disposal there, of which you may be confident.

I formerly writ you that the traders desired some kind of regulation in the Canary trade, but they meant not to limit any man for matter of quantity, only in price they would, so that you may clear yourselves of those doubts.

Mr Holle advises me this instant of a great Fleming's arrival from Tenerife at Nantes laden with hides, sugars and a great parcel of *leña noel*, and intended to load wheat back again for Tenerife. But he writes me the people will not suffer more corn to be shipped out by reason they have had very much drought of late, and we here have had the like.

Here is ships arrived from Barbados since it was surrendered to Sir

George Ayscue. Mr Body's and Stephen's ship, which they sent there with wines, is arrived to a great market. Have sold all his wines at 16 cwt sugar per pipe. Of this I saw a letter from Barbados.

As yet Mr Holle hath not advised me the sum of what hath laden aboard [at Nantes] for your accounts on the *Blessing*. When have his advice shall make insurance according to your order.

61e. I shall now give you a brief account of the prices of West India goods: West India hides at 7d per lb; Havana sugar white, £6 10s per cwt; ditto muscovado, £4 5s per cwt; ginger garbled, £3 15s per cwt; good cochineal, 27s per lb; campechena, 5s per lb; sylvester, 2s 10d per lb if good; indigo Guatemala, not hard-backed, 4s 6d per lb; good Varinas tobacco, 6s 6d per lb; Palma sugars, £8 per cwt; logwood, £10 per t aboard ship. But none of these commodities are comparable to good Canaries. Though you give high prices for them next vintage, yet if good the market here will make you a means for all.

If the *Swan* come home [from Tenerife to London] with any considerable cargo for our accounts, it would be necessary that you give me advice per all vias whereby I may make a further insurance, which will be now done very reasonable. I have formerly writ you how there's £1,000 done upon the general account per month in trade.

I here send you a bill of rates which I received this day from Rouen. My correspondent there, his name is Humphrey Wilkings; if you have occasion to, make use of him.

I hope, God sending the *Swan* well, that we shall have above £1,500 in other goods besides Negroes, especially if she went for the Bight [of Benin], for then half our iron and the copper bars will buy 300 Negroes. I desired Mr Jewell to invest the overplus in elephants' teeth, which is a very good commodity here, and beeswax, which is very plentiful at Gambia, which is a current commodity with you. I pray see that there come no private adventures, for I told Mr Jewell I should except against that. I wonder that you did not look better after that of our Barbary voyage but to let others bring ⅓ part of our ship's lading free of freight. These things will soon make a rich factor and poor principals. I do not write this in any way to deprive Richard Jewell of his right, but I would have Caesar to have his due. Since we run great risks and pay great freights and the like, it may be worth looking after such things. ...

[P.S.] If any ship should arrive at the Islands from Caracas, I would wish you to buy those hides before Havana or Santo Domingo though you give 4 or 6Rs per hide more. They turn better to account than others by reason we sell them by weight here. Capt. Garvis Russell is now in the States' service with his frigate [the *Katherine*]; hath 26 guns, 85 men. We [as shareholders] have £280 per month, which is a good rate. I here send you a book which Mr Kilvert hath set forth of late [see **61c**]. You are all beholding to that man.

62. to William Clerke   25 May 1652
... The bearer hereof is one Thomas Leigh, now your apprentice, having sealed his indenture this day to serve you 7 years, to which purpose I have his mother's bond for £1,000 per his truth. He carries over with him

a true copy of his indenture in parchment which you are to seal to him and send it home unto one Mr Thomas Leigh here.

I have endeavoured what in me lies to procure you a pretty youth, which I hope this will prove so. He is a very good scholar and writes a pretty school hand, both Italian and Spanish hands, which he will improve daily by his practice, you having a little patience for 6 months. His father [Richard] was a very eminent merchant, ... in London, and his mother lives in very good rank and quality. ... [The] young man hath £200 per annum in as good land as any in England, besides, I believe, some money left him. His land comes into his hands when he is 21 years of age. I have not any way undervalued you, in that I have advanced your interest as much as though it were my own case. You are to have £220 with him, to say £120 in a month and the other £100 at 12 months hence. As yet I have not given Mrs Leigh a grant that I will stay so long for the £100. Per next you shall know what is done in it.

This office which you have put me upon in taking a servant is a very unthankful office, as it proves many times. For if you like not the man or the man you, I shall be sure to hear of it, but I hope otherwise. Of this I make no question, if he behave himself civilly, but you will use him accordingly. Though I am not engaged by writing, yet I have passed my word for your performance in his good usage, which question not but will be beyond his friends' expectations. The sum which they give, you cannot deny but is more than you would have asked. Therefore they expect that you will have a special care over him and see that he be well clothed. I have recommended him unto Mr James Cowes of Palma to send him over unto you in the first boat, and what charge he is out to draw its value upon you, which pray see discharged. I shall desire you to advise me 2 lines how you like the youth.

I would not have you to be too fearful of the Holland difference, for be assured we shall beat them to nothing in a short time if we have wars with them, which God forbid. ...

63. to Gowen Paynter and William Clerke   5 Nov. 1652

a. I have received yours of 18 and 21 June, since which time have had no fit opportunity to answer them until now. I have been this 2 months absent from hence in the western parts [Devon, see **64c**], which hath been the chief cause of my silence.

About 2 months since here arrived a ship from Barbados, in which ship came home one of our ship *Swan*'s company, who came passenger from Guinea in Capt. Powell's ship and declares that on 3 March the ship *Swan* was cast away coming out of Rio del Rey, alias Calabar, in the Bight [of Biafra], having then aboard her above 200 Negroes, some elephants' teeth, wax, skins, and some gold, and above £500 of the goods she carried out of England. Mr Jewell died suddenly after the ship went from river Gambia so that Mr Pulman and Thomas Dixon managed the business and bought all the Negroes. And about a month before the ship was cast away, they both died so that the whole charge of ship and goods was left to one Carnaby who was chief mate to Mr Pulman, who, as I am informed, did presumptuously cast away the ship. Most of the Negroes were saved and sold by ditto Carnaby to other English ships that were there trading, for a trifle. Only 30 Negroes were put aboard the pinnace [the *Turned-out*], who did intend to carry them for the Canaries and says that a few of the goods were saved, which Carnaby carried for Barbados and is there arrived, as I am informed. But I cannot hear a word of his proceedings so I do conclude that what was saved we shall be cheated of all.

I do now intend to renounce my interest to the insurers speedily, there being £1,000 insured, the policy being valued at £2,000, so that the insurers must pay their losses. And what goods is saved, if we can get anything, the one-half is ours and the other the insurers', which must be cast into an average. Likewise the insurers will have the one-half of the pinnace's Negroes, being taken out of the *Swan*'s cargo, but I am doubtful she is miscarried in regard have no news of her all the time. I am doubtful shall have a suit of law with the owners. The seamen will recover their wages without question, but I am resolved to try the title with the owners rather than pay a farthing freight.

Thus, in brief, I have given you an account of our Negro voyage. I have had sufficient trouble about it, you well know, and yet I doubt the worst is to come. The seamen's wives do protest they will bring their children and lie at my doors by reason they cannot receive their husbands' wages, which does not concern me to pay a farthing; but those kind of people will not understand reason. God grant I may be so happy as to see an end of this unfortunate business. I hope for future shall be more cautious how I undertake any such business. Your advice about making a full insurance upon the *Swan* came to my hand after the news of her being cast away. The insurers have had great losses of late so doubt must stay some time for their monies. My diligence shall not be wanting to further your interest in that or anything else which you commit to my charge. Richard Jewell made a will and left me his overseer and withal left me ⅕ part of his estate, the rest to other of his friends and kindred, which I doubt will come to a small dividend in the end.

63b. I have received a letter, 5 Sept., Lisbon, from Mr Ralph Standish [supercargo on the *Blessing*, Capt. William Webber] who was then newly arrived there to a bad market with your hides. I wrote you per Mr Price [the *Judeth*] to forbear sending any that way, which advice came time enough to have hindered your design. I believe it had been better you had sent them here and sold at 7d per lb. I wish you may have some good returns [in cargo from Lisbon to Tenerife] to make amends, otherwise I doubt you will make a bad voyage. I shall not enlarge upon this, supposing the ship will arrive with you long ere this comes to hand. Whereas you desired to have £1,500 insured on her for your accounts, I conceive you are not ignorant of the dangers nowadays. I could not have done [insurance] to all of those places you write of under 40 per cent. I thought the voyage would not bear it made me forbear, so that you have run a greater adventure than you thought of. God send her well to arrive with you, I hope you will load her with good *malvasías* which is at present and will be all this year the very best commodity that can be sent for England. Had I but certain notice of her coming home, I would endeavour to get some insurance for your accounts, though at excessive high rates (cannot be done under 15 per cent), but the commodity will bear it if prove good. I conceive I need not hint unto you the inconveniency of bad wines, you having had sufficient experience last year to your cost and my sorrow.

Mr Holle's letter for Nantes I did not send forward for reasons formerly writ you. If ever you send any ship that way, it will be necessary you send a man upon her. Per advice from Mr Holle, wheat is worth 200 *livres* per t, rye 120.

Our States' ships have lately taken 8 men-of-war and 5 fire ships of the King of France coming to relieve Dunkirk, by which means it was surrendered up immediately to the Spaniard; so that the King of France hath made an embargo in all his ports upon English ships and goods.

What ginger you have in Palma may dispose of it there again, though at loss; for here is above 500 ts of ditto commodity come from Barbados, besides the Islands', which is more than will be spent this 7 years. Worth at present 30s per cwt; such a fall never the like was known.

63c. The Portuguese ambassador [Penaguião] is here at present treating for peace, which it's thought will be suddenly concluded, at which the Spanish ambassador seems to be much distasted. Besides, our ships have brought in 6 or 7 Hollanders laden with wools for the *asentistas'* [the Spanish king's creditors'] accounts of Madrid, which goods have been detained here this 3 months and for ought I see are like to stay 3 more. It's worth above £200,000. And the last week Gen. Blake surprised a great Hamburger of 36 guns, which ship hath aboard her above £200,000 in bars of silver and pieces of eight, all pretended to be the King of Spain's money and *asentistas'* of Madrid. The ship came from Calais. All which is a very high aggravation to the Spaniard, insomuch that if there be not a speedy restoration the ambassador gives out that his master the King will embargo Englishmen's goods in his dominions for satisfaction, which, if should do, you at the Canaries will be in the saddest condition of all men because all your estates is in goods and debts; will not be able to save the tenth part. Of this I thought good to give you timely advice whereby you may be the better prepared if such things should come to pass and that you may see the danger we nowadays live in. In my opinion it's no wisdom to remain with a great estate there.

You see our States care not to quarrel with any king or prince in the world upon a sudden, as Portugal, Holland; and now the King of Denmark hath embargoed all our ships in the Sound and merchants' goods ashore, taking the Hollander's part. And we look daily when the Swede, Hamburger and Lubecker will declare against us upon the same score, so that we are like to have wars with all these northern nations. God in mercy look upon us and send us his peace within. The Hollanders' fleet and Gen. Blake have met twice within this 10 weeks, about 60 or 70 sail at a time. But the Hollander never stands to it; always run away. We at both times have sunk and taken some of their ships and not one of ours lost. Besides, have taken above 200 sail of their merchantmen since these wars, which are computed to be worth above £1,000,000. Very few escape through our Channel. If it so continue, the Hollander will be ruined in a few years. They have taken very few of our merchantmen, only some colliers from Newcastle.

63d. Thus I have given you a brief narration of the passages here at home. I shall now come to our business, which is that on sight hereof you buy up a good large parcel of wines, always provided they be sound and agreeable, otherwise he that hath fewest will be best to pass. Of foreign commodities none so much in request as good Canary wines. I verily believe a man might sell a ship's lading at £30 per pipe, which is price enough. Malaga wines prove but ordinary this year, there being some arrived at Plymouth. Sherries scarce and bad, as they write from San Lucar.

Mr George Clerke [William Clerke's brother] and myself have found out a way to ship out some English wheat, being under the statute, which few men, I conceive, pry into yet. Abovesaid Mr Clerke is now in Kent shipping some aboard this ship *Agreement*, whereof Nicholas Harwood is commander. The quantity certain I cannot inform you, referring you to his advice and bill of lading. The ⅔ part is for his account and company, and the ⅓ part for mine and company. We have agreed to buy up 200 ts. The rest shall go in the next ships, which may be ready a month hence. We durst not adventure too much in one bottom these dangerous times. When other men come to know that we have shipped this corn, I doubt they will spoil our market by sending great quantities. If you send home Webber [the *Blessing*], peradventure may return him you back with corn. I only want money when this corn comes to your hands. Pray dispose of it speedily at the price current, for without question great quantities will come after, which may serve per advice.

I have taken 10 ts in this ship homewards upon account of this wheat, which pray see laden in good wines. We must pay but £4 per t though all other ships have let for £5 per t. Were I certain wines would prove right, I would charge you with 100 ts, but I durst not adventure till I hear from you.

Pray God send Webber well home. The ship proves but [a] leaky trow. Pray send home an account of what have paid ditto master that I may make an end, otherwise I shall be vexed with his multiplicity of words.

There are at least 12 sail of great ships freighted for the Canaries, which intend to go all in a fleet out, so that you may do well to buy up your wines ere they arrive, otherwise will pay dearly. ...

[P.S.] May please to take notice that I have got £1,000 to be insured on the *Blessing* from the Canaries to London at 12 per cent for your accounts in equal halves, at which price I purpose to get above £500 more underwritten speedily. This ship is to stop 4 days at Santa Cruz in Barbary [Agadir]. Pray dispose of the corn she carries speedily after it's ashore for our design is discovered per some who will send quantities.

64. to William Clerke   15 Nov. 1652
a. I have yours of 1 May, 15 June, 15 and 30 July. I have presented Mr Richard King the affidavit you sent me, who objects in it that it specifies for charges of 24 chests [of tobacco], and there does not concern them but 20 chests, as by your account. Which nicety pray clear per first, until

which be done will not yield up my obligation. He says hath written you about it. I shall take occasion to speak with Mr Thomas Boone, the Parliament man, about the 933*Rs* he owes you, but I doubt will be to little purpose per what I could understand per Mr Christopher Boone. He pretends you overcharged him in the hides you sent him. It would be necessary you writ him 2 lines yourself about it.

I have received of Antonio Fernandez [Carvajal] £150 upon Duarte Enríques [Alvarez's] bill of exchange and have paid £300 per order of Mr Henry Lee for your account.

As touching the *Swan* business, it proves unfortunate. I have written you at large in my joint letter, to which refer you. By your several proffers I could very well have freed myself of my interest, but to take a burthen off my own shoulders and put it upon yours, I scorn it, though I protest had no intelligence of any loss when your first proffer came to hand, only of Richard Jewell's death. Though I did in several write you to make provision against the ship's arrival there [in Tenerife] and about the freight, yet my intent was not to clear myself of the voyage, in which you did very much misconstrue my meaning. Had she come well I believe we should have made a good voyage, but I have observed that generally these Negro designs seldom prosper. Pyle writes home to Mr Bulkley that will force me to pay freight for the time the ship served us, so that I do daily look when they will begin with me. I hope you will bear me out in the business. I am resolved to oppose him.

I am shortly to meet the insurers about our loss. Our custom is to abate 10 per cent. If they stand upon more, must go to law with them, so that I shall not want trouble ere I clear this unfortunate business. I deal really with you, I would not undertake the like in every respect if would give me £500.

64b. West India goods are low at present: hides, 6½d per lb; ginger, £2 per cwt; logwood, £12 per t, clear aboard ship; Varinas tobacco, if right, worth 6s per lb; cochineal, 25s per lb; campechena, 5s per lb; sylvester, 2s 4d per lb; indigo Guatemala of the best, 4s 8d per lb; Havana sugars white, £6 per cwt; ditto muscovado, £3 10s per cwt; Palma sugars sorted [good whites] £7 per cwt.

Upon Mr Taylor's arrival here there came several passengers on him from Tenerife who brought letters and reported that James Cowse had embargoed your goods at Palma which went upon Webber [the *Blessing*, to Lisbon], which was very frequently reported upon the Exchange in an undervaluing way as though you had not been able to pay your debts. Which scandal did much redound to your disparagement but that I quashed the business by daring any man to avouch it, so that I hope you will vindicate yourself upon Mr Cowse who hath been the occasion of this aspersion cast upon you. I could not but give you a hint of it though you never gave me notice of your difference.

I pray you give me notice how your business stands with Mr Richard Lant [William Clerke's former master], who threatens that he will attach your estate next vintage, whereby I may be prepared to defend his malice, for I verily believe it's nothing else. In anything that concerns your reputation or interest, I shall stand by you to the utmost of my poor ability.

I have received £100 of Mrs Leigh and hath promised me the rest shortly. [See **62**.] I should be glad to hear your youth [Thomas Leigh] proves to your content. I shall pay Mr Shorton the money which you drew [by bill of exchange] in favour of Capt. Diego Benitez at all demands. So much you may certify him.

64c. I have been this 10 weeks in Devonshire from whence I writ my father-in-law a few hasty lines per a small Fowey man. Had but 2 hours' warning, otherwise had writ you. Wherefore I pray excuse me. My servant Peter Browne gives me an account hath shipped aboard the *Agreement* the coach for Don Carlos before I came home, which, I hope, will give you and him content. I could with less trouble have bought up a cargazon of £2,000 than done that. I cannot as yet give you an exact account of the costs, but I have very much exceeded the commission, being about £100 as I guess. And whereas you desire those drugs for curing your breasts, I went to Mr Mullines, whose advice I took in choosing them, which cost 6 times more than you write of, at which I did admire, but the mistake is in yourself. I shall send you the apothecary's bill which Mr Mullines and others approve of to be reasonable. I have endeavoured to buy you a Turkey carpet of the length and breadth you write of, but cannot find any such in London. Your couch shall get made with expedition. And for the rest of your *encomiendas*, shall get ready speedily, which will take up much time providing. The candles have cleared that were formerly seized on in Price [the *Judeth*], which cost dearly.

I know not of certain what quantity of wheat is laden aboard Mr Harwood [the *Agreement*], your brother being at present in the Downs putting it aboard, to whose advice refer you. The remainder which we have shall go in James Blake [the *Constant John*] and another ship.

God send Webber well home. I hope to dispose of your wines at good rates if prove right. I shall speedily return him to you with wheat, being worth under £10 per t at present, which is very cheap. Had I effects of yours and order, now is the time to get more, but I doubt too many will follow the design; hereafter will be worth nothing. Of this 2 lines.

All kind of woollen goods are 20 per cent cheaper than formerly. I am doubtful your Azores ship [the *Elizabeth and John*, Capt. Thomas Waight] will not be admitted to load corn, though it's very plenty there, per reason of the *fianza*.[1] I pray let me hear from you per all vias.

The Hollander at present hath few men-of-war out. Our frigates do make them keep in. If they do not make their peace speedily, we shall ruin their trade, being few of their merchantmen do escape through our Channel. ...

1. ? for lack of a bond guaranteeing that the ship will not carry the wheat to enemy, i.e. Spanish, ports.

65. to Gowen Paynter and William Clerke   23 Nov. 1652

I have received yours of 22 Oct. per the *Turned-out* frigate who is safe arrived at Tenby in Wales 8 instant, where the master [Capt. Nicholas Straw] writes me is in a sad condition, the vessel proving very leaky and wines there are a drug and at Bristol, and the owners will sue the penalty of charter-party against me if do not bring her here. What I shall do in this condition as yet know not.

Pray send me home per first an account of what goods Mr Straw left with you of the *Swan*'s cargo because I must give the insurers an account of it, having renounced unto them. Besides, Mr Jewell's father hath preferred a bill in Chancery against me, wherein sets forth how I have a great estate of his son's deceased of the proceeds of the voyage. Indeed I am much money in disburse but as yet not received a groat nor God knows when shall. I thought my trouble of this unhappy voyage had been over, but I doubt the worst is to come. Pray speed home abovesaid account very authentic, for until that come they will not pay a farthing. Likewise send me home the frigate's expenses at Tenerife, in English.

Per next shall be larger. The frigate's putting into Tenby is £100 out of our way in the sale of those few wines, besides the charge we are at, men's wages, victuals and freight. The voyage hath proved unfortunate from the first, and I doubt it will so end. Carnaby, the master's mate of the *Swan*, is at Barbados. Several ships have come from thence but not a line from him.

Wines that prove good will be in extraordinary esteem here. I have insured on the *Blessing* for your accounts in equal halves £1,000 from Lisbon to the Canaries and from thence to London £1,350, the first at 6 per cent and the other at 12 per cent. If you can get freight, may do well to send home wines. ...

[P.S.] I cannot answer yours per the *Turned-out* frigate at present, but per James Blake [the *Constant John*] shall write you at large, who is now at Gravesend with 8 ships more all bound for the Canaries to load wines. In which ship we shall ship more wheat. You need not send your ships anywhere else for ditto commodity. Here is free liberty and very cheap, which may serve per advice. The peace with the Portuguese ambassador is upon the matter concluded, and I am really of the opinion we shall quarrel with the Spaniard. Few days will produce strange alterations; therefore, I beseech you, slight not my advice.

66. to William Clerke   4 Jan. 1653

a. My last unto you was per Capt. Harwood [the *Agreement*] of 15 Nov., to which crave reference. Since, I have received yours of 22 Oct. per the *Turned-out* frigate. I have paid up Shorton £10 for account of Diego Benitez per your bill of exchange. I here send you the apothecary's bill by which you may see what those medicines amount unto, as also I send you the account of what Don Carlos' coach cost here first penny. You may charge him with freight, insurance and my commission. I hope it will be little inferior to the [Capt.] General's coach which cost £50 more. It hath cost me no small trouble to have all things exact according to order. I have bought you a large carpet which shall send over per first.

I should be very glad to hear that you had bought up a round quantity of wines as you writ me would do suddenly after Mr Straw's [the *Turned-out*'s] dispatch, which, if you had given me advice thereof per Mr Webber [the *Blessing*], I would have adventured to charge you with some tonnage in this ship [the *Golden Star*, Capt. John Holman]. But not knowing your mind makes me forbear doing it. I have taken 80 ts in this ship to carry away a parcel of rye which I bought in Plymouth about 3 months since. Mr Rowland Wilson hath 70 ts and Mr Canham 40 ts. Now in case the ship carry any more than abovesaid tonnage, then my father-in-law hath privilege to load it. I have written him 2 words to that purpose that he spare you room for 20 or 30 pipes if possible he can, for I know this ship is 220 ts. Of this I thought good to give you a hint by reason there is now an opportunity to get money by wines which there may not be another year. I hope you have reserved some of the Duraxno wines to send home for your account.

66b. I have in my former letters given you an account of what insured for you in the *Blessing*. Though you had not written me of it, it should have been done. I am half resolved to insure £600 or £700 for your and Mr Paynter's account on your Azores ship [the *Elizabeth and John*] though have no order, of which shall advise you the certainty in my next.

I have had some discourse with some of Mr [William] Elam's [English merchant in Genoa] principals here who have monies lying in Genoa, so that shall endeavour to get a credit upon ditto Elam that so he furnish your order with £500 and draw it upon me here. The reason why I do not remit the money according to your order is because I hope you will better consider of it and desist the design, for I see you are not sensible of the great danger in those parts, all which is for want of advice. You may take notice that this 10 weeks all our merchant ships in the Straits above Alicante have been blocked up with 8 of our States' men-of-war by 30 sail of Holland men-of-war, insomuch that we durst not stir from one port to another. And there they must lie until our State send out a great fleet to relieve them, which 'tis thought will not be till May next. Here are above 20 sail of gallant ships now in the river laden for several ports in the Straits which durst not adventure thither but stay for convoy. And whereas you desire to have insurance made upon ditto design, I went yesterday to the office purposely and proposed the voyage from Tenerife to Genoa, or any port thereabouts, and back to Canaries. Many would not write at any rate; the rest asked no less than 60 per cent. You need not go so far afield for corn; if once our Channel were clear, it might be shipped from hence upon better terms. You may do therein as you think fit, but as a friend and well-wisher to your affairs, I may advise you forbear going upon many designs these dangerous times. Both here and in Holland there [are] scarce any ships fitting to go out as merchantmen but all for men-of-war. The Hollanders since the last encounter with our fleet [off Dungeness] have reigned masters of our seas and are at present very potent. Our fleet is retreated into Lee road whereby to gather greater strength to fight the enemy, which, I doubt, will not be this 6 weeks.

66c. How I shall get up Webber from Falmouth I know not. I doubt must make further insurance upon him from thence, which will cost 10 per cent, which you will admire at and well may. I shall resolve speedily to take some course about him, for the wines will take wrong in lying so long aboard; besides, monthly pay is chargeable. Pray God direct me for the best. Were you here yourself, could do no otherwise than I have. I have written you and my father-in-law at large jointly per this conveyance, to which refer you.

I am ashamed that you should write me so often about your account, which is much against my grain. I must now deal really with you. The first and second years which I did your business I lived in one Mr Robert Turner's house, who did enter my goods and received some monies and paid out for charges, assisting me in my business, for which I allowed him half commission. And to this day I cannot get an account from him. The man is able and I do intend to make him honest, if the law will do it. All what I want is some charges from him and some bills of exchange which he paid. The rest I have in my own books. It is just in the same manner with me and my father-in-law. I wish that I had given £500 that I had never seen him [Turner]. It makes you and others think I am very backwards in my accounts, which with much reason you may. But though I lost £100 by it, I will send over your account this summer. In the meantime, pray have patience and judge charitably, for none desires to be more punctual in those things than myself, however it pleases God to cross me in that thing which I desire to be most exact. ...

67. to William Clerke   1 Feb. 1653
a. I have written you at large per this conveyance, to which crave reference. Have since received yours, 16 Dec., per Mr Thomas Warren, which cannot answer at present so fully as could wish, being straitened with time.

Your brother [George] and myself writ you and my father-in-law a few lines giving you notice how we have freighted the *Mary* frigate, burthen 120 ts, which ship is now ready to take in her lading of corn, only expecting our Parliament's fleet to go forth, which I doubt will not be this 20 days, so that you may not mistrust in case she tarry a little. For we are fully resolved, by God's assistance, that she shall proceed the voyage, therefore intreat you to provide her lading of the best liquors that Island affords. I do engage for $\frac{3}{8}$ parts of her lading out and home, whereof I interest you $\frac{1}{8}$ part, and the like my father-in-law and myself $\frac{1}{8}$ part. The rest your brother and friends have. I hear of several ships now laden and lading of wheat upon the same design, which makes me doubt it will be a drug with you.

I shall not be able to send you the *Blessing* so soon as thought. Mr Webber writes me she must have much work by carpenters done unto her, which will require a long time. And for other ships, the times are such that no owners will let any per month, so that you may expect none from me until I hear further from you. I was yesterday in company with some friends where I saw £80 per month proffered for a ship of 80 ts, and it was not accepted of. All kinds of cordage, provisions and men's wages are at present 50 per cent dearer than formerly, besides great dangers; so that except you have very hopeful designs, the freight will devour the principal.

As for your Genoa design, I writ you at large in my last wishing you as my friend to desist from it. You must pay here 5s 4d for every piece of eight there, if I remit any money for you, which is near 20 per cent loss unto you by exchange.

67b. In my former gave you notice how was in suit of law with the owners of the *Turned-out* frigate; and since, we referred our differences unto two arbitrators, Mr Stephen Slaney being for me. They have ended the business and awarded me to pay £146 besides what you disbursed upon the vessel at Tenerife, the owners to receive the vessel at Bristol, which is not worth £50, so that they will never see the money she cost them. So that you need not send over the accounts in English; only pray fail not to send me an account of those things which appertain to the *Swan*'s cargazon, for the insurers will not end till they see it.

Though I have no particular order from you touching insurance on the *Elizabeth and John*, yet I have adventured to insure £600 on her from the Azores to the Canaries at 6½ per cent, for your and Mr Paynter's account in equal halves. The thing which conduced me to do it was that I received a letter from Terceira how she was to load corn for your accounts, and hearing of those 2 Holland men-of-war about your Islands made me fearful of her. I hope you will approve of what I have herein done.

Pray answer Mr [Richard] King's objection, which I formerly writ you of, that I may have up my obligation to cancel it.

Whereas you desire some ozenbrigs to be sent you, may take notice that our Hamburg trade is blocked up since these wars with Holland, so that at present there's not 2,000 ells in this city. And as for your necessaries for house, I have the major part bought long ago. Per the first ship shall send them.

Here is great preparations making, both here and in Holland. I doubt this will prove a bloody summer, for I see no hope of any peace.

As yet Mr Webber [the *Blessing*] not come up. Mr Warren and the rest interested in the *Morocco Merchant* have unladen their wines, which prove pretty green, rising wines, some few agreeable. They have sold most part at £33 10s and £34 per pipe; and the next ship's will sell better if the wines prove answerable, which is price enough. But they have near 20 per cent leakage, which is merely through bad cask and not being well rabbeted. Webber's not coming up troubles me, and yet we cannot help ourselves. ...

[P.S.] I have ordered Matthew Phillips to deliver you half a dozen barrels oysters, which pray call for.

68. to Gowen Paynter and William Clerke   1 March 1653
a. Since the arrival of the *Morocco Merchant*, have not received one from you. As yet no news of Mr Lawrence's arrival in the ship *Recovery*, which is much doubted. These are chiefly to acquaint you how I have discharged the ship *Blessing* the 28th past and have sold all [160 pipes of] your wines without any choice at £35 13s 4d per pipe, ⅓ money, 3 and 3 months' time [see **11b** note]. Such a price was never given before. The vintners do exclaim against me sufficiently for getting the price, but I had rather they should do so than pity me. When I have delivered the wines, shall give you an account of the leakage, which I hope will come out very reasonably. At the delivery I shall take particular notice of the proofs of each man's wines; but in general I find them sound except 2 pipes, most part wise green, rising wines, pretty bodies, and about one-quarter part

especially agreeable. Mr Clarke, which came from Guinea, is now unladen. That ship brought about 300 pipes which prove for the most part but mean wines, green and thin bodies and flashy. Though there be a great scarcity, yet the vintners will not look upon them, they being not fit for their draughts. Thus you may see the difference between good wines and ordinary, the one esteemed as gold, the other as dross.

Mr Chalk [the *Mary*] is at present in Faversham creek above half laden with wheat. I hope will be full laden within this 5 days. Here is at present great press for seamen, yet I make no question but we shall get him away with the first opportunity though others may be stopped. Therefore, I beseech you, provide his wines before his arrival and such as may be fit for this market. I thought to have returned you the *Blessing* with corn, but she cannot be made ready this 10 weeks. I doubt the owners and we shall not agree.

I have about 10 days past given the insurers upon the *Swan* a dinner at tavern, where I found them inclining to reason. Made me close with them: I am to abate them 13 per cent, and they are to resign up all hopes of goods saved unto me, which I think is the best agreement I have made this many days. After this agreement was made, it pleased God to take away one of the insurers who was in £200, Alderman [William] Berkeley by name, so that I doubt shall be kept out of that money this 12 months. We have a law here that all executors have 12 months' and a day's time to pay debts; besides, there's no will can be proved at present, being no judge in the Prerogative Court, which breeds confusion.

68b. I am now to give you notice how on 18 Feb. Generals Blake, Deane and Monk, with about 30 sail of our men-of-war, off Portland came up with Van Tromp who hath about 80 sail men-of-war and 200 merchantmen in his company which loaded salt and wines at Nantes, Rochelle and Bordeaux. Our men-of-war and theirs engaged most desperately all that day, and likewise the 19th began again and fought all day, and the 20th continued fighting. But Van Tromp began to run and our ships pursued him, not regarding the merchantmen. The Battle of Lepanto was not comparable to this, by all men's opinions. There was never the like battle fought upon the salt waters since the creation of the world. Our men fought like true Englishmen. The Hollander sank one of our men-of-war named the *Sampson*, 32 guns, and we have sunk 14 of their men-of-war, whereof one vice-admiral and another rear-admiral, and have taken 6 of their men-of-war, whereof one is vice-admiral of Zeeland and another rear-admiral, a ship of 1,200 tons. We have likewise taken 70 sail of their merchantmen, and our fleet remain masters of the seas. By this you may see the Lord hath been pleased to own us and crown our endeavours with a mighty victory. The Lord make us truly thankful. Had our enemies prevailed this time over us, we had been in a sad condition. I am informed there's above 3,000 men slain on both sides, whereof we have about 1,200, as 'tis said. I think Hans will scarce face our Channel this 6 months for this bout's sake. I am sorry there should be so much Christian blood spilt; hope this may be a means to bring peace in the end. Our States are hastening out another great fleet with expedition. I believe by the beginning of May we may have 140 sail men-of-war out. Here enclosed I send you Capt. Garvis Russell's letter, who relates something of the fight in brief, to which refer you.[1]

This goes via Dartmouth by a ship which goes consigned to Messrs. Stephens and Throckmorton. I had but short warning, therefore crave excuse. Cannot write you particularly at present, desiring you to buy up some good wines to come home in Chalk, which will come to a better market than the *Blessing* if good. ...

1. Russell and his ship, the *Katherine*, in which Paige, Paynter and Clerke owned shares, served the State during the Dutch war. Cf. **61e**, **77c**.

69. to William Clerke   8 March 1653

May take notice have written you and my father-in-law jointly per this conveyance at large and delivered the letter to Mr Hardin, as my friend writes me from Dartmouth, wherein have writ the needful, giving you advice how have sold the *Blessing*'s whole lading of wines at £35 13s 4d per pipe. Mr Chalk [the *Mary*] was yesterday full laden with wheat. May expect him within 3 days after this ship arrives.

These are chiefly to give you notice how on 28 Feb. our friend Mr Stephen Slaney was taken very ill of a fever, who is at present even at death's door, given over by all doctors for a dead man. I am doubtful shall never see him go abroad again. The Lord fit us all for him. He was a very likely man to live as any I knew. ...

70. to William Clerke   12 March 1653

I have written you and Mr Paynter at large for what concerns your joint affairs, to which crave reference. These are chiefly to give you notice how with much trouble and difficulty I have got your 5 boxes of candles which were formerly seized on. The charge and composition comes to above half as much as they first cost. And now once more have adventured to ship them again in the *Mary* frigate, William Chalk commander. Have likewise sent you a hamper of ginger aboard. The particulars shall give you underneath. Have likewise laden aboard this ship the ⅛ part of her full lading of wheat for your proper account and have charged the like proportion of tonnage for your account homeward in ditto ship.

Our loving friend Mr Stephen Slaney departed this world the 10th instant. The Lord fit us for him. I daily expect to hear from you. The *Susan* [Capt. Giles Paynter] is arrived at Penzance in Mount's Bay, who reports that Capt. Harwood [the *Agreement*] came away 2 days before him. ...

[P.S.] The mark and number of 5 boxes and one hamper aboard the *Mary* frigate, William Chalk, viz. 5 boxes of candles, one hamper containing 2 dripping pans, one pair cob-irons, one pair andirons, one Turkey carpet packed in a trunk of Mr Paynter's which you may demand.

71. to Gowen Paynter and William Clerke   12 March 1653

a. ... [H]ave given you a full account of the last engagement between our fleet and Van Tromp, who with much difficulty got into Amsterdam with part of his fleet much torn and shattered. Nevertheless, they are now providing a new fleet to come forth, which may be ready about 1 May. Our fleet is at present scouring the Channel, consisting about 80 sail men-of-war; and here is now another great fleet providing to come forth, about 50 sail more, which may be ready within a month. It's generally conceived we shall have a bloody summer of it. Both states do make it their whole work to carry on this war with a high hand. We have now 30 sail new frigates upon the stocks, which will carry from 50 to 60 guns, not to be paralleled in the whole world. I find our seamen are much encouraged with this great overthrow we have given the Dutch. Without any partiality, I am of the opinion we shall bang them soundly this summer. The King of Denmark just before last fight hath declared war against our nation and will assist the Hollander in this war. I doubt all the rest those northern nations will do the like very suddenly, as the Swede, Hamburger, etc., so that we shall be much straitened for want of hemp and tar and masts, etc. Here is such an extraordinary great pressing of men that it's a difficult thing to get out a ship. Mr Chalk [the *Mary*] hath made many hard shifts, fain to send his men down to Dover by land.

71b. The wines which came in the *Blessing* have delivered and taken particular notice of their proofs. Those of HP proved above 30s per pipe better than those of JP. The uppermost wines of this last mark proved very poor, thin bodied and green wines, which pulled down the price. By what I can learn they were those which came from Garachico, the most part. Those which lay in the second and lower tier, of ditto mark, proved fine rising liquors, which I suppose to be *el marca de campo* [i.e. *el maestre de campo*, Canarian military official] Lorenzo Pereyra's wines of the Duraxno. But Don Juan de Aponte's wines were above all, and Don Antonio de Lugo's; those of Don Benito and the *embusteros* [?tricksters] were pretty rising wines. But those of the steward of Don Luis Benitez were as bad as the Garachico wines. Thus I have given you an account particularly of their proofs to the best of mine and my cooper's judgement, without any partiality. There are 2 pipes in the parcel which are not sound, which I am to allow them £10 and am to give them a feast, which they say does cost them dearly. Had it pleased God that the ship had not been so stopped in the West Country, the wines had proved far smoother, but then I had not obtained the price I now sold for. The *Morocco Merchant*'s coming up before the *Blessing* was £300 in your way. To give them their due, they were pretty kindly wines, free from the *vidueño*.

As yet Mr Webber [the *Blessing*] and I have not come to account, being newly discharged. Except the rest of the owners join with me, cannot put him out. The ship wants great repair; cannot make ready this 2 months. As for the money which you furnished him during his being abroad, may not expect any advance, it being my promise to furnish him with needful expenses for the ship's use. Touching the Newfoundland bills, he utterly denied all. He is very well rewarded per Mr Campion for taking his corn from Mr Clerke. The wines which he hath sent him are not worth £15 per pipe. Except Adam Wyles go in the ship, I am resolved to buy or sell, of which you shall hear more hereafter.

71c. Whereas you advise to have this ship returned back with wheat, or some other in her room, for 8 months certain and 20 months if occasion, I believe a man can scarce get a ship to go per month in these times. Both masters and seamen are much altered within this 6 months; having much encouragement in the State's service, care not for merchant voyages, finding much plunder and the like stories. Besides, weighing all things, I find much corn gone from England to the Islands, which makes me doubt it will lower much in price. So shall forbear until I hear a little further from you. Were not the master of this ship a very diligent man, we could never have got out the ship. Besides, it's a very dangerous thing to freight a ship and load her with corn as the times now govern, for on a sudden comes an embargo for a month or 2 and then it will be fit to throw to the hogs.

You may please to take notice that Mr George Clerke [William Clerke's brother], late of Lisbon, and myself have freighted this ship, the *Mary*, whereof William Chalk is master, in equal halves to go from hence to any of the Canary Islands, there to stay 35 days to unload and take into her all such goods as you shall load aboard her, and from thence to return directly for London, for which we are to give £4 10s per t and a gratuity of £5 to the master. We have ordered that Mr Goldsmith should load aboard her 600 quarters of the best wheat could get for money, which is 120 ts. The just costs thereof know not, having not received the account, invoice, nor bill of lading. I have interested you, Mr Gowen Paynter, $\frac{1}{8}$ part, and Mr William Clerke, $\frac{1}{8}$ part, and Mr Canham, partowner, $\frac{1}{8}$, and myself, $\frac{1}{8}$. The other $\frac{1}{8}$ is for Mr George Clerke and friend's account. I should have interested you a quarter each, but could not obtain the grant, being part of the owners bear a share. I hope long before her arrival you have provided her lading of wines, and of the best, which will come to so good a market as at first of year. I conceive it needless for me to press you to lade good liquors, you being sensible of their esteem here. ...

72. to Gowen Paynter and William Clerke   25 March 1653
... [T]he *Mary* frigate, William Chalk master, ... went out of the Downs 14 instant; hope will be arrived long ere this comes to your hands. ... I have received a bill of lading for 500 quarters wheat which shipped aboard the *Mary* frigate for the account aforementioned. I expected Mr Chalk would have taken in 100 quarters more for ditto accounts, knowing the ship would very well have carried it, but I doubt it goes upon some private adventures; wherefore my desire is that you take particular notice what corn the ship carries besides ours.

May please to take notice Capt. Harwood in the ship *Agreement* is safe arrived at Falmouth some 10 days past, and as yet no letters come up, which does much trouble me that I cannot answer them per this conveyance. Capt. Harwood had a hot dispute with a Holland man-of-war the next day after he went out of Santa Cruz [de Tenerife], but, blessed be God, he foiled him. And coming near our Channel, ditto Harwood met with a Hollander of 120 ts, laden with Virginia tobacco and a good quantity of beaver skins, which he surprised. She is computed to be worth £5,000. The *Recovery* and *Susan* are arrived in Plymouth. How their wines prove, know not; but sure I am they come to a great occasion. And so will all those that come after, which may serve per advice.

West India goods are very low here at present: hides, 6½d per lb; ginger, £2 per cwt; logwood, £12 per t aboard ship, the buyer paying custom and other charges; Varinas tobacco, if good and new, 5s 6d per lb; cochineal mesteque, 20s per lb; campechena, 5s per lb; indigo Guatemala, 4s 6d per lb; Havana sugars white, £6 per cwt.

Pray send me per first, affidavit what quantity of corn and other goods you landed out of Mr Waight [the *Elizabeth and John*] for your joint accounts, and send me home a just account of the sale thereof because the insurers are to have the benefit of all goods so landed.[1] Of this, I pray, fail not to send me very punctual and authentic whereby there may be no obstacle in the business here. Otherwise the insurers will have a commission granted them to examine witnesses there and prolong the time.

The ship *Golden Star* [Capt. John Holman], which I freighted to go for Tenerife from Plymouth, is taken [by a Dutch man-of-war] and brought into Nantes. No remedy but patience. This is the fruit of our unhappy war. …

1. Capt. Thomas Waight later testified that after the *Elizabeth and John* had arrived from the Azores foul weather forced her from the roadstead Puerto de la Cruz before all the cargo was unloaded and that she was then taken prize by a Dutch man-of-war (H.C.A. 13/67, 2 May 1653).

73. to William Clerke   1 April 1653

a. I have yours, 16 Jan. and 17 Feb. For what concerns your joint affairs I have written you and Mr Gowen Paynter the needful per this conveyance, to which crave reference. I perceive upon Don Cristóbal de [Alvarado] Bracamonte's arrival wines did rise, being then in expectation of several ships from London. But upon mine, 11 Dec., the factors were much discouraged by reason of the defeat given us per the Hollanders, at which time both you and my father-in-law had a very good opportunity to buy up some wines. But I doubt you did not avail yourselves of the good occasion. I much question wherever you will have the like occasion as long as ever you live in the Island. What is past cannot be recalled.

My last unto you was of 12 March where I wrote you at large; but Mr Chalk [the *Mary*] being nimble and the wind came fair, left my letters behind, in which ship there goes ⅛ part of 500 quarters of wheat for your proper account. And the like you have in the ship's tonnage homewards, which I hope you will load in good liquors. When not, cannot want to let it out to freight for more money than you are to pay. Had your advice come per the *Agreement* 2 days sooner, we would have endeavoured to have persuaded the owners that Mr Chalk might have touched at Safi, but it came too late.

I formerly writ you at large per the ship *Golden Star* [Capt. John Holman] of Plymouth, of 4 Jan., the copy of which I sent you per Mr Steniquer who, I understand, is safe arrived at Oratava. I then sent you an invoice of Don Carlos' coach, as also of those syrups, which papers are miscarried in that the ship is taken per a Holland man-of-war and brought into Nantes. So now I return you the copies. You may add my commission, freight and insurance to the coach if you think fit. I likewise send you an invoice of goods on the *Mary* frigate. With much difficulty, trouble and charge, I have cleared the candles which were given over per all men for loss, there being so strict prohibition against the shipping of them out, as also butter, cheese, bacon, beef and all other victualling commodities.

73b. I take notice of your intention as to your coming home next year. I wish with my heart you may be serious in your resolution and make it your whole work, not thinking upon any other business. I am glad your mind is altered from proceeding on your Genoa design which was somewhat desperate considering the great danger now in the Straits whilst by Dutch men-of-war and some by French we have scarce a ship of late escapes them. When your contradicting order came to my hands, I had not remitted any money in regard was confident that you would not proceed on ditto design when you heard of the danger. Whereas you have given Mr Abraham Lee of San Lucar order to value himself on me here for £400 sterling for your account, whenever his bills come to hand, shall find punctual payment, of which you may rest confident.

Pray fail not send home an account of the sales of those goods Straw [Capt. of the *Turned-out*] left you for account of the interested in the ship *Swan*. In case you have not sold them, pray value them at an indifferent rate, for until that come I cannot adjust the business of that voyage nor pay Mr Jewell's legacies. Likewise, I pray, send me an answer to Mr Richard King's letter, for I cannot get in your agreement. Concerning your brother's [George Clerke's] 15 ts in Capt. Harwood [the *Agreement*], my confidence in your brother's promise made me neglect taking a paper under his hand. Had not you and my father-in-law done me justice therein, it might have prejudiced me above £150 as the year falls out; but I am glad you have ordered it as you did to prevent misunderstandings at home. I should have been glad to have received 2 lines touching the coach. Your silence therein makes me doubt that all things are not as they should be. If so, must impute it to ignorance, for really I did do all things according to the best of my knowledge, and moreover I took the approbation of several judicious men in the contriving of all things. If any man would lay me down £20, I would not undertake the like business.

73c. I take notice there's one West Indiaman arrived at Palma with 6,000 Caracas hides and 400 chests [of] tobacco and another at Santa Cruz [de Tenerife] from ditto place who, it seems, ask high rates for their goods. I shall not encourage you to buy any except can have them very reasonable and upon easy terms of payment. But I must tell you I account Caracas hides better worth 40*Rs* than Havana or Santo Domingo [at] 34*Rs*. At Cadiz there's arrived a frigate with 2,600 chests [of] Varinas tobacco, most part new and sold at 5s and 5s 6d per lb. The ordinary will not yield 3s, such is the difference in that commodity. Hides worth here 6½d per lb; ginger £2 per cwt; cochineal, 22s per lb; campechena, 5s per lb; sylvester, 2s per lb; indigo Guatemala, 4s 6d per lb; Havana sugars white, £6 per cwt; muscovado per rate. No commodity so staple and vendible as hides, which may serve per advice. Logwood, £18 per t; £13 per t aboard ship.

Pray let me hear from you per all vias, and give me timely advice what you will have done against next vintage, for as the times govern at present, all negotiations are difficult. Therefore it requires the larger warning, especially freighting of ships by reason of the great press for seamen to go in the States' men-of-war. And after that trouble's gone, then many times comes an embargo to stop all ships; as soon as that is over, the Hollander, he is out with a fleet and stops on the other side. Such are the hard tasks that poor merchants are put to in these times of trial. We have at present 80 men-of-war of our States' keeping the Channel, and there are now 50 sail more coming forth within 20 days. The Hollander is making great preparation to set out a great fleet which may come forth within a month. I believe this will prove a bloody summer.

As soon as I have made an end with the Guinea business [i.e. the *Swan*'s voyage], I will draw out your account. ... Capt. Harwood [the *Agreement*] is now at Gravesend. ...

74. to William Clerke   11 April 1653

... May please to take notice I have put aboard this ship, the *Matthew*, John Brampton master, a large Russia leather couch, matted up, which I should be glad may be to your liking. The just cost thereof I cannot advise you. In regard it's for so small a matter, I do not send you a bill of lading. The master I know will deliver it you at all demands.

Yesterday I writ Mr Andrews [English merchant at Terceira] a few lines directing my letters to Terceira. I admire you had not sent him per Capt. Harwood [the *Agreement*] a letter whereby I might have sent it him and given him order what he should do in your business. What I writ him was the ill news of the ship's [the *Elizabeth and John*'s] being taken and how corn next harvest was like to be very cheap with you. I understand he owes several men monies in those Islands [the Azores], so that I doubt your estates must go to pay his debts.

Mr Carnaby, who was master of the *Swan* after Mr Pulman's decease, is here at present, who hath near £200 in gold of ours, as he acknowledges, of which I have witness, being the money made of our Negroes. But he brings me in for £90 for his wages, 18 months', and charges, diet, etc., which I will not allow but part, so that I purpose speedily to arrest him in £2,000 action, conceiving that he may not get bail for such a sum, so peradventure that way shall bring him to reason. But there's one obstacle in the business, which is that I have no letter of attorney from you, and the action must be entered in all the interesteds' names. So that if they question it we may chance to be nonsuited. Besides, if you chance to have a loss by way of insurance, I cannot sue any man without your letter of attorney. Therefore it's most absolute necessary you send one over, either to me or any other that you can repose trust unto.

Since the death of Mr [Stephen] Slaney, I have heard that he should have £3,000 in your hands. How that can be you best know; but I do not believe half the money, for I understand that you were interested one-quarter part in all the wines which you have sent him these late years. Those which you have now laden in the *Agreement* prove but mean wines; a great many are mixed with *vidueño*, they being very foul, besides extraordinary bad cask. Such hath my father-in-law laden me that of 80 pipes I doubt will not make 55 pipes [because of leakage]. ...

75. to Gowen Paynter and William Clerke   11 April 1653
... Speed me home a just account of what corn you unloaded out of Mr Waight [the *Elizabeth and John*] for your joint accounts, as also the charges and sales thereof; otherwise the insurers will have a commission granted them to examine the business there upon oath, which will be a means to prolong time, if you do not prevent them by sending the account beforehand. I have formerly writ you how had insured for your account £600 on ditto ship, but we must use the insurers Christian-like. I have spoken with Mr Waight who came home, passing in Capt. Harwood. I purpose, God permitting, to have him examined in the Admiralty Court next week to prove the loss. I do expect that you will allow me £20 to buy me a gelding for my extraordinary care in this insurance.

The French ambassador and our State are upon the matter agreed for a peace, so that consequently we shall have a free trade with France. Here is at present above 3,000 ts of French wines brought in as prize, taken from the Hollander, yet I do not find that it lowers the Spanish wines a farthing. The Spanish ambassador doth rage at those passages that Portugal and France should make a peace with us, being his mortal enemies. I doubt it will provoke him to quarrel with us.

Here is great talk of a hopeful vintage next year at the Canaries, as though the grapes were near ripe already. The noise of £36 and £37 per pipe makes all men to come in for Canary merchants. Some send goods for Spain, others for Bilbao, and so draw it thither [i.e. draw by bills of exchange on credits in peninsular Spain in order to buy Canary wines]. Others say they will send pieces of eight from hence. No trade so much cried up, so that I foresee you will not want ships next year to bring home your expected plentiful vintage, if the State do not hinder them. Of this I thought good to give you a hint. ...
[P.S.] Pray let me hear from you per all vias, as Bilbao and Holland. Though we have wars yet the post comes every week from thence duly.

76. to William Clerke   26 July 1653
a. I have yours, 29 March, 24 April, 4 May and 12 June, which I cannot answer at full, having but 24 hours' warning of this vessel's departure, being far from hence and quickly ready. I come now to give you notice how have paid Mr Abraham Lee [of San Lucar] his order, £400 sterling, for your account. Touching Elias de Bulacia, you may be confident is not come for Holland, I having made inquiry for him. Mr Richard King hath delivered up my obligation. Mr Christopher Boone is here at present. I purpose now to demand the balance of your account of Mr Thomas Boone, he being one of those which General Cromwell turned out of the Parliament. I shall speedily make up your account with Mr Chalk [the *Mary*] about his freight, where shall see that you have no wrong done you. In yours of 12 June you advise sent me the costs and charges of 30 pipes of wines laden aboard the *Turned-out* frigate, but I find no such papers in your packet, neither the account of the sales of corn out of the *Elizabeth and John* nor the letter of attorney, all which papers want very much. Cannot finish the business without them.

Mr John Andrewes is newly come home from Terceira. I have demanded an account of him, though have [no] such power from you, who hath delivered it me. I find he hath left 340 *milréis* in the hands of Mr William Searchfield, which is all that you and Mr Paynter may expect as the proceeds of your corn sold. Of this I shall be more larger in my next. I shall endeavour what I can in the interim to make further inquiry after the business. I have written Messrs. Ackland and Davies of Bilbao that whensoever they draw the £400 on me for your account I shall honour their bills with punctual payment, on which you may rest confident. Mr Waight [Capt. of the *Elizabeth and John*] denies that he has received anything in account of his freight from you. Therefore, pray send the particulars. I shall order Mr Searchfield to send home your money or else to employ it in sugars.

76b. I cannot dispose of your part of the *Blessing* except should sell it under £20. She is now ready, bound for the Canaries. I have taken 60 ts in her. Mr Webber [formerly master of the *Blessing*] is in a Flemish ship of 300 ts now bound for Rochelle, so I have put in for present Mr Charles Bradick for commander, I think an honest man. But I believe when she comes home Webber will go in her again.

The generality of the wine which came in the 5 last ships proves very poor wines, being all unladen and not a pipe sold that I hear of. Wines are fallen above £6 per pipe. Here is very great preparation making for the vintage, many ships already freighted, great quantities of goods bought to go in them, and abundance of credits. And if the ships get out, of necessity will raise the price of wines higher than last year, and here must not expect the prices as formerly. Of this I thought good to give a hint, that if you intend to buy any wines, stay not till the ships arrive. I shall follow your order in not charging you with any tonnage.

In my last via Palma I wrote you of the dissolution of the old Parliament. I now give you notice how there is a new Parliament chosen by my lord General Cromwell and his Council, which sit now at Westminster.

On 2 June last our fleet met with Van Tromp and his fleet off Dunkirk, being equal in number, having about 110 sail each fleet. They fought 2 days and in the end the Hollanders run for it, insomuch that our whole fleet chased them most shamefully into Zeeland. In which fight we took 14 gallant men-of-war of theirs and sunk and burnt 8 sail more without the loss of one ship on our side, which will seem strange to you, but it's very true. Ever since our fleet have ridden upon their coast, Van Tromp is daily expected to come forth with a fleet of 140 men-of-war. I make no question but our fleet will be able to receive him. Here are 4 Holland ambassadors at present; cannot do nothing as to a peace, so will return home. ...

77. to William Clerke   26 Aug. 1653
a. ... [H]ave received yours, 24 June, per Mr Pitchers, with your letter of attorney, as also all such papers as concern the ship *Elizabeth and John* which I find to be very authentic, and without them I could not have done nothing. I am now speedily to give the insurers a dinner, when hope shall

make a good end for you. At least I shall use my best endeavours and give you a speedy account thereof.

Likewise I have received an invoice of those wines laden on *Turned-out* frigate. After a great deal of trouble I thought now should have seen an end to that unhappy voyage. Some of the seamen of late have entered their actions against Capt. Pyle and owners [of the *Swan*]; and likewise those seamen's wives which died in the voyage have done the like and have yesterday obtained a sentence against the owners for their full wages, notwithstanding ship cast away, so that they are resolved to appeal to the Delegates, which is the Chancery of the Admiralty. And withal they told me this day that by the same rule I must pay them freight, desiring me to give in bail to their action, for their counsel tells them that they shall recover freight for 6 months. I have been with Dr Walker to know his approbation concerning the business, showing him the charter-party, who, I'll promise you, is very doubtful and is accounted as able a lawyer as any in England, which makes me beside myself. But I am resolved to oppose them, cost what it may, for, in my weak judgement, in justice, equity, or a good conscience, we ought to pay none, sufficient we lost our goods. Thus you may see how I am like to be plunged into a vexatious suit which will hinder me from my business. I believe if did give Pyle £100 in secret might do much, but I shall not do it. I think you will say the charter-party is as well made as ever you saw any. The words run thus: that I shall pay 6 months' freight at the expiration of 8 months. But my lawyer replies for objection that clause does not cut off the owners from receiving any freight in case the ship do not serve out full 8 months or should be lost within the time. I shall take the advice of one or 2 more, being resolved not to starve the cause. In the meantime I shall put some friends that have a power over Pyle to dissuade him from proceeding this way, if it be possible. I pray with the first let me have your advice. In the meantime, be sure shall lose nothing that may be advantageous unto us. I shall so order it that they shall not bring it to trial this 9 months. Capt. Pyle is the stickler because was forced to pay the wages. As yet there stands out owing £300 per insurance on our general policy. Alderman Berkeley, who died, owes £200, and his sons are in law who shall take out the administration, so know not whom to sue. There's £100 more owing by 2 or 3, which hope shall speedily get in. Likewise, Alderman Berkeley is in £100 loss upon the *Elizabeth and John*. The man left a good estate as I am credibly informed.

77b. Mr Jewell's father and I cannot agree. He endeavours to make his son's will null and void, pretending he was not in his true senses when made it, and so consequently will cut off all legacies. [See **63a**.] For my own part, I value them not; only seeing it was his love, I am resolved will have it. But my resolution is to bestow it on Mr Pulman's 2 children who are left, poor souls, in a very sad condition. Had not Capt. Pyle troubled me, was resolved to have given Mrs Pulman £20 out of the joint stock, but now must not be too liberal, fearing the worst. I have near finished your account. Had I but settled this unhappy business, I should have sent it per the vintage ships; but in case I see no hopes of composure, then I will send you account of the rest and leave that to be perfected hereafter.

Mr Perryman from Palma, laden for account of Mr Bradick and Mr Spicer, was taken last week off our Land's End by a Flemish man-of-war and carried into Brest. Sugars and all sort of West India goods are low at present; only hides a good commodity, worth 7d per lb. I understand there lies a good parcel at Palma of Caracas hides unsold, which might be money gotten by them. They are worth 26 *livres* per hide now in Rouen, a great price, and like to rise both here and there for I know of none to come. Campeachy wood begins to rise now, worth at present £18 or £19 per t. If cheap, send a quantity. For all other India goods, meddle not with them.

Good wines will be in request this year, I mean Canaries, for there lies at Cadiz, Gibraltar and Malaga 20 sail of Holland men-of-war which intend to take up their abode there for this winter. So consequently, they will block up those ports that we shall scarce have any Jerez or Malaga wines, which will advance Canaries, which may serve per advice. Here are many ships providing for your vintage, only want men to carry them out.

77c. Here enclosed I send you a coranto which I received this week from Rouen, to which refer you. Mrs Mary Leigh entreated me to take for her 20 ts freight for the Canaries and so home, which I have done upon the *Charles* of London, burthen 160 ts, whereof Charles Saunders is master. You are to pay per charter-party £5 per t. For the disposal thereof I refer you to her advice, supposing it's upon account of what Mr Fernando Body and company owes her in her behalf. I pray do the part of a friend in getting in what you can for her, she being a gentlewoman, that her condition is somewhat to be pitied, having scarce a faithful friend that she can trust unto. I should be glad to have 2 lines from you how Thomas Leigh [Clerke's apprentice] behaves himself and how you like him.

I do now daily expect Messrs. Davies' and Ackland's bills for the £400 for your account, which shall be punctually paid when due, of which rest confident. I have not spoken with Mr John Andrews this month. There's money due upon your particular account besides the 340 *milréis* in Mr Searchfield's hands, which he should pay here. But of late he appears not. He is a very poor man. I doubt shall scarce get anything more of him. Rather than fail, I'll give him 12 months and a day for payment so can get security, though I have no such order from you. Here enclosed I send you a letter which he sent me days past, for I sent him word I would arrest him if did not come and give me satisfaction.

I do forbear to give you the particulars of the great fight between our fleet, consisting of 120, and the Hollanders, about 112 sail, on 2 Aug. [off the Texel], referring you to Mr Lambell and Capt. Russell. But, in brief, they fought most desperately on both sides, never the like fight since the creation, by all men's reports. We sunk, burnt and destroyed all the men-of-war which we took of theirs in the fight, which were near 30 sail, took 1,200 men prisoners, killed Van Tromp, their general, and beat them into their ports. We lost 2 ships and about 1,000 men killed and more hurt, our ships very much tattered and torn, but now are made ready again, the most part. We have at present 120 sail which will be ready all within a week. The Hollander hath a great fleet making ready which will be speedily out; no hopes of any composure. Capt. Russell [of the *Katherine*] will give you an account what the State owes us besides £380 which he shared days past. ...

[P.S.] Per Pedro Ribete shall send you your case of rich spirits, etc., who may be ready next week.

78. to Gowen Paynter and William Clerke   18 Nov. 1653

a. I shall now answer yours of 20 June. At Mr John Andrews' first arrival here [from Terceira], I demanded an account of him in your names by virtue of those procurations I have from you, who with much ado gave me one, the true copy thereof I here send you. The original thought fit to keep here, on which he owes you 104,669 *réis*, reduced into sterling at 10s per *milréis* is £52 5s 5d, besides 23½ hannecks of wheat which Mr Waight [the *Elizabeth and John*] took, pretending to be his when it was yours, for which he allows £22 6s 6d. So that in all he owes you £74 11s 6d as appears per the account which I here send you. The day after we adjusted it he came to me and pretended that he was short of money and had not £10 to command in England, upon which I was so reasonable, considering the man's poverty, as to give him 12 months' time for payment thereof, provided he gave me his bond with good security, which he promised would do. But from this day to that I never saw him nor cannot hear of him, but I am credibly informed he is not worth a groat, so that you may put this debt on the backside of your day-book. The reason why he came short upon this account was that he paid some of his debts at the Azores with your monies. As I formerly writ you, he hath delivered me an obligation under Mr William Searchfield's hand for 334,775 *réis*, which money I have ordered ditto Searchfield to invest in Brazil sugars and to send it me home per first ships.

I shall now give you an account of what passeth about your £600 which was insured on ditto ship from the Azores to the Canaries. Upon Mr Waight's arrival I caused him and one of his men [Thomas Grey] to be examined in the Admiralty [Court] whereby to prove the loss, and, having order to take out the depositions, perusing them with my counsel, Dr Exton, the policy being for your accounts. And Waight and the other man, whether ignorantly or wilfully, they have sworn positively the corn to be for my account, not so much as mentioning you, which is clear contrary to the assurance. So that I durst not go to a trial for their evidence will overthrow our cause. Thus you may see how knaves may ruin a man. Ever since that time I cannot see Waight; I am informed is gone for Barbados. What to do in this business I know not. The insurers will take advantage upon their depositions. Now in case they had sworn the truth, that the corn was yours, yet we could not have recovered the £600 because it was not a loss but an average, by reason some corn was landed. At first I could not believe any such thing, but since I have been better informed and am convinced it's so by the ablest merchants that walk the Exchange and my counsel. Besides, there's several precedents of the very same nature upon record in the Insurance Court, which undoubtedly they will judge this accordingly. So that all you can expect to recover from the insurers is, viz. first, the policy is valued at £1,200 sterling, and there's insured £600, so that now we must produce an account what the cost [was] of those goods which were aboard the ship at her departure from the Azores, and the one-half thereof must be paid by the insurers, and the other half you must bear yourselves by reason the valuation was £1,200. So that this insurance will come very short of what you or I expected at first. Had you landed no corn, there had been no dispute, but had recovered the whole, so that by your own diligence getting goods ashore you are prejudiced. Though it be law, I am sure it's not equity. I shall advise you hereafter what passeth in this business. In the meantime, if possible, I'll see where can bring the insurers to any agreement. I wish had 30 per cent of what is insured. You may imagine this is no small trouble to me, however be confident no diligence shall be wanting in me to promote your interest.

78b. There's £200 yet not recovered of that insurance made on the *Swan* which Alderman Berkeley's executors owe. Capt. Pyle and I am like to have a trial next term in the Admiralty Court about £900 freight which he demands for 6 months, a thing very unjust. The seamen's wives which died in the voyage, being 14, have recovered wages of him, else I believe he would not have minded to sue me. I sent you a copy of our charter-party. I think you will say it's as authentic a one as ever you saw. The advantage which they find in it is in these words following: 'provided that if the ship be well, and in the service of the said merchant at the expiration of 8 months, and not coming home, that then upon certificate or certain advice the said merchant shall pay 6 months' pay'. To which I answer that the ship was not well nor in my service at the 6 months' end, ergo no freight due. Upon this I have been with 2 of the ablest lawyers in the Admiralty and given them large fees whereby to deal really with me, and they both conclude that Pyle will receive freight of me, first because they have condemned him to pay men's wages, though he proved in Court that he shipped them upon the same terms as he let the ship to freight, to have no wages due till 8 months were expired. But the judges are very favourable to the seamen nowadays by reason the State have occasion to make use of them in this juncture of time, having wars with Holland. My counsel gave for reason thus: that though it were certain I had freighted the ship for 8 months, yet the charter-party does not say positively that in case the ship be cast away within the expiration of that time that the owners shall have no freight; ergo it lies in the judge's breast, from which God deliver us. They say the same law which condemned Pyle to pay wages will me to pay freight, so that we are like to make a black voyage of it. If possible, I shall get the difference to be arbitrated rather than stand to a trial, though I have no such order from you. This Guinea voyage hath from the beginning been to me a vexatious business. God grant I may once see an end to it [so that] I may be able to perfect that account.

78c. We have had very stormy weather of late, NW winds which are bad for the coast of Holland. The Dutch have 14 sail of their men-of-war cast away which ride in the Texel, besides many others torn and some cut their masts by the board, which hath somewhat disabled them for coming out so suddenly as we expected. Upon which our States have disembargoed all ships; otherwise they had not gone hence till after Christmas, I mean the vintage ships which remained here.

We shall speedily have 100 sail men-of-war forth. The Hollanders have 4 ambassadors here at present; as yet have concluded upon nothing, nor do I think they will, so that consequently we are like to have a bloody summer and very dangerous. Here's news there lie 10 sail of Holland men-of-war at the Strait's mouth, which have taken several of our merchant ships and 'tis like[ly] will do further mischief. I doubt poor William Chalk [Capt. of the *Mary*] will hardly escape them, being bound for Malaga from thence [Tenerife].

Here are letters of 20 Oct. [from Malaga] where they writ have a very short vintage, not half so much wines as last year. Here is some newly arrived which proves some good and some bad, much inferior to last year's wines, as yet none sold. Canaries will not yield above £30 per pipe this year except they are very rare indeed. As yet no ship arrived from thence. West India goods do now begin to rise: hides worth 7d per lb; logwood, £19 per t, a great charge upon it; cochineal, 30s per lb; campechena, 6s per lb; indigo, if not hardbacked, worth 5s per lb; Varinas tobacco, if right, 6s per lb. ...

79. to Gowen Paynter and William Clerke   10 Dec. 1653
I have written you at large per Mr Jenkins [the *Sarah*] and sent the copy per Capt. Wall, to which crave reference. These are chiefly to advise you how within this 20 days logwood is risen £10 per t, worth at present £28 per t and like to rise, a thing contrary to the expectations of all men. But of late here have come orders for the buying up of above 150 ts to send for Rouen where it's worth 30 *livres* per kt. Now I am informed per an Indian which came in the Biscayner how there's great quantities of Campeachy wood in Tenerife to be sold, which, if so, now is the time for you to make an engagement for a good quantity, 3,000 or 4,000 kts, by which there will be money enough gotten by it, and I suppose their order of payment will be accommodating. Besides, if you are not minded to adventure it home within a month's time, when the general advice of all men comes there, I am confident they will give you good profit there for it again in the Island. You need not fear of any to come here to lower this market for at San Lucar and Cadiz there's not 100 kts as per advice. Perhaps may get more money by it than if had laden 1,000 pipes wines for your accounts this year. You may do therein as you think fit. Were I there I would employ all that I have in the world in ditto commodity. If you buy any, I shall take it as a favour you will interest me a part with you. Advise me where shall send you a ship, per whom shall send you what effects you think needful. Campechena worth 6s 6d per lb; indigo, 5s per lb. If you do anything, you must be nimble. ...
[P.S.] Hides worth 7½d [per lb]. In Rouen those of Caracas, 28 *livres* [per hide], ditto Havana or Santo Domingo, 22 *livres*. Campechena, 6 *livres* per lb.

80. to William Clerke   22 Jan. 1654
I have written you per several ships this vintage at large, to which crave

reference. But as yet have not had the happiness to receive a line from you, at which I do not much admire in regard I hear you were at Gran Canaria. Here are several passengers come from Dartmouth by land from the *Peter*, Capt. Pedro Ribete, who is safe arrived there about 25 days since and as yet not come into the river but hourly expected. I am told Pedro Ribete hath letters for me but told the passengers would deliver them by his own hand. I have a great desire to have a few lines from you. I hope you are not angry with me, though I confess I have not been so good as my word with you about your account.

This small vessel [the *Agreement*, Capt. John Mourton] I bought between me and Mr Thomas Warren in halves; and having a few pilchards in the West, by great chance, I have ordered them to be sent in this vessel, seeming could get no other in all the West Country for to carry the fish away, being about 120 hhds, which were all that I could get for love or money.

The wines in general from Orotava and Rambla prove this year very miserable stuff, such trash as I never saw the like. Only those from Garachico being made before the rain fell prove pretty wines, especially those which came in Hedgethorn's and Bean's [ships] laden by Mr [Henry] Negus and Mr George Webber and company. I had a few from my father-in-law in Capt. Garvis Russell [the *Katherine*] which proved very ordinary, but I took my first chapman and have sold them at £33 5s per pipe and most men's wines unsold. Within this 20 days wines are fallen above £4 per pipe. I leave you to judge what a market Steward and the rest will come to. I am glad you were so judicious as to foresee the palpable loss which most men are like to sustain this year. I account myself a happy man that I have sold my wines. Were they to sell now, really they would not yield the money by £500 in the parcel.

There is a small vessel now in Plymouth which is to touch in Santa Cruz [de Tenerife] by whom shall write you more at large. In the interim I hope shall receive my letters per Pedro Ribete. West India goods bear great prices: hides, 7¼d per lb; logwood, £27 per t; indigo, 5s 6d; cochineal, 27s per lb; campechena, 6s 6d per lb; Varinas tobacco, if good, 6s per lb; Caracas hides in Rouen worth 27 *livres*, ditto Santo Domingo or Havana, 21 *livres* per hide; Campeachy wood, 26 *livres* per kt; campechena, 6 *livres* per lb as per advice from thence [Rouen] at last post, which may serve per advice.

Little hopes of any peace with Holland. Here is great preparation making for a summer fleet to consist of 200 sail of men-of-war and to lie and block up Amsterdam and Flushing as last summer. The Hollander durst not encounter our fleet. I look upon them as in a sadder condition than we by far.

I have made a final end with Capt. Pyle. Per next shall give you the particulars. ...

81. to William Clerke   10 Feb. 1654
a. I have written you at large of 22 Jan. per Mr Mourton [the *Agreement*] via St Sebastian, a small vessel which took in 100 hhds of pilchards which I sent my father-in-law. And since, I have received yours of 2 and 4 Dec.

per Pedro Ribete who was a month in the West Country and did not send up his letter, being in hopes every day to get up and deliver them himself, as he pretends.

Considering how the year proves, you have done very prudently in not buying a pipe. Those gentlemen which have their wines now coming home will be sufficiently soaped, else I am very much mistaken in my judgement. Wines are fallen £5 per pipe of what they were worth 2 months since. Mr Christopher Boone sold 50 pipes of Don Luis Benitez' wines yesterday at £24 per pipe, which once was proffered £30 for them. Indeed they were trash. Antonio Fernandez [Carvajal] hath sold this day 40 pipes of wines out of a cellar of 70 pipes at £28 per pipe. The refuse which they leave will not make £10 per pipe. I will not excuse Don Balthazar [de Vergara Grimón] and that gang for 10,000 Ds loss this year upon their wines, of what they cost them put here with all charges. Such may be their success henceforward. I shall not give you more particulars, but by this you may judge a little more or less what the trade of Canary wines will be for this year. Indeed there are some few men which had indifferent good wines from Garachico, as Mr Bonfoy and others, which have sold at good prices. Amongst all I have not sold at the worst price, £33 5s per pipe.

81b. I have written you and Mr Paynter at large concerning your insurance on Mr Waight's ship [the *Elizabeth and John*] and in what a condition it lies that I durst not meddle further as yet. Here is a ship arrived from Terceira, but not a penny return for your account [due from John Andrews], nor so much as a letter from Mr William Searchfield, at which I admire. The world is grown to that pass that it is a rare thing to find an honest man. I shall write Mr Searchfield per next conveyance; and if do not answer that, must send a procuration over to some for its recovery. Since my last, no news of Mr John Andrews, your debtor, nor the master [of the *Elizabeth and John*, Thomas Waight]. And as for Daniel Coult, he was taken by the Turks going over in the *Blessing*. So much for that unfortunate business.

I shall now come to give you an account of our Guinea business. As yet cannot get a penny of Alderman William Berkeley, [i.e.] his executors, for the £200 he is in by assurance. Since my last joint letter writ you and Mr Paynter, I have endeavoured by several means and ways to bring Capt. Pyle [partowner of the *Swan*] to a right understanding of our difference, sometimes by friends' persuasion and other times by threatenings. And at last, I thank God, have brought my designs to take effect. To tell you the particulars, it would be too tedious, but such was my condition with vexation that I could scarce rest at night, that after we had lost almost all should pay freight, and such a considerable sum, which could not have been avoided had he put it to a trial. It cost me above £5 in counsel about the charter-party, and all the lawyers that ever saw it told me that I must pay it. It would make you laugh if you knew which way I got off, which I am enjoined to be private though you be most concerned in it, neither do I think you will be so curious as to know when you hear the end. In fine I have got in my charter-party and cancelled it. I shall be very cautious how I bruise wax another time. And it cost me but £40 which I paid Capt. Pyle, which, had he stood upon terms, really I would have given him £200 rather than gone to trial. But there are times and seasons for all things. I got him in the mood and did business, and since, I am sure, he hath repented, and his owner [William] Bulkley is very much vexed with him. And thus in brief I have given you an account of our Guinea business.

81c. Be pleased to take notice I have paid Mr Ackland's and Davies' [of Bilbao] order, £400, for your account. They put 12 per cent premium to your account, but that do not concern me. Only, as you are my friend whose interest I do esteem as my own, give me leave to acquaint you that therein they do you wrong, except you have absolutely agreed so with them, for at present, and anytime this 12 months, the exchange hath gone *plata* for sterling at 4s per piece of eight. As for example, a piece of eight, being 8*Rs*, it's brought here, and, if [of] Mexico or Seville [stamp], it's worth 4s 4d; then, deducting out freight charges and insurance, etc., it makes not out above 3s 10d per piece of eight. As for the money I received of Mr [Christopher] Boone and [Richard] King, I make you good the same value in sterling. I wonder you do not order me to send goods for Seville whereby to have effects there and to make advance outwards upon your goods. It would be far more advantageous to you than drawing the money [on London via Bilbao]. You may do therein as you think fit.

I am glad to see you go recovering in your debts. There's some hopes of your personal appearance here shortly. I could wish my father-in-law would take the same course, but instead of that, I doubt he makes more [i.e. sales on credit] daily. You shall not be many months without your account. I should be sorry I should occasion your stay there upon that score.

I perceive you were about buying a large parcel of West India goods. If you went through with the bargain, blame me for giving such encouragement if you suffer thereby. India goods have not been so high in England and France since I have resided here: hides worth 7½d per lb; logwood, £26 per t; cochineal mesteque, 26s per lb; campechena, 6s per lb; indigo, 5s 4d per lb; Varinas tobacco, if good, 6s per lb; Caracas hides worth in Rouen 27 *livres* [per hide]; ditto Havana or Santo Domingo, 22 *livres*; logwood, 26 *livres* per kt. Mr James Cowes is newly arrived at Falmouth with most of aforesaid commodities, which come to a very great occasion. Though there come 6,000 hides, it cannot fall the market.

81d. I perceive you and my father-in-law have had some discourse about a design, viz. to have me send you a ship against Lent with about 300 hhds of pilchards, which had your advice come sooner, I could not have effected it because no pilchards to be had this 3 months, and those which I sent at the first of the year in the *Blessing* cost 9s per m. These which I sent in Mr Mourton [the *Agreement*] were taken since Christmas unexpected, and for my life I could not get a hhd more than she carries. This ship carries 50 hhds or thereabouts which my cousin [John] Paige of Plymouth hath been 2 months laying up for his own account. Now to freight you a pretty vessel per month, I think really I shall not be able to get one from hence. The times are so difficult owners care not to let their ships. Mr

Chalk [the *Mary*] is now arrived from Malaga, of which ship I own part. She is about 100 ts. The owners will not let her a farthing under £120 per month which I will never give. I proffered £100 and they make slight of it. Neither will they oblige to carry the ship into the Downs by such a day, nor that she shall go full-manned by reason of the great difficulty of getting men in these times of trial to men's patience, so that I am resolved to desist to do anything till next ships come from the Canaries, per whom hope shall hear from you. ...

[P.S.] Mr Boone and your brother [George] have promised to me that we may discourse and end your differences very speedily. You may please to take notice that I paid [Capt.] James Blake £12 9s for your account towards the setting out of your $\frac{1}{16}$ part of the *Constant John*, Mr [Richard] Lant refusing to pay it and hath delivered up your bill of sale unto your brother. Be pleased to order therein as you think fit.

82. to William Clerke   10 March 1654

I have written you at large per the *Agreement*, Mr Mourton, and likewise per the *Golden Cock*, but the former per accident came too late so both went per the *Golden Cock*. I have now received yours of 28 Jan. per Mr Smyth, by which perceive you have bought a considerable parcel of West India goods in Santa Cruz [de Tenerife], hides, logwood and most part campechena and sylvester. The last is not a commodity to send here, being not worth anything. The 3 first sort commodities as hides worth 8d per lb; logwood, £25 per t; campechena, 6s per lb; indigo, 5s per lb; Varinas tobacco, 6s per lb if good; ginger a very drug, not worth 30s per cwt and at Lisbon not worth 4 *milréis* per kt of 132 lbs, as per advice, there being 150 ts arrived there. Genoa is the best market you can send that commodity to.

If you draw the £600 on me, I shall see your bills honoured and paid. You desire to have a ship of 120 ts freighted between you and my father-in-law per month, which I cannot procure a pretty vessel except give an extraordinary rate never known. Now I am informed there's a ship arrived [at Tenerife] from Spain of 160 ts which comes to seek a freight, so I know not where you may furnish yourself there or no. Besides, I have sent my father-in-law a small vessel of 75 ts [the *Agreement*], so that in one or other I conceive you may send home some goods. So that I shall desist freighting a ship till I hear further from you. But if any ship go from hence per t to return home, as I suppose there will within a month, then I shall take 50 ts freight in her and charge upon you, upon which you may depend. If the Havana man arrive, you may do well to buy up her hides especially, for they are a staple commodity here at all times.

Capt. Wall's letters are not as yet come up, he being in Plymouth. ...

83. to William Clerke   1 April 1654

a. My last unto you was of 11 Feb. via Plymouth, to which crave reference for what then proffered. Since which have received yours of 27 and 29 Jan. The last came to my hands but lately. You there desire me to freight a ship of 120 ts for your account and my father-in-law's per month, which I cannot get, as the times now govern, none upon those terms except I would take some ordinary or old vessel which I know will not be fit for your turn. And those ask unreasonable prices, no less than 20s per month for every t, a rate which I shall not give. I would fain have had Mr Chalk [the *Mary*] or Brampton [the *Matthew*], but neither would go except per t, and now both are freighted. Now seeing I sent out a small vessel [the *Agreement*] to my father-in-law about 7 weeks since with a few pilchards, I suppose he will load home his West India goods upon ditto, so that I shall not adventure to charge him with any tonnage till hear of her arrival and how disposes of her. I perceive you have bought a large parcel of West India goods in Santa Cruz [de Tenerife] and, seeing you depend upon my sending a ship to fetch it away, I have this day freighted a pretty new frigate [the *Peter and Anne*, Capt. William Chamlett] of 80 ts, 10 guns, to go from hence to Tenerife and so home at £5 per t, and with much entreaty. In which vessel I shall charge you with 40 ts for your account; the rest Antonio Fernandez Carvajal takes. Which vessel, I conceive, will be ready within 15 days, but it will be a very difficult thing to get her out in these vexatious times. Never was the like pressing as at present. Here are 3 Holland ambassadors now treating with the Lord Protector, but I doubt whether they will agree. The vessel's sudden departure will, I doubt, prevent me sending goods for your account, yet I shall endeavour to send you something, though you never sent me a memory, nor my father-in-law, until Mr Lambell came home, which is not 15 days since.

83b. What money you draw upon me I shall see your bill [of exchange] punctually paid. It had been better you had ordered me to send goods for Spain and to have advanced upon your goods and not to have drawn sterling money at 12 per cent loss as Mr [John] Wheake of Bilbao puts to your account, which is very disadvantageous to you.

I am credibly informed Mr Henry Lee of San Lucar, your correspondent, is going for Barbados, being much engaged in the country and likewise here, so that he is looked upon as an insolvent man, which I thought fit to give you a hint of. In case you want an able man to do your business in Cadiz, make use of Mr Richard Ducke, of whom I have had sufficient experience. I believe in discourse of time you will give me thanks for recommending you to him.

Pray per first advise me where you will comply with this tonnage and what shall insure for your account homewards. Hides worth 7½d per lb, the only staple commodity of all West India goods; Campeachy wood worth £24 per t; campechena, if good, 6s per lb; cochineal, 28s per lb; sylvester, a very drug, not worth 20d per lb; ginger, 30s per cwt; new Varinas tobacco, 6s per lb. You cannot send too many hides for they are a great commodity in Rouen. I would have charged you with 10 or 20 ts more in this pretty frigate [the *Peter and Anne*], but could not get it.

Canary wines prove very bad in general. Only Steward's wines prove good, and another small vessel which Mr [John] Turner laded; most part sold for £35 per pipe. I am confident there will be above £10,000 loss upon wines this year from the Canaries. Some men cannot get £18 for their parcel round, Mr John Bewley for one, Mr Richard King for another. Don Balthazar [de Vergara Grimón] will lose above £3,000 this year by his wines, besides several others which will be too tedious to particularise. I understand you have had much rain this year. If so, I hope a plentiful vintage will ensue. In case you intend to have any tonnage at vintage charged on you, it will be necessary that you give timely advice, else it will be impossible to get a ship out in these difficult times. Seamen's wages are at 50s per month. ...

[P.S.] This goes via Dunkirk per a Spanish ship.

84. to William Clerke   25 April 1654

a. ... I have received yours of 28 and 29 Jan., 15 and 17 March. Thereby perceive you have bought a very considerable parcel of West India goods and that you desire a ship per month. But before your advice came to my hand, I had sent my father-in-law a small vessel [the *Agreement*] with some pilchards, which I conceive would bring away his goods, upon which consideration I did forbear. Besides, at that time I could not get a complete frigate as I know you expected, the times being dangerous and men not to be got for money. Now whereas you desire to hear from me what market will be most proper and beneficial for your West India goods, indeed I know none like England at present, and next to that Rouen. As for Lisbon, it's very bad, hides not worth above 2,700 *réis*; ginger, 4,000 *réis* per kt. Now you must note that [Portuguese] money is as bad as *vellon* in Spain, so that considering all things, you had as good have a ship freighted per t to come for London as to have one per month and not to have your goods lie there till the markets lower, which, in all probability, they may hereafter.

Now you may please to take notice how I have taken 40 ts freight or the one-half of this frigate called the *Peter and Anne*, whereof William Chamlett is master, at £5 per t, to return for London. She is to go to any of the Islands. The other half is freighted by *Señor* Antonio Fernandez Carvajal who loads his part in wines. Now in case the ship's days be out before she reaches Santa Cruz [de Tenerife] then in such case they are to pay half demurrage. For by particular agreement between the freighters, you are to have the ship as many days in Santa Cruz, etc., as they [Fernandez Carvajal's factors] in Orotava or Garachico. But I hope there will no occasion be of these things, conceiving you will dispatch her away long before the days are expired, being summer season.

84b. You writ me your parcel consists of hides, wood, campechena and sylvester, the most part of the 2 last commodities. You may do well to load home your hides in this ship and what wants to fill up with wood and campechena and some sylvester, assorted, but most hides, which are now worth 8d per lb; Campeachy wood, £23 per t; campechena, 6s per lb and sylvester, 2s 8d per lb to 3s if very good. Here enclosed I send you a coranto which I received from Rouen where those goods bear good prices but not altogether so much as the bill specifies. You may please to give my father-in-law a view thereof. If any hides chance to come in from Havana or Caracas, you may do well to buy a parcel. No India commodity so staple as that. Here is come and expect a great quantity of Campeachy wood, which I doubt will somewhat lower the price, though not much. I am sorry you are so plagued with a rigorous Judge [of the Indies]. I doubt he will undo the [West] Indians and cause them to forsake the Islands, which will be a great hindrance unto that trade.

I cannot do anything as to the insurances made on Mr Waight's ship [the *Elizabeth and John*]. In my former gave you notice how had made an end with Capt. Pyle about the *Swan*'s charter-party. Alderman Berkeley, which owes us £200 by insurance upon ditto voyage and £100 upon Waight, he being dead, is now found to be a beggar, so that I do despair ever seeing a penny of that money. It is not I alone that am thus injured. He owes for losses above £8,000.

By yours, 15 March, I perceive you do not take it well that had none of mine by the *Agreement*. It was unhappily left behind. Had your letter per Capt. Pedro Ribete's ship been sent me up immediately upon the ship's arrival in the West Country, assuredly I had interested you in the *Agreement*'s pilchards, for there was never anything that you desired in that way since our first correspondency that ever I scrupled or denied you an interest in where you desired it. Likewise your letter per Capt. Wall was not delivered me in above a month after the ship arrived in Plymouth and Falmouth, and when a man taxes them for their neglect, their excuse is that your grand charge is that they deliver them by their own hands. Therefore, for future, pray order them to send up their letters per post in case they stop in the West Country, which is a very sure conveyance.

84c. In my last via Plymouth I gave you an account of the state of your business with Mr John Andrews, who is gone God knows where. I will not give you a groat for all your debts, only that which remains in the hands of Mr William Searchfield. I shall now once more give order to have it come home in Mr Brampton [the *Matthew*] who is bound that way. You writ though Waight has made a bad affidavit that things may be put to rights by those papers as invoice, account, etc. To which I answer that it's not worth a rush in law except oath be made. Were the insurers honest men, it's possible your papers might be credited, but they are wrangling knaves. [See **78a.**]

The peace with Holland is now concluded and tomorrow it's proclaimed. Seeing I send you no ship per month, I conceive it needless to write my correspondents' names. However, seeing you desire it, I shall not omit it: at Lisbon, Mr Edward Chappell; at Rouen, Mr Humphrey Wilkings; at Amsterdam, John Schanternell; at Nantes, Mr [Lewis] Ackland, as Mr Holle [who is leaving Nantes for London] hath advised you. I am now sorry I had not taken this whole vessel [the *Peter and Anne*] to have brought away all your goods. If you can get tonnage, may do well to send it home, for without question now will be the best market. Your bill [of exchange] of £400 payable to Mr John Turner's order is come to hand and likewise the other of £250 payable to Mr William Cary, both which have accepted and shall be duly paid when grow due. I have likewise sent you a small parcel of goods in this ship for your account, as per invoice and bill of lading appears, which goes in another letter written you per this conveyance, to which refer you. I would have sent you a few ozenbrigs but could not get you a *vara* for money at present. In case you will have any tonnage taken against vintage, pray give your orders in time, for good ships will be taken up by 1 July at furthest. As yet no news

106

of the *Agreement*, God send her well home. I am now making insurance on her.

I have put above £1,000 worth of goods aboard this ship for the account of my father-in-law and myself, which hath been bought most part this 4 months. It goes upon your tonnage out, seeing the ship would have gone empty. I hope you will be so favourable as to take no freight, when not, I leave it to you to do therein as you think convenient. I shall be ready to do you the civility at any time.

I have received yours by Mr Fernando Body and, according to your commands, I have tendered him my service in a real way and what else he wants and shall be very ready to do him any civil office that my mean capacity reaches unto, for he is a person that I ever have esteemed deserving. I received a letter from cousin Mr David Stephens [Body's partner] to the same effect, which I cannot answer at present, but you may please to certify him my readiness as to that particular. ...

[P.S.] Here enclosed I send you a copy of the charter-party. You may clear your goods of the contraband upon my father-in-law's certificate sent him.

85. to William Clerke   27 May 1654

My last unto you was of 25 April per the *Peter and Anne*, since which I have not heard from you, which makes me brief at present. We are now in expectation of Mr Mucco, Mr Mourton [the *Agreement*] and Capt. Knowles who do now begin to tarry. I do much fear your new Judge [of the Indies] hath mounted some mischievous demur to their dispatches. I wish my jealousies do not prove true in the end.

Since my last here are now strange designs in agitation. As 'tis generally conceived, we have at least 40 sail of men-of-war now sheeted and may be ready within a month to proceed their design. It's affirmed they are to go against the Spaniard, to lie off Cadiz in July to meet the *galeones* and from thence for the West Indies. Now the thing which does the more confirm these jealousies is that last week there came down an order from the Council at Whitehall to the Commissioners of the Prize Office to make sale of all such goods as they had under seizure of the Spaniards, as well that which was freed by decree in [the High Court of] Admiralty, as also that which was not condemned at all, a thing not to be parallized [i.e. paralleled] in England this many years. But since the peace with Holland, most men cry up war with Spain, saying the fleet and army must be kept in employment and no place worth their attempting like unto the West Indies. And the Spanish ambassador is now in little esteem and seems to be very melancholy at these actings. A short time will produce the reality of these kind of affairs.

I am now sorry I did not charge you with more tonnage in Hyatt, I say Chamlett [the *Peter and Anne*]. I hope he is new laden by this time. The goods will come to a pretty good occasion in my opinion: hides worth 8d per lb; Campeachy wood, £21 per t; cochineal, 24s per lb; campechena, 6s per lb; sylvester now begins to be in request, worth 3s per lb at least; Varinas tobacco, if right, 6s per lb; but no commodity like hides at all times; indigo, 5s per lb.

Here enclosed I remit you the articles of peace printed here between us and the Hollander, which pray be pleased to give my father-in-law a view thereof. The last week there was a letter of marque granted against the Spaniard in satisfaction of some injuries done above 15 years since, which is an ill omen. You may please to make use of this advice as you think fit, but pray impart it to no man. ...

86. to [William Clerke]   1 June 1654

... [I]f you intend to have any tonnage at vintage, give me your advice in time. Except I find much danger, I shall not insure anything for you from the Canaries upon Mr Chamlett [the *Peter and Anne*]. Here is news of Mr [Thomas] Hiway's arrival at Barbados from river Gambia with 20 Negroes. He brought out 60 but they rose against the seamen who killed 40 of them, so they are like to lose half the principal. ...

87. to William Clerke   11 July 1654

My last unto you was of 27 May per Mr Hyatt, the copy thereof sent via Palma, to which crave reference. Since which have not received any from you, so have little subject to insist on at present. This day is come certain news from Galicia how on 27 April Capt. Knowles with another small vessel in his company, supposed to be Mr Mucco, were taken near our Land's End by 3 Holland men-of-war and carried into Vigo, so they are prize, being taken within the limited time of the articles of peace which was 4 May. As yet no news of my small vessel [the *Agreement*], Mr Mourton, so now I do conclude she is miscarried likewise. Before this news came, I supposed the Judge of the Indies had detained them [at the Canaries]. I do now begin to look out for Mr Chamlett [the *Peter and Anne*], God send him safe. I do not apprehend at present any danger of men-of-war, therefore as yet have not insured anything for your accounts upon her. Neither shall I except she stay a month longer.

Your India goods will come to a very good occasion, else my judgement fails me. Hides worth $8\frac{1}{2}$d per lb; logwood, £21 per t; campechena, 6s per lb; sylvester, 3s 4d per lb, if good; indigo, 5s per lb; cochineal, 23s per lb; Varinas tobacco, if good, 6s per lb (none good arrived in Spain, so it's like to rise); ginger, 35s per cwt. No such vendible commodity as hides; it will prove far better return than any other goods you can send.

Here are at least 20 ships freighted for the Canaries to load home with wines at vintage. I shall not take you a t except I receive your further order. Except wines prove very rare next year, they will be a very drug next year, for here are above 2,000 pipes this day unsold, which will not yield £15 the one with the other, I may justly say less, by which there will be above £20,000 loss, whosoever's share it falls to.

Our fleet of men-of-war bound to the southward are now near ready. Their preparations and provision do daily discover more and more that they are bound for the West Indies, in that they have bought up all the eager wines for beverage, with 300 ts cider, great quantities of strong waters and French brandies, all which are unproper provisions for the Straits or anywhere else. Their design is kept very private; not any commander knows of certain where they shall go.

The Portuguese ambassador [Penaguião] hath concluded a peace with the Lord Protector and yesterday signed the articles of peace, which very day his brother [Dom Pantaleon Sa] was beheaded upon Tower Hill for murdering a man some 6 months since. His brother the ambassador solicited a pardon very much but could not obtain it, upon which he is gone very much discontented but his business finished. The French ambassador is very earnest in his treaty, and it's supposed will conclude a peace very suddenly. ...

88. to William Clerke   17 July 1654

My last unto you was of the 11th current under covert Mr Fernando Body. Since which time I have certain news my ship *Agreement* [Capt. Mourton] is taken, being one of those carried into Galicia, which was formerly conceived to be Mr Mucco, of whom there's no news as yet. Both your letters and my father-in-law's are all lost, so I am much straitened for want of advice. I do now hourly expect Mr Chamlett [the *Peter and Anne*], on whom I have insured for your account £700 at 4 per cent. You writ me to charge you with 25 ts per Lawrence Browning and to make you no insurance; but, seeing I charged you with 40 ts, I thought good to secure something and the rather because last post I received a letter from Falmouth where they writ me there came in 9 Flemings which ran away in their boat and left their ship within 20 leagues of Scilly where they met with 4 Turks, men-of-war. Besides, the Brest rogues have taken several ships of late. So I hope you will approve of what I have done herein. If your goods arrive safe, the market will bear higher insurance.

The miscarriage of the Canary men makes logwood to rise, worth at present £23 per t. I shall not charge you with any tonnage at vintage except receive your further orders hereafter. By Mr Mourton I understand you have the half of 60 bags of ginger, which was more than you intimated unto me, so that you will be a sufferer as well as my father-in-law and self. No remedy but patience. The Lord restore it us some other way if it be His good will and pleasure. ...

[P.S.] This letter was left behind, the ship being departed, so send it per covert Mr Spicer.

89. to William Clerke   18 Aug. 1654

a. I have yours, 3 July, per the *Peter and Anne*, William Chamlett. Have received out of her all according to bill of lading excepting 4 hides which the master pretends were washed overboard, being stowed upon deck. I have opened the 10 skins of sylvester and find them to prove very good, and have likewise bared every chest of the campechena, which for the most part proves not very good. The news of the *galeones'* arrival in Spain makes the salters hang off buying any at present, being they expect great quantities will come home in Capt. Pyle's [ship], who is now at Cadiz. If they do not buy it, I am resolved to send 6 chests next ship for Rouen, and if find that to turn to account, shall send the rest in small parcels (it will be better for sales). Besides, our peace with France is somewhat dubious; we take all their ships at sea that we meet with, and they many times procure orders from Paris to embargo Englishmen's goods for satisfaction, which makes me somewhat timorous at present. And though men do trade upon these kinds of disadvantageous terms, yet there does not want them that will adventure.

Your hides I have rather chosen to dispose of them here than send them for Rouen for the aforegoing reasons. I have sold them all at 10d per lb, a price not known in England this many years. There came home at the same time a small vessel to Mr Spicer and Bulkley which brought 900 hides; they sold theirs at 8¾d and 9d per lb. Your hides weighed in all 9,300 lbs, which was far less than I expected by above 5 lbs in a hide. I could wish you had 1,000 more to supply this good market, but I doubt it will not hold very long at these rates. Yet I believe when lowest they will yield 8d or more all this winter, which is a very good price. There's great quantities of indigo come in the *galeones*, which falls here to 4s per lb; logwood worth at present £24 per t, but that is a commodity that will hold long at a certain price if there come above 120 ts, of which you may take notice. Cochineal worth 25s per lb, which commodity being so cheap is a means to pull down the price of campechena, but for all, I hope I shall be able to give you a good sale of yours, though not so suddenly as I expected for it's a commodity little spent in winter. Here enclosed I send you one of John Day's bills of prices, to which refer you for other commodities.

89b. Mr Richard Lant refused to pay the master [Chamlett of the *Peter and Anne*] freight for the 30 ts you let Mr Leonard Clerke. He pretends to have 20 cwt English weight per t, whereas for the 12 ts which came upon the Spanish tonnage he hath paid that at 20 Island [Canarian] kts and £5 per t. It seems it was expressed in a bill of lading, but yours is obscure, as he pretends. Now the masters and owners will come upon me as being obliged per charter-party to pay according to custom, which indeed is 20 Island kts per t. Seeing Mr Lant and you are at variance, you should have been so much the more cautious to have prevented such pretences. A short time will either produce a conclusion or else a suit at law. I have incurred anger about this business for he and I have had very hot discourse about it. I am very confident both your intent in letting and Mr [Leonard] Clerke's intent taking the tonnage was at 20 kts to the t, as he gave the Spaniard. Besides, you lose 20s per t and they have the full freight as it was let out here.

I have paid Mr Holle [formerly Paige's correspondent at Nantes] £120 and am to adjust with him within 3 days. You require 35 per cent for the exchange at that time, which he makes you good but 25 per cent in account. Besides, you quote his own letter for it, to which he answers if have any such advice it's an error. But waiving all that, I have been with several of our best exchangers and seen their books how the exchange run that very week he passed the money upon me. And in reality I find it went but at 25 per cent. However, I shall not allow him the 10 per cent without your further order, of which 2 lines in your next. I find the man to be very fair and honest, but I believe no great matter of estate.

I perceive for future you desire to have nothing acted here in your business but what [I] have your order for, which I shall duly observe to the best of my mean capacity. But sure I am you will soon be weary of [this] and be of another mind in a short time, for alas such are the difficulties of times that many things happen out here you know not of there. But to prevent misinterpretations for future, pray give in your orders in full and ample advice that I not be at a stand, for so long as I am limited I shall not act beyond your order. Since I have done your business, I can make appear I have got you £500 by what I have done without your order, but to the best of my remembrance, I never lost you £50 by anything I did without your advice. I am very glad you have taken up this resolve. To me it will be a great deal of ease and quietness of mind.

89c. When I freighted Mr Chamlett [the *Peter and Anne*], it was upon good grounds. First you writ to charge you 25 ts upon any ship, so that I exceeded 15 ts, which was upon this very ground that you writ me, [that you] had a very considerable parcel of India goods upon your hands; and here being a rumour we should quarrel with the Spaniards, I think was a sufficient conducement to make me do what I did, if you really consider all circumstances. Besides, if these goods had remained there to come home at vintage, you had lost your market for hides and perhaps something in the other goods. And seeing Mr Chamlett stayed so long and he had a tedious passage northwards, above 5 weeks, I began to doubt him. All which I communicated unto Mr Body, your friend, whom I told you would have above £1,500 in him [Chamlett's ship, the *Peter and Anne*], who concluded with me it was very requisite that some insurance were made in regard at that time there were Turkish men-of-war off Asilah which took some Flemings and likewise Brest men-of-war which took several Englishmen at that time. Upon which I insured £700 for your account on her at 4 per cent, which I hope you will approve thereof, for therein I did for you as if it had been for [my] own self.

I perceive by yours you desire to have me buy a ship of about 160 ts and to put in her 14 guns, sheeted and completely victualled for 12 months. Though there have been many prizes taken of late, that trade [of buying prize ships] is now over, and at this present most ships are taken up for vintage and other voyages. So it's the worst time of year to buy that can be. Besides, a ship of those dimensions as you writ of, etc., will cost at least £1,400 set to sea. I doubt I shall not be able to get one to my mind till the vintage ships return. I have been all the Thames over and set friends to give me notice, but cannot find any. I would wish you to consider that in my opinion it's better to freight [rather than buy] a ship and ditto money [equal to the purchase price] employed in goods will turn you far better to account. I have freighted part of [the *Matthew*] John Crampe [*recte* Brampton; cf. **93a, 96a**] for Malaga, who is now at Gravesend, I suppose may be home 1 Dec. He tells me will build a new frigate at his return and dispose of the *Matthew* which is a pretty-conditioned vessel but now begins to be old, yet will not be set to sea under £1,000 sheeted and victualled as you desire. And a hired ship per month will be as much at your command as one of your own, being well tied in charter-party. Besides, to have the whole ship and her cargo, it will be a great interest in one bottom. But you best know your own business.

89d. I shall go on investing the money of your hides in linens, which are 40 per cent dearer than they were when you had Barber [the *Blessing*] from Nantes [in July, 1649]. The reason is this 3 years they have scarce

111

gathered any flax in France by reason of great drought and, secondly, their civil wars. I have not as yet had much discourse with Mr Standish about your business, he having been in the country and I somewhat busy. But I purpose, God willing, shortly to have some further conference with him. The linens you writ for will cost a great deal [of] time to lay them up. They must all be brought here, for whereas you desire to have the ship go for Nantes and fill up with pipestaves, you may take notice there's a prohibition. None shall be shipped off from thence. Besides, they are worth 200 *livres* per m, insomuch there have been several ships consigned there with their lading of pipestaves from the East country. Now by this you may find how times do alter trade. You limit me to send a ship for Nantes, prefixing upon that place and no other for staves. It's true, formerly they were to be laden, but now they are not. If my time were short, what could I do in such case but stay for your further order? In the meantime your design might be overthrown.

Now whereas you desire to have my correspondents' name in Barbados, Ireland and Bristol, I shall in due time give you them. But ere you proceed further, take your friends' counsel. Should you send that ship laden with Santa Cruz [de Tenerife] wines, which you write me for, to any of aforesaid places, I am sure you would lose above half your principal, especially at Bristol and Ireland, for those parts are not able to vend above 100 pipes each. And for Barbados, they are drugs there; besides, there's Mr Mucco gone there. Capt. Feeney, the *Morocco Merchant*, a ship that Mr Lambell hath, now gone out, and at Plymouth there's one that is to touch [at] Santa Cruz [de Tenerife] and take in 120 pipes which Mr Spicer hath sold at £10 10s per pipe, to be paid here upon exchange. Had you writ me of any such thing, I could have sold them for you before Mr Spicer, or else you should have ordered me to freight 2 small vessels, one for Barbados and the other for Ireland at first of year. But now it's too late. You may [do] well to put off your wines in truck of West India goods if possible, but to go the other way the remedy will be worse than the disease. You had better dispose of them in the country [in Tenerife] at low rates and know your loss at first.

89e. I read your joint letter to Mr Chamlett about the freighting of his vessel [the *Peter and Anne*] for 14 months, who answered that you had some kind of discourse about it, but coming to acquaint his owners, they by no means will not [sic] let her per month if you would give £85 per month. So what you treated with the master is even come to nothing. Neither do I send any in his room, having no order from Mr Paynter. I have only charged you with 25 ts in this ship *Mary*, whereof William Chalk is master, which pray see complied withal in rare wines, else you had better let out the tonnage and load none. And although good, yet we must expect no high prices this year, per advice. Pray on your part give him a quick dispatch and load good cask, well rabbeted. Here are above 1,500 pipes of ordinary green Canaries this day unsold, which I am confident will never yield the money they cost at the Canaries besides leakage, freight, custom, petty charges and racking, which is above £10 in every pipe, an unsufferable loss. Such is the fruits of hedge wines.

I shall inform myself about the permission you writ about. I doubt it

112

will hardly be obtained except from Seville where have been several granted to bring linens for Cadiz or San Lucar. I have received 3 chests of sugar from Mr William Searchfield [at Terceira], in part your debt and Mr Paynter's; but does not so much as give me a reason why did not send the full. I shall not be wanting to write him per every via. I have paid Mr Chamlett per your order £30 and have accepted your bill [of exchange] of £100 payable to Mr John Webber or order, which shall be punctually paid when grows due. I am very sorry to hear how discourteously Mr Abraham Lee of San Lucar hath dealt with you. If he chances to come this way, I shall observe your commands, but I doubt will not travel this way because owes a great deal of money to several men here. According to your desire, I went and acquainted Mr Goldsmith, as soon as I received your letter, how if he had any goods to remit you, might freely send them aboard [the *Industry*], Capt. Sidrake Blake, which was a gallant ship where I have taken 130 ts. He gave me thanks but never made use of my proffer. I have received of Mr James Blake £25 for the dividend of your $\frac{1}{16}$ part of the *Constant John*, his Straits voyage, for which I have given your account credit. By a letter I understand you were pleased to favour me with a token of sweetmeats from Palma per the *Agreement*, as Mr Lang advises me, for which I render you many thanks. I have sent you a small token per Capt. Blake's ship, which pray accept thereof as a remembrance of my best respects to your good self. It is a keg of sturgeon and a box with a dozen of neats' tongues, both marked W[illiam] C[lerke], which you may demand of one John Heamens, quartermaster of ditto ship, unto whose custody I committed them with some other things for my father-in-law. I have ordered Mr Arundell likewise to put aboard this ship [the *Mary*], Mr Chalk, 2 dozen barrels of oysters for you, which pray demand of the master upon his arrival.

We are now in expectation of Capt. Pyle's arrival from Cadiz every day, who will bring near 350 ts of West India goods. Till know what sorts they are, can scarce give you ample advice as to the market prices of West India goods here. In the interim, if any good parcel offer, I would wish you to secure it, especially hides, which commodity I had rather have than wines at vintage. But you must not expect such a market as had for those in Mr Chamlett [the *Peter and Anne*], for right I know as long as ere I live.

Not a penny to be got of Alderman Berkeley's debt, neither have I any hopes for future.

89f. This very instant is come an extraordinary post from the King of France to his ambassador here, how his armies have routed the Spanish forces which lay at the siege of Arras. They have killed 5,000 Spaniards and taken 3,000 more prisoners, besides all their train of artillery, and dispersed their army. Such an overthrow the Spaniards have not had this 7 years. Upon this the French will go near to overrun most part of Flanders. I look upon the Spaniards as a lost nation in those northern parts. The Prince of Condé and his army was joined with the Spaniard in this battle.

Our fleet designed for the West Indies is now ready but is detained till the new Parliament sits, which will be 5 Sept. next. Here is daily expected an extraordinary ambassador from Madrid. I could wish he were here at present. If it should so fall out that he conclude a peace, without question we shall have very honourable articles on our [part as] ever nation had. Therefore, it would be necessary that you with some friends would draw up a particular of such laws or customs in that country as do prejudice you in your negotiation, whereby they may be rectified, as assizes upon all victuals, paying custom from island to island, and that all men's estates be liable to pay their debts without any pretence of dowry made over to their wives, which generally is used to cheat their creditors. Several of abuses there are which I know you have them fresher in memory than I can have.

Your account shall be sent per Mr Standish without further delays. ... [P.S.] Since the writing of abovesaid, Mr Richard Lant and Mr Chamlett [the *Peter and Anne*] are agreed upon the tonnage of the logwood, abating [Mr Lant] $1\frac{1}{3}$ t in the whole, at 20 kts per t.

90. to William Clerke   1 Sept. 1654

I have written you at large per the *Mary* frigate whereof William Chalk is master, to which crave reference. A copy thereof intended per Capt. [Sidrake] Blake but unfortunately came a little too late; my correspondent at Dover writes me will send it per first.

As yet I have not sold any of your grain, the salters being all combined together, but I hope in the end I shall come off with credit. To edge them on I have now sent 4 chests of the worst campechena for Rouen for your account, which will not produce so good a price there as I could wish, as per the enclosed coranto you may see, which I received this instant. You may rest assured there shall be no diligence wanting in me to advance your interest. Here enclosed I remit you a letter which came this day to my hands per which you may see the prices of linens there and pipestaves.

Per Mr Chamlett [the *Peter and Anne*] I shall enlarge, who most discourteously hath gone and let his ship unto Mr Robert Sweeting for Tenerife and Palma at £5 10s per t, denying that ever he made any agreement with you and Mr Paynter before Mr Standish, and avouches that he never asked you under £80 per month, under which rate he would not go, and to be paid his freight at every port of discharge. In fine he finds this freight of Mr Sweeting to turn him best to account, which he embraces. Such is the word of most seamen.

Indigo is much fallen here, worth but 4d per lb. ...
[P.S.] Here is hourly expected Capt. Pyle from Cadiz who brings 800 chests of Varinas tobacco which cost but *6Rs plata* per lb. I have some in him at ditto rate. I doubt it will fall much here.

91. to William Clerke   20 Sept. 1654

a. My last unto you was per Mr Chalke [the *Mary*] of 18 Aug. Its copy was intended to go per Mr Sidrake Blake [the *Industry*] but unfortunately left behind; he went through the Downs without anchoring. Since which I have 3 days past received yours of 22 July via Palma per the *Giant*, who is now at the Isle of Wight. In my former I gave you notice how had sold your hides in a nick of time, they being now fallen to 8d per lb. Capt. Pyle is now arrived from Cadiz very rich—brings as per advice £50,000 in silver; 1,200 chests of tobacco, cost 6 *Rs plata* per lb; 2,600 Caracas hides, cost 40 *Rs* aboard; 100 bags of cochineal, cost 80 *Rs* per *arroba*; 250 chests Honduras indigo, cost at 6 *Rs* per lb; 1,500 kts Campeachy wood, cost clear aboard 22 *Rs* per kt. I cannot understand of any quantity of campechena nor sylvester that he brings. Within a few days shall know the certainty. Here is more cochineal in town than will be spent this half 7 years. It's not worth above 20s per lb, which commodity being so low consequently pulls down the price of campechena and sylvester, for one lb of cochineal will strike a better colour and go further than 4 lbs of campechena. As yet I have not sold one chest; have sent 4 chests for your account via Dieppe to Mr Humphrey Wilkings of Rouen. When they arrive there, will fall the price above 15 per cent. Besides, you must take notice there's 13 per cent loss in weight, which is material. I shall use my best endeavour to dispose of your grain as speedily as I may, whereby to invest the proceeds in linens according to your desire as near I can.

I have now accepted your bill [of exchange] of £70 payable to Mr Throckmorton's order, which with the other bill payable to Mr [John] Webber and the money paid Mr Chamlett [the *Peter and Anne*], with the freight and custom of your goods in ditto comes to as much as the money of your hides, all which will lessen your cargazon. Your account shall be sent per ditto ship and its full balance, which is as much as you can desire, and of that you shall not fail of.

Now days past I received in company with Mr Body a letter from a merchant of Bilbao who writes a large narration about a permission [to import French linens, see **89e**] which you should desire him to procure, but before he does anything must remit him to the value of £300 to procure it, which I shall not do, for I know he is a very unfit man to act any such thing, and I wonder you make choice of him for such a business. I have written to Seville about it, but at last I believe a gift of 4,000 *Rs* [to an official] in the Islands will do better than all, being they ask 10 per cent in regard the quantity is small. Mr Body informs me hath not paid above 2 per cent. I have given order to give 8 per cent for 10,500 *Rs* permission. I cannot find by Mr Standish that he intends to put in any such sum as you wrote me, so your cargazon will not be so great as you expect.

91b. I perceive you have notice how Capt. Knowles and Mr Mourton [the *Agreement*] were taken and carried into Galicia. You desire to know where made insurance on your and Mr Paynter's ginger. To which I answer that I knew not of a *real*'s value that you had in the goods aboard [the *Agreement*] before Mr Sweeting and the master told me of it upon the Exchange. Besides, had I known it, without your precise order, should not have done a penny upon that commodity for the market here would not bear it. Had it come safe you had never seen 15s per cwt clear of freight, custom and petty charge and garbling with breakage. Not worth at present above 28s per cwt. Besides, had I done anything that way, you might have expected that I had given you advice thereof per Mr Chamlett, Hyatt or Cowse, as I did my father-in-law for what I insured for your accounts equally, which advice he can produce, if you desire, for your better satisfaction.

I perceive the West Indiaman from Cartagena is at last admitted and how you have thought to make an agreement with them [for West India goods] and to put off your 200 pipes wines [in exchange]. I wish you continue in that resolution, for if you send them to Barbados, Bristol or Ireland, remember these lines of mine: you shall never see half your principal. Mr Chamlett's son bought 2 chests of tobacco out of that West Indiaman and brought them home, which proved pretty good, and sold them for 6s per lb, far better than that which came from Spain. If you deal in that commodity, you must have a mighty care, for they come false packed of late, which causes great loss when they come home. There's no commodity so vendible and staple as hides. I believe between this and Christmas they will be a good commodity. I do expect to hear from you per the first vintage ships when I suppose you will alter your resolution as to buy any ship. You may see per my former part how West India goods are bought above 20 per cent cheaper at Cadiz and San Lucar than at your Islands. I have not else to enlarge at present. The fleet intended for the West Indies is now ready, only waits the new Parliament's resolutions, which is conceived will be suddenly. ...

92. to William Clerke   8 Nov. 1654

I have written you at large per our vintage ships. Since have not heard from you, makes me brief at present, and more especially in that I did not hear of this conveyance an hour since. I am now to give you notice how I have sold 12 chests of your campechena grain at 6s 10d per lb, to be paid at Christmas, which, if get it 2 months after, will be well. I have sent 4 chests for Rouen which as yet is not sold. I have likewise sent 6 skins of sylvester grain there which lies unsold. That market is far worse at present than this. I shall use my best endeavour to put off the rest of both sorts that lies unsold in my hands. When done, I shall immediately invest their proceeds according to your orders. In all things you may be confident I shall do my utmost endeavour.

Here enclosed I remit you a bill of rates which I received from Rouen last post. Hides do still bear a good price both there and here, 9d per lb; good Varinas tobacco, 5s 6d per lb; logwood, £20 per t; indigo, 5s per lb; campechena against the spring will be in request; cochineal, 24s per lb; sylvester, 3s 4d per lb. No commodity so vendible as hides at all times. If there come 10,000 the market will not be cloyed, which may serve per advice.

Here is news come this instant of 20 Malaga men arrived in one fleet in the Downs laden with fruit and wines. By the fruit there will be above 35 per cent loss. The wines prove very good; cost 1,700 *Rs* per butt *vellon*. If Canaries prove right, I hope we shall sell them at £28 per pipe, I mean rare parcels.

Excuse brevity. I shall speedily write you by another conveyance which I know of. ...

93. to William Clerke   14 Dec. 1654

a. I have yours, 1 and 22 Nov., which I find too large for me to answer in full at present in that I have been ill this 14 days, never out of my chamber. But, blessed be God, I am at present pretty well recovered and hope within 2 or 3 days to go abroad about my business whereby to comply with your commands as near as the times will give me leave.

Since my last unto you by Mr Bulkley's vessel, I have sold no more of your grain, nor do I hear of any sold at Rouen, so I hope there's no linens bought for your account, my order being as soon as he [Humphrey Wilkings at Rouen] sold to invest it in the sort of roans you writ for. I think you have saved £500 by giving over your first proposed design. I was almost confident that you would contradict it, which made me the slower in the prosecution thereof. I find now you desire to have a ship of 120 ts freighted per month, particularizing Mr Brampton [the *Matthew*] above all others, who is at Malaga and not expected home this month (I have 30 ts in him), so I doubt will come too late to serve your occasions. So I purpose, God willing, to look for another and, please God, to dispatch her hence by the fine of Jan. with the pipestaves and goods you writ for, whereby she may return home in due time to go for Newfoundland, which, if be performed by all June, will be barely enough. Therefore, pray make preparation for her sudden dispatch. Were she to go directly from the Canaries to Newfoundland, I would not send her out till 1 May, for there's never no price broken here for codfish till after Easter Day, so she cannot carry any orders for her lading if she go away so soon.

Mr Standish, I understand, is in the country at his brother's. Tomorrow I purpose, God willing, to send for your cousin [Charles] Goldsmith to speak with him about your business. I am informed he is bound for Smyrna, but I doubt not but shall use such means as may persuade him to comply with your desires in some measure, though I believe he may not be overlarge. You may rest assured I shall leave no stone unturned to promote your interest herein, for I perceive it highly concerns your affairs, being very sensible of the prejudice it hath done you in disappointing you thereof.

93b. I have this day bought you 20,000 pipestaves at £11 per m first penny. I think in all London there's not so many unsold, so that those which come after, I believe, will be disappointed. Wheat cannot be shipped off at your limited price by 3 *Rs* per *fanega*, so may expect none. I have paid all your bills [of exchange] and now accepted another payable to Mr Samuel Wilson for £150, though you writ me it's £200. To this day I have not received a farthing [from sales] of your grain neither do I expect it this 2 months at least. I would not [get] for £50 [per m] the pipestaves were now to buy again. If I go through for any ship while this ship is windbound in the Downs, you may expect to hear from me. Be assured I shall lose no time whereby to comply with your earnest desire, but I doubt shall have a hard task to get a complete ship and master, for most owners care not to let their ships upon monthly voyages, especially in regard mariners are at such exorbitant rates, 40s per month a common man.

Here at present 14 sail of Canarymen now in the river unloading all at once such miserable trash as never came the like from the Canaries, by what my cooper informs me. Capt. [Sidrake] Blake [the *Industry*] arrived in the river as soon as Chalk [the *Mary*], who are now both unloading. Orotava wines prove miserable, not one good [pipe] in 10. I doubt the vintners will this year crush us. Garachico wines pretty well, especially

117

Newman's lading. A short time will discover what our doom will be; I fear a fatal year. I hope I shall fare no worse than my neighbours. Excuse brevity. Per next shall be more larger.

Hides are worth 9½d per lb; logwood, £20 per t; indigo, 5s per lb; Varinas tobacco, 5s per lb, if right; cochineal, 23s per lb; campechena at spring I hope will yield 6s 10d per lb; sylvester, 3s 4d per lb; sugars very low.

Mr Lambell's Santa Cruz wines proved pretty wines, but I cannot give you any encouragement to send any; no hopes now selling [for] you any [of your *vidueño*] wines to be paid here [for export to Barbados, see **91b**], there being orders given to several for above 2,000 pipes, but I conceive few will take effect. ...

[P.S.] Your brother Mr George Clerke is newly married to a gentlewoman of good quality. I writ your cousin Goldsmith a note about your business, who sends me word will send your goods by the ship I send, without fail.

94. to William Clerke   25 Dec. 1654

a. I have written you at large per this conveyance already, to which refer you. Understanding this vessel is windbound in the Downs makes me adventure these few lines per post, hoping they may come in season.

Since my going abroad I have spoken with your cousin Goldsmith touching the business you recommended to my care. And, after a great deal of discourse, he promised me to send you the full of what hath in his hands of yours and to invest it in all such goods as you advise in your memory to him except ozenbrigs and Hampshire kersies, which indeed are not to be gotten for money at present. He says will make them all ready by 5 Jan. to be shipped, at farthest, which I hope he will comply withal. In the interim he shall not want all the solicitation that may be from me in your behalf. And for these goods you writ me for, shall have according to memory except the corn and Hampshire kersies.

I have been all the Thames over and for my life cannot get a vessel to my mind for you. Those ships which are new and pretty, commonly their owners give them employment. I have proffered £100 per month for Chalk [the *Mary*], but my partners will not let him as they say. If I find one of £100, it's too little and then perhaps hath 4 or 6 guns and one drake; and if chance to meet with one of 12 or 14 guns, then she is too big, perhaps 160 or 180 ts. So I know not what to do. I have freighted many ships since I came home but was never put to such a nonplus as at present, for I find it very difficult in that owners are loath to let ships per month, men's wages being so unreasonable. But one or other, I purpose, God willing, to go through with all the next week at farthest.

94b. I am now to give you notice how on 12 instant, Gen. Penn's rear-admiral [George Dakins] with a squadron of 12 frigates went out of Portsmouth to touch at Barbados, there to get in readiness 4,000 planters against Gen. Penn's arrival there with his whole fleet, which consists of 40 sail and carries 6,000 soldiers from hence. And this day it's written from Portsmouth how Gen. Penn is gone with the rest of his fleet, so that now we know for certain they are bound for the West Indies against the

Spaniards and carry such provisions of war as never did any fleet out of England before. Gen. Blake with his fleet lies at Gibraltar, supposing to wait till the galleons come home, as it's said.

I am sorry these, my lines, should be the messenger of such unhappy tidings unto you, but in such cases it's good to be free with one's friend. I would wish you on sight hereof to prepare yourself for a storm, for surely it's near at hand. Some of our great ones give out that this fleet had gone out in June last but was delayed merely that the merchants might get home their vintage ships and estates, which indeed I am of opinion it's really so. Gen. Penn carrieth most of the ablest commanders for the West Indies coast that could get in England. Of all the merchants that reside in the King of Spain's dominions, I pity you at the Canaries, as knowing you are in that saddest condition of all men when an embargo comes, for $\frac{3}{4}$ part of your estates there is in debts and drugs, which are visible things to be all lost. Now whether the King of Spain may suspend seizing of Englishmen's estates until hears of an absolute break on our side, it's not known; but his ambassador from hence cannot but give him notice of all passages, and I am of opinion he will lose no opportunity as to a sudden embargo. Such is the sad condition of poor merchants. The Lord endow us with patience to endure such afflictions in these times of trial. I shall desire you will be private as to this particular, supposing it concerns you to be so. Were it not your positive order, I should not send you a pack of goods, but I shall no ways presume to contradict it. When it arrives there, if you have no need of it, you may keep it aboard and return it (it's but insuring it back, which may be done for a small matter) or send part for Madeira.

I have not further to trouble you at present. I should be glad you had gone through for the West India goods whereby you may dispatch home the ship I send you that so you may get some things off before this news be too public abroad. For wines, I know you can have none good, and for bad, here are too many already, to all our grief. ...

95. to William Clerke   3 Feb. 1655

... I gave you notice had freighted Mr Chalk [the *Mary*] for you, who was to be ready the first of this month. But one of our wrangling owners made some unjust exceptions to our agreement which caused a demur upon our proceedings as to the making ready of our ship. But considering the present times, I thought it rather prudence to condescend to that which was none of our bargain than to contend and spend time. So have now once more agreed for her and hope she may be ready within 10 days, where you may expect Mr Goldsmith's goods for what he owes you and likewise all according to the memory sent me, except Hampshire kersies and corn which cannot be bought at your limited price. So that you may do well to make provision against the ship's arrival. You writ me to insure £500 upon her out and home, which I shall see performed for your account. But by all your letters I cannot find you have gone through for the parcel of West India goods in Santa Cruz, which, if omitted, have done ill as times now govern in that I doubt others will carry it from you. Mr Chalk will not carry the orders for the Newfoundland fish in that no man will sell till past Our Lady Day, 25 March, next.

Now in regard we are like to quarrel with the Spaniards speedily, I suppose your design will be over. So that by the very first conveyance I desire to know what you will have done as to the fish business and how you will dispose of Mr Chalk's ship, that I may order your business in the best manner I can in these uncertain times. If you can get up 50 pipes of the best sort of Santa Cruz *malvasías*, it will be better to send them than leave your estate there to be seized, as I am confident it will come to that very suddenly, here being no longer than yesterday letters of marque granted against the Spaniard for £20,000 and, besides that, an absolute peace concluded between our Lord Protector and the French ambassador here. And the Genoese ambassador which is here desires our protection against the Spaniard. Here are now 10 merchantmen laden with provisions and 5 men-of-war which go as convoys. They are to follow Gen. Penn for the West Indies, so that as you are my very good friend and I a well-wisher to your affairs, on sight hereof secure what you can. Per Mr Chalk shall be more larger. The owners have bound me the ship shall not go for Guinea, Barbados or the West Indies. ...

96. to William Clerke   8 March 1655

a. I have now received yours of 11 and 14 Feb. per Mr Cowse, unto which shall give full answer. Only in the first place, I shall give you an account how about 1 Feb., according to your earnest desire, I freighted a ship for your account to be ready to depart from Gravesend 15 ditto, which was Mr Chalk [the *Mary*]. But after a week's time, when I thought the ship was near ready, depending upon her and no other, there wanted not an unjust partner that objected against the agreement who drew one another or 2 to side with him and declared positively the ship should not go to sea. Which unhappy business hath caused such a demur to the design as it hath lost above a month's time. The chief thing objected against was that whereas I had freighted the ship for 10 months certain and at the determination of said time I was to pay 8 months' freight, and if in case the ship should miscarry within aforesaid time, no freight to be due. Now I took the advice of a civilian in the Admiralty Court who told me my agreement was firm, but then it would be 3 months ere I could bring it to a trial. So considering the remedy to be worse than the disease, I thought fit rather to condescend to that which was none of our agreement than to spend time and hinder your intended design. So now I am bound to pay 4 months' freight after 6 months' service, and so accordingly for a longer time, as by the charter-party will appear, to which refer you, desiring you to see all things therein complied withal on your part. I have had a great deal of trouble about her with the owners. With some I shall scarce have any dealings as long as I live again. And had I not secured this ship, I know not in all the Thames where to have furnished myself with one so fit for your turn.

Mr Brampton [the *Matthew*] is now newly arrived from Malaga, being 3 months from thence sprung a leak at sea and was forced to bear up for Lisbon. That vessel hath seen the best of her days, being now ancient. Mr Brampton hath sold her and is now resolved to build a new frigate of 200 ts.

96b. I have written you a few hasty lines of 6 current, chiefly imports the covert of the charter-party, which you may demand of the master. I have laden aboard this ship, the *Mary* frigate, William Chalk master, a parcel of goods for your account, according to the memory you sent me, importing £529 1s 1d, which I hope upon their receipt will be to your liking. As for wheat, I send none in that cannot procure any on your limited price. Hampshire kersies, there's none made of late. My father-in-law wrote me 4 months since for 50 pieces, but I cannot get them, only half a score I have had by me ever since Nov. last. And as for your wrought paragons you writ for, no Norwich man knows any such stuff, neither could Mr Standish tell what you meant thereby.[1] There's 5 pieces of Welsh plains more than you writ for and a small parcel of statute-lace which was merely to fill up the trunk of stockings, no. 6, the key of which I delivered Mr Chalk, which you may please to demand of him. I here remit you an invoice of said goods and a bill of lading, as also a certificate for all your goods aboard, as well mine as your cousin Charles Goldsmith's, who would fain have had the £100 you ordered him from me, which I proffered him several times provided he did but show me you were so much indebted unto him, which was but reason. But he refused it several times, and at last upon better consideration he accepted of my reasonable proposition; and upon view of the account I found but £88 9s 6d due unto him, which I immediately paid him, for which sum have made your account debit. I understand he is bound away suddenly for the East Indies. I am glad you have a full return, though long first, he was troubled that I should be made acquainted with his non-compliance, and for doing you a friendly office I have gone near to insure his ill-will. I have according to your order paid Mr Ralph Standish £50 for your account, for which have made you debit.

1. In the 1640s John Turner at Tenerife had imported red Turkey paragons which he described as a 'new stuff' much used in Tenerife to make riding jackets (C. 110/151, J. Turner to R. Wilson, Sr and M. Bradgate, 25 Feb. 1646).

96c. I have in my former letters per my cousin [Richard] Chappell, Mr Mourton and others given you ample advice of the affairs between us and Spain, to which crave reference. Only I must needs acquaint you how daily affairs do represent themselves in a far worse manner than formerly, and undoubtedly there will not pass many months ere there be a general embargo in all the King of Spain's dominions upon poor English merchants' estates. To tell you my author, it's not proper, but I write it with the more confidence in that I have it from the second or third man now in England, I mean for government, which I thought fit to hint to you. Moreover you may take notice here are now 6 ships freighted to carry soldiers, ammunition and provisions to Gen. Penn's fleet, to touch at Barbados and from thence for the Bay of Mexico. The news you had from Cadiz how Gen. Blake had destroyed the French fleet is mere flames. We have notice he is now coming for Cadiz, it's thought to intercept the *galeones* that are expected and likewise those bound out. They write from Seville, Cadiz, Madrid and Bilbao that since the Spaniards have heard of Penn's departure for the Indies they will not pay any of their debts, saying there will come a time speedily to balance them. I wish you may find the Islanders to be of another mind.

I have endeavoured all what possible I can to dispose of some *vidueño* wines here for your account but cannot effect it by no means. Your orders came too late by above 3 months, and every man hath the same from their friends. Some have proffered to load off wines at £33 per pipe since Mr Cowse's arrival, who brings advice that *vidueños* are to be had for a song.

Mr Humphrey Wilkings of Rouen gives me advice this post how hath sold your sylvester grain at 52 *livres* per lb. Only one seron, no. 8, proves to be very much damnified, for which is fain to abate 20 *livres* per lb upon that seron. It's a very mean price. The campechena is not sold. I think to return it hither again. I have now sold 2 chests at 7s 6d, so there remain 2 chests in cellar, one of which is very much damnified. Mr Standish told me it was let fall in the sea embarking at Santa Cruz [de Tenerife]. Mr Standish sold his 2 chests of campechena at 6s and 6s 8d per lb.

96d. Now whereas you desire me to send per this ship [the *Mary*] a credit for 2,000 kts of Newfoundland fish, you may take notice the price of ditto commodity is never broken till Easter Monday, so that I cannot buy any till that time. And to send you a credit, it's uncertain, for in case fish should be scarce, then every ship will first deliver what they catch to their sacks, and so your ship may return empty. Now I hope you may so order your business as that this ship may return home in time enough to proceed for Newfoundland from hence. In such case, for brevity of dispatch, you may order her to unload at Dover so as she be there by the fine of June. It's time enough, for no man will oblige himself by covenant to deliver a kt of fish in the land before 25 Aug. at soonest, so that I shall not adventure positively to buy any fish till the ship return or at leastwise I hear from you. But this I will do: get a credit from my cousin John Paige of Plymouth under hand and seal, or 2, and send them for Newfoundland, there to meet the ship, in case I hear not from you in the interim, which I hope I shall. Besides, I fear when you receive my letters by Richard Chappell you will alter your fish design for Bilbao, for as things now govern, no man will engage upon any such design. I know not how you will approve of my acting herein. Let the success be what it will, I am sure my intentions are very cordial as to your interests. But these uncertain times put all men at a distraction in their affairs.

I shall, according to your order, insure £500 out and home upon this ship for your account in hopes she will come home. If do, I pray spare my father-in-law a little tonnage if he need it. And whereas you were pleased to give me order to permit my father-in-law to have 10,000 pipestaves in your ship, I find they take up much bulk, insomuch cannot carry but 15,000 of your own. Instead of that favour, I have put aboard this ship 30 odd small packs, I may say half-bales, for him, which is goods I bought ever since Nov. last and lying upon my hand here and proper for no other place but the Canaries. I have adventured to send it per this ship in hopes to sell it for ready money and so to have the proceeds in ditto ship returned, when not, to send the goods home again. For it's a madness to land any except you are certain of a speedy disposal. Don Cristóbal de Alvarado [Bracamonte] hath 5 small bales, for which you are to receive 80 *Rs plata*.

96e. I take notice of the parcel of sugar you bought. It's none of the best commodities here. I am sorry the Caracas vessel was not permitted. Tobacco, if good and new, is worth at present 7s per lb; hides, 10d per lb; Campeachy wood, £25 per t; campechena, 7s; sylvester, 3s 4d; cochineal, 28s; indigo, 5s. Wines a very drug here. Here I send you a coranto from Rouen, to which refer you.

Not else at present. Being doubtful the wind will come fair and Mr Standish left behind, makes me abbreviate, referring you in many things to his relating, who is able to give you an account thereof. ...

[P.S.] I have not time to write my father-in-law at present. In case the ship should depart without his letters, pray impart unto him your advice, wherein I shall be much obliged.

97. to William Clerke   20 March 1655

... [Y]esterday here came letters from Bilbao of 10 current where the factors in general write their correspondents here to forbear sending any more goods in that the natives begin to deny payment of their debts and threaten them besides, upon which the merchants now trading there have sent an express to the Isle of Wight to stop a ship which they have bound there laden with above 500 bales of goods.

I fear a short time now will produce a sad alteration in that yesterday here came letters from Barbados of Gen. Penn's arrival there with his whole fleet, who was to carry from the Caribbee Islands 12,000 men, besides 7,000 soldiers he carried from hence.[1] It's conceived is bound for Veracruz or Portobello. Therefore look about yourself and prevent what in you lieth.

I would wish you to send home Mr Chalk [the *Mary*] though let out part of him. However, in prosecution of your former order, I shall not fail to send credits to Newfoundland to meet the ship there, though I think you would scarce proceed upon that design, especially for Bilbao, except you have a mind to lose all. Now in case Chalk come home [from Tenerife] and that you have no further employment for him, then in such case you may give me order to dispose of him here, which I make no question but shall do without a farthing loss to you. All which I thought fit to signify unto you that so accordingly you may proceed upon your business as reason shall best guide you. I have insured upon the *Mary* frigate from hence to the Canaries £500 for your account at 3 per cent. I shall hereafter do the like sum homeward upon her for your account as you order me. ...

1. Penn had about 7,000 regulars, but raised only about 1,200 additional troops in the Lesser Antilles (*The Narrative of General Venables*, ed. C. H. Firth (Camden Society, new series, 60, 1900), xxviii, 122).

98. to William Clerke   4 April 1655

Per this ship I shall send you a credit for 2,000 kts of Newfoundland fish, under the hand and seal of my cousin Mr John Paige of Plymouth, which I hope will come in due time to go by Mr Chalk [the *Mary*]. When not, you may take notice I shall send another directly from hence to be left in Newfoundland against his arrival, of the same tenor, which will be sufficient were it for 10,000 kts. But if Mr Chalk proceed that voyage, you must order him some other where, for at Bilbao I fear all will be naught ere that time.

Here enclosed goes a letter for your cook from his wife, unto whom I have paid £5 for last quarter by the direction of Mr Charles Goldsmith, so I shall desire your approbation thereunto else I shall pay no more. The other pray deliver Mr John Campion in his own hand, it being from a good friend of mine. ...

99. to William Clerke   14 April 1655
a. My last to you was of 20 March per Mr Phillip Hyatt, since which have not heard from you, which makes me the briefer at present. I have advice Mr Chalk [the *Mary*] went out of Falmouth in good company 28 past, so I hope may be safe arrived with you ere this. Upon which ship I loaded you a small parcel of goods according to memory sent me except the corn and Hampshire kersies, as also there went the goods you expected from your cousin Goldsmith who is now gone for Surat in East India under one Mr King who hath formerly lived in those parts.

I do very much long to hear where you are resolved to send Mr Chalk for Newfoundland. If he goes directly from the Islands, will arrive there as soon as the ships which went to catch the fish, for the Newfoundland men went away with the same wind that carried Mr Chalk out of the Channel. As yet I cannot hear of any fish bought, but it's like to be very low in that few or no buyers appear as in other years. Men being afraid of wars with Spain will not adventure upon such a perishing commodity in such uncertain times. I believe it will be sold for 20 *Rs* per kt, which is very cheap. Now to prevent the worst, I have procured 3 credits of one tenor from my cousin John Paige of Plymouth to furnish Mr Chalk with 2,000 kts of fish, which is sufficient were it for 10,000 kts. One of which I here send you. The other 2 I shall send per the first ships that are bound for Newfoundland. Now if I receive any answers of my letters written you by my cousin Richard Chappell how you are fully resolved to send Mr Chalk for Newfoundland, notwithstanding the danger with Spain, then, and in such case, I'll immediately buy the fish here, provided I hear from you between this and 20 June next, which I hope shall. When not, I shall conclude Mr Chalk comes not home. Nevertheless I shall insure according to your order £500 homeward, not knowing what interest you may have in her. I have insured £500 in ditto ship upon your goods from hence to the Canaries at 3 per cent, which may serve per advice.
99b. As to the affairs between us and Spain, I cannot write you more than have formerly done, only every day produces things plainer as to a breach. Here are several merchantmen freighted to carry provisions and ammunition to Gen. Penn, whose charter-parties I have seen contracted by the States, to say for Barbados at 50s per t, if for Santo Domingo, £4 per t, and if for the Bay of Mexico at £6 per t. In all probability in the month of June we may hear what place they assaulted, upon which undoubtedly you may expect an embargo.

The frigate which touched at Gran Canaria and could not be admitted by that villainous Judge [of the Indies] is now arrived at Cadiz. She brings 1,800 chests of true Varinas tobacco. Here are 13 chests come home in a small Orange vessel which I saw and tasted. It proves excellent. They are sold at 7s per lb; hides, 10d per lb; logwood, £25 per t; cochineal, 25s per lb; campechena, 7s [per lb]; sylvester, 3s 4d per lb; indigo, if good, 4s 6d per lb; ginger, 26s per cwt; Havana sugars, £4 per cwt at most.

I do very much desire to hear from you how you intend to order your business. Though a plentiful vintage may much tempt you, yet I would not have you to soothe yourself with vain hopes as to think you will see another vintage go over your heads with peace. Days past there was an embargo in most parts of France upon all English goods and ships, but now all is over. Though it was in Rouen, yet my correspondent's [Humphrey Wilkings'] care was such as neither your sylvester nor campechena was meddled withal. However, I have given him order to dispose of your campechena grain, which I doubt will not yield £5, far less than it's worth here.

Undoubtedly if you land your goods out of Chalk [the *Mary*] and do not speedily convert them into ready money, you will lose them all. I cannot sell a pipe of wine for your account, there being so many [wines] bound for Barbados and the fleet and New England that I doubt they will never see half their principal at the end of 2 or 3 years' time. Rather than I would go upon such indirect designs, I should even run the hazard to have them embargoed by the Spaniards. ...

100. to William Clerke   10 May 1655
a. ... The pipestaves which I bought for you and my father-in-law, being 25,000, whereof you have 15,000 of them in Chalk [the *Mary*], when I came to adjust the account with the yard-keeper of whom I bought them, by his master's order, whereas I absolutely made a plain bargain between him and me as I then advised you at £11 per m, the villain now affirms, and offers to swear it, that he sold them me at £11 10s per m, whose oath will condemn me, as being a person of no interest in them, though it be as false as God is true, which does not a little trouble me that we should be so cheated and know not how or which way to remedy ourselves by our laws here.

Mr Abraham Lee of San Lucar is now come home, who, as they write me, had not parted from those parts but that necessity drove him away from thence. And truly it appears to be so here, in that I think hath scarce money to put himself into English clothes. Yesterday I took an occasion to signify unto him what I thought needful as to the injuries done you about the protesting your bills, who acknowledged he had done you more wrong than it was possible ever to make you restitution. To be brief, I demanded satisfaction, or at leastwise good security; when not, in plain English, I must enter an action against him as being your order. To which he answered with many protestations and vows that no man should have satisfaction before you, pretending a great sum due to him at Barbados, which I scarce believe as liable, for there's little credit to be given to persons that have once lost their credit and reputation. Now if I should put him in prison, I have no articulation against him nor papers, as the bills protested, nor any of his letters. So that undoubtedly he will nonsuit me if I put not in a declaration against him the first term. Besides, if I could do all what might be desired as to the proof, really I see little probability of recovery, so that I shall expect your further order until I meddle with him, except I can discover that he hath anything or that he be refractory in denying you a bond or the like. Of this, more in my next. In the interim, I desire your advice and papers as to this business.

100b. I intend now to send away a second credit for Newfoundland for the buying of Mr Chalk's [the *Mary*'s] fish where I believe you will have it very cheap, under 20 *Rs* per kt. However, if I hear not from you by the fine of this month, I shall insure £500 on him from Tenerife to London according to your former order, which as yet you never contradicted it.

Here's now come the Marqués de Lede, Governor of Dunkirk, at Dover as extraordinary ambassador from the King of Spain unto our Lord Protector, they say merely to give him the compliments of his government. If for peace, I doubt comes too late. Gen. Penn was setting sail with 35 sail of ships from Barbados 28 March, it's said bound for Havana first. He carries from the Caribbee Islands 8,000 planters besides 6,000 soldiers from hence [See **97**]. And now here are 8 gallant men-of-war going to him with some soldiers for a second supply, so that you may see our Protector is resolved to carry on his design vigorously, as indeed he does most what he takes in hand. Here is letters from Madrid where they write the dispatch ship is arrived at Cadiz 17 April and left the *galeones* and *flota* within 80 leagues of aforesaid port, which is good news. I could wish you at Tenerife had 2 or 3 of their ships there whereby you might be able to make home something in these dangerous times. Indigo not worth 3s 10d per lb; cochineal, 22s per lb; hides, 9½d per lb; Campeachy wood, £22 per t.

I am now about your account, only want one from Mr [Robert] Turner [Paige's former landlord and bookkeeper], whom by fair means cannot get any from him. It hath so troubled me that I have not answered your expectations in that particular, or that you should write so often for it, that of late I have even pined away with mere vexation. Now that you may not fail of it speedily and that I may not omit to make you good everything sent and remitted me, I desire you to send me a charge of all which you needed not to have done had Mr Turner perfected with me. ...

101. to William Clerke   25 May 1655

Since the writing of my [last] letter, here is come a contradiction of the *galeones'* coming this season, as I question not but you have heard of the same per Mr Hussy who, as I understand, is bound from Cadiz to the Islands. All sorts of West India goods do rise very much at present upon the said news: hides, 10d per lb; Campeachy wood, £26 per t; cochineal, 30s per lb; campechena, 7s; sylvester, 3s 6d; indigo low, being great quantities come from East India, 4s per lb; Varinas tobacco, if new, 6s per lb; ginger and sugar very low.

I have sent per Giles Paynter another credit for 2,000 kts codfish to deliver unto Mr Chalk [the *Mary*] at Newfoundland, as being a trusty friend. You need not fear it will be far more to your advantage than if I had bought the fish here. ...

102. to Gowen Paynter and William Clerke   31 May 1655

These are chiefly to give you notice how yesterday Mr Chalk [the *Mary*] is safely arrived at Dover and how I intend, according to Mr. Clerke's order, to dispatch him away for Newfoundland within this 8 days, to load fish and so for Bilbao. I have likewise news of Mr Mourton's [the *Agreement*'s] arrival at Dublin where there's no market for his wines, so I have ordered him to come for London. I have not time at present to write you particularly, but if this ship be windbound in the Downs any longer, I shall next post. ...

103. to William Clerke   1 June 1655

I have yours per Mr Mourton [the *Agreement*] and Mr William Chalk in the *Mary* frigate who, thanks be to God, is safe arrived in Dover 3 days since, where I have given my correspondent, Mr Michael de Haze, order to unload all such goods as you have aboard, which I hope will be speedily done. Only for want of invoice I know not how to give direction for an entry of your sugars, you not mentioning the quality of them, how many whites and muscovados, which will put us to some trouble. According to your order I have given Mr Chalk direction to make ready his ship whereby to be ready 10 current to proceed for Newfoundland. I am at present upon buying his fish and hope to get it at 20 *Rs* per kt, which is 15 per cent cheaper than other years. In all things I shall promote your interest as if it were really mine own, of which rest confident. Your sugars come to a low market, and I am informed by a man of judgement that your sarsaparilla is of a wild sort. If so, it will yield little. Three days hence I purpose to make a journey for Dover when I shall carry with me his [Chalk's] dispatches for Newfoundland. As yet no sacks are gone out of England, so I hope Mr Chalk will be gone one of the first. Mr Chalk sent me your order to have it priced, out of which I observe some necessary things for my better government. As to your affairs, your not sending me a particular memory of what goods and money are aboard does put me to a nonplus. As yet the master hath sent me none. I have given Mr Chalk order to deliver no money chest, trunk, nor box until I come down, for I doubt there's more money than you writ of and it's no reason the ship should be other men's carrier for nothing.

I hear the Governor [and Capt. General of the Canaries, Don Alonso Dávila y Guzmán] hath sent for you prisoner. I doubt it will be a troublesome business to you. Though you are no ways faulty, yet it must needs cost you money. I am vexed that Mr Chalk should so carry himself like a fool, being an ancient commander and knowing the dangers of such things.[1] Your bill of £120 I have accepted to Mr John Thomas, which shall be duly paid at the time.

Our fleet went from Barbados 30 March consisting in all 70 sail. We expect to hear of their success about the middle of next month, at which time I doubt you will see sad alterations.

Mr Chalk did arrive here before I expected him. The same day I heard of his arrival I caused a policy to be made upon him for you. But by good chance there was nothing underwritten, so you have so much money saved. Yet I must confess I do not deserve thanks for it, but rather to be chided in not doing it sooner. ...

1. Clerke had been imprisoned at Tenerife apparently because Spanish officials had discovered that Capt. Chalk was loading silver for London. Cf. **118**.

104. to William Clerke   Dover, 8 June 1655

I have written you already per this conveyance, to which crave reference. I formerly gave order to my correspondent here, Mr Michael de Haze to unload your goods out of Mr Chalk [the *Mary*] and send them me for London, which is this day completed. I came yesterday to this post merely to give Mr Chalk his dispatches for the Newfoundland, which I have now done with an additional order to yours in that the other I find not to be so full as the present occasion requires, times being dangerous. I have bought [of George Kennicot and company] for your account 1,500 kts of fish to be delivered at Newfoundland 10 Aug. 1655 at 19 *Rs* per kt. The rest I have given Mr Chalk credit to buy at price current of the country, which I verily believe will be very reasonable in regard of the probability of a war with Spain. All men are fearful to deal in the commodity, which makes it low at present, as you may well perceive at the price I have bought at, which is above 15 per cent cheaper than any year since I came to England.

I have ordered Mr Chalk to go for Santoña first and there to give notice of his arrival, and to know how squares [i.e. the game] go from some of our nation before undertaking to go over the bar of Bilbao. For though you are assured your fish may be free though a war, yet I must tell you as an owner that we know in such case our ship will be lost, so in prudence we hold it fit to prevent the worst.

I have perused your order to Mr Chalk, which utterly denies that he did anything without your order and admires you would offer to put pen to paper to write any such thing when as you sent part of Mr Rawdon's things aboard in your bark, which is his answer. [Cf. **103**, **118**.] ...

[P.S.] If you will have anything insured on Chalk from Newfoundland to Bilbao, advise me. And likewise it would be necessary you writ me 2 lines which way Mr Chalk shall go in case of war, as I doubt it will be. Your wines aboard Chalk prove miserable trash, and your sarsaparilla is of a wild sort so will yield little, which may serve per advice.

105. to William Clerke   14 June 1655

... I have bought [of George Kennicot and company] 1,500 kts of Newfoundland fish for your account at 19 *Rs* per kt to be delivered Mr Chalk [the *Mary*] 10 Aug., which is the soonest of most men's. What he shall want more to fill up his ship I have given him a credit of my cousin John Paige of Plymouth for 2,000 kts in case the ship which I have bought abovesaid fish of should miscarry. According to your desire I rid post down to Dover last week to give Mr Chalk his dispatches for Newfoundland, with an additional order to yours, which I did accomplish and left him ready to depart with the first opportunity of wind and weather that should present. But being contrary, is now gone into the Downs where will have good company out Channel. He will be one of the first sacks out of England if please God send a speedy fair wind.

Your sugars, wine and sarsaparilla are now come into the river in 2 small barks which brought it up from Dover. All which comes to a very bad market. The sugars are generally coarse and moist, and the wines miserable trash, and your sarsaparilla of a wild sort, as I am informed. So that I fear all will lie upon my hands unsold this long time. And from Newfoundland I must expect £1,000 in bills of exchange upon me for the fish and £400 for freight of 6 months. And your campechena in Rouen unsold, so that I shall find myself short in cash. Nevertheless, God sending me health, all things shall be complied withal. Only I would desire you to draw no more money upon me for the reasons abovesaid.

It would be necessary you write Lazaro de Ormacho [at Bilbao] and me 2 lines which way Mr Chalk shall proceed with his fish in case we should have a war before he arrives at Santoña, which in all probability we shall. In such case you know the ship cannot go in over the bar of Bilbao with safety. Therefore it concerns you to give timely notice about it. I writ you a few hasty lines from Dover of 8 current per Mr Crispe to this purpose, unto which crave reference.

Our new Spanish ambassador extraordinary, the Marqués de Lede, is to go home for Flanders next week without doing anything with our Lord Protector, all which tells us that we shall have a sudden change. I can now speak it of a certain how our fleet are gone first for Santo Domingo and from thence proceed for some part of the Main. I believe both the King of Spain and we here shall have notice of their success ere next month pass over our heads.

Methinks you at the Canaries are very confident of getting off next vintage fruits, else you would not act as you do, which I fear you will be much frustrated of your expectations. Advise me where you will have anything insured upon Chalk's cargo of fish. If it should so fall out that you abide there in peace till vintage, seeing you are resolved to load home Chalk with wines, let them be very excellent else you had better knock out their heads, for I think here are bad wines enough for this 3 years already. Never stand for 2 or 3 ducats in a pipe nor a little extraordinary order of payment. The market here will pay for all if prove good, which may serve per advice.

All sorts of West India goods are dear at present: hides, 10d per lb; logwood, £30 per t; cochineal, 30s [per lb]; campechena, 7s [per lb]; sylvester, 3s [per lb]; indigo, 4s 6d [per lb]; Varinas tobacco, if new and right, 5s 6d per lb; ginger, 3s per lb. ...

106. to William Clerke   7 Aug. 1655
a. My last unto you was per Mr William Cowse who went from Falmouth about 5 weeks since, in whose company Mr Chalk [the *Mary*] went out the Channel, with whom was above a month windbound in the Downs, yet he [Chalk] went away with the fleet of sacks bound for Newfoundland, and I hope he will get there in a very seasonable time to take in his fish. They are bound to deliver it 10 instant, and undoubtedly he is there ere this time, so that his coming home will not any way hinder your fish design.

I have now made sale of your white sugars which find to be 60 chests, I say 62 chests, at £4 8s per cwt, I paying the excise which is 5 per cent, to be paid for them at 3 months' time, which I look upon as no bad sale considering the quality of them. They were very damp, miserable ware. I believe you will say the same. For want of an invoice I was very much pushed for their tares, so we are agreed to allow the same as Mr Nicholas Warren did give upon Mr John Webber's parcel, which I conceive were of the same sugars. Now there remained 52 chests of your parcel which prove to be muscovados, which are no vendible commodity here, Barbados sugars worth but 37s per cwt. Upon which I resolved to send them for Amsterdam where, I thank God, they are safe arrived, as per advice from thence this very post. I have ordered my correspondent, Mr John Schanternell, to make sale of them if can make out but 56s per cwt sterling money, considering the exchange. For here is now arrived above 1,000 ts of sugars from Barbados, and many whites, and here is daily more expected. It's a thing scarce to be credited that little island loaded off above 10,000 ts per annum which cloys most parts of Europe. As for your sarsaparilla, it's of a wild sort. I believe I shall never make so much off it as to pay freight, custom and charges.

I have now paid your bill of exchange for £120. Pray draw no more at present for I shall have bills on me for your account for Chalk's cargo of fish and freight to the value of £1,500 or thereabouts, which I must get money in a readiness to pay in Oct. next. As yet not any of campechena at Rouen sold, neither does it advance in price 5 *livres* per lb. I have received an account of the sylvester [sold at Rouen] which does by no means please me. The custom and charges are extravagant. No more there if I may have my way. I shall now give him [Humphrey Wilkings at Rouen] order to sell the campechena grain whereby I may have monies in a readiness against the Newfoundland bills come. In all things I shall promote your interest as if it were really my own.

106b. I wish when Mr Chalk comes to Bilbao he find no embargo there. But I ordered him to stay at Santoña before he venture off the bar. I have perused your orders to the master but do not find any proviso in case troubles at Bilbao that cannot have pratique, or embargoes, to what other place he shall proceed unto, which had been a very necessary clause. Gen. Blake lies now off Cape Santa Maria with his fleet, supposed waiting for the *galeones*, which, do molest them, undoubtedly an embargo will suddenly follow. The fear of which hath caused no less than 30 factors to come away from Cadiz, San Lucar and Seville, who are now arrived here and at Plymouth, with whom I have had some discourse, demanding the reasons of their coming away, who give for answer that if Gen. Blake meet the *galeones* and take but one of them, common people's rage are such as that their lives will run a great hazard. If they come this year, either they are safe in Spain or taken by our fleet ere this time, so a short time will discover what passeth as to that grand danger.

Our fleet under the command of Gen. Penn landed their forces near Santo Domingo 13 May, who unexpectedly were shamefully repulsed by an inconsiderable number of the Spaniards, so were forced to retreat aboard ship. And from thence they went to a little island 80 leagues to leeward called Jamaica which they have taken and are there. So I fear our hopeful design will not be crowned with that victory as most men expected.

Here are freighted many ships for the vintage, so you may do well to provide your parcel in time, for I can tell you peradventure more than you know there. Assuredly you will have a great crowd when the vintage ships arrive there. I wish Mr Chalk's design may prove successful to you. But in my weak judgement, to deal in a perishing commodity in an uncertain time as this is, there cannot be much ground for it. Besides, though you have never so quick dispatch at Bilbao, yet you cannot have her [the *Mary*] there to load home the first wines. And at the best of markets, though you sell for 50 *Rs vellon* per kt, yet you shall scarce see your money, considering the freight of the ship, as you have her per month.

Here are letters via Dunkirk of 4 July where several men write of Mr Campion's death and likewise how wickedly poor Mr [John] Chickley and Robert Smith were butchered by those villains. God grant you and the rest get safe away from them. It hath not been my happiness to receive a line from you nor my father-in-law per ditto via, at which I admire at. Capt. Russell is come from the East Indies [on the *Katherine*]. Hath made us a good voyage. I have [heard] we shall clear £100 per each $\frac{1}{16}$. I have freighted him for the vintage. I hope if Chalk come there in time, you and my father-in-law will come home in the *Katherine* frigate. This vessel [the *Agreement*, Capt. Mourton] I send my father-in-law, being our own, with a few pilchards which cost near 11s per m—a shame to write of such a thing. ...

[P.S.] If you will have anything insured on the *Mary* frigate from the Canaries to London, advise me.

107. to William Clerke   13 Sept. 1655

I have written you at large per Mr Mourton [the *Agreement*] and Capt. Garvis Russell [the *Katherine*], to which crave reference. In my last gave you notice how with much difficulty and entreaty, as Mr Humphrey Isham can inform you, I had the promise of 25 ts in this ship *Prosperous* whereof Christopher [*recte* Matthew] Smith is master; but when came to seal charter-party, I could obtain but 20 ts, which they are obliged to take in. Which tonnage I charge upon you for your own proper account, and accordingly I desire you to see it complied withal. There wants 30 ts to make up the 50 which you advised for, which I make no question but you will have enough there were it for a greater quantity and upon reasonabler terms than I am to give for this, which is £4 15s per t.

I have laden aboard ditto ship for your account 6,000 of pipestaves, excellent good as ever I saw. I had entered 6 ends of goods upon her for your account and sent them for Gravesend after the ship, but Mr [Humphrey] Isham [a mariner on Smith's *Prosperous*], contrary to his promise, went away half a day before they came down, so are returned me again. And here at present I know of no ship bound that way, which troubles me that after I have taken a great deal of pains, having but 14 days to dye and make them ready, and most of that time was rainy weather so that I could not get the goods dry. There's 2 bales Welsh cottons, one bale Welsh plains, 2 bales bays, and the calicoes; ozenbrigs nor Hampshire kersies not to be got upon so short warning.

Here is news from Newfoundland of 30 July where they write the ships have made very bad voyages and fish at 23 *Rs* per kt. By what I gather Mr Chalk [the *Mary*] is arrived there. They writ from Bilbao this post abundance of Basques arrived with fish there. You may do well to provide Chalk's lading of wines in time.

[P.S.] Here is arrived Capt. Crispe but not a line from you.

108. to William Clerke   28 Sept. 1655

a. ... [I] have written you per Mr Christopher [*recte* Matthew] Smith master of the ship *Prosperous*, which ship is gone out of the Downs about 10 days since, notwithstanding the freighters gave him notice of the embargoes which were laid upon all Englishmen's estates in Bilbao and San Sebastian 10 current and conceived to be all over the King of Spain's dominions. So that he and all the rest which were at that time in the Isle of Wight, about 16 sail bound for the Canaries, which had likewise notice thereof, do even deserve to have no freight, it being one of the most wilfullest acts that ever was committed by men to go away in that manner against sense or reason when they were sufficiently forewarned of the embargo and how impossible it was for any man to comply with their tonnage in such dangerous times.

I have received a letter from Mr Chalk [the *Mary*] of 9 Aug., from Newfoundland, which was the very day he arrived there, where he writes me had notice of the ship which he was to receive 1,500 kts fish of by contract, which seems was 50 leagues from him, where he intended to ply with the first wind, not losing any time. Neither if he had arrived sooner could have been sooner dispatched in that the fish generally was then scarce ready to be delivered. He writes me the ships have made, most of them, bad voyages and fish worth there 23 to 24 *Rs* per kt, a thing very unexpected. I did once think it would have been bought in the land under 18 *Rs* in regard there went but few sacks this year. I conceive he may be near Bilbao by this time.

I conceive he will stop at Santoña before he goes in over the bar and know how squares [i.e. the game] go. I wish you may have given such ample orders there to your correspondent as that there may be a right understanding in the business. I cannot find by those orders which you gave Mr Chalk that in case of war you make any proviso where else to go, which I could wish you had inserted something to that purpose. For if he go in over the bar, the ship will be lost; and if he stay at Santoña, I question where they will admit him pratique as to land his fish there. Besides, that will be a dangerous place to ride for San Sebastian men-of-war, as most men say it, know the place. God direct them for the best. Really it troubles me as much as if were my own interest. If I hear that Mr Chalk delivers the fish at Bilbao or thereabouts unto your order and proceeds for the Canaries to you, then according to your order I shall get insured £1,000 on him homewards for your account, which I fear will be at high rates as times now govern, for undoubtedly there will be a great many men-of-war out from Dunkirk, Ostend, and San Sebastian, besides

Brest. So that if you take my counsel, it will not be amiss to insure more, in regard there will be a good sum due for freight which must be paid though she miscarry, as per the charter-party you may see, every 6 months.

But I cannot imagine how you can have pratique to unload her fish nor load wines except you have more than ordinary favour; which, if you chance to obtain and load him with wines, they will come to an extraordinary occasion here, for since the news of the embargo wines are risen £5 per pipe. I have 120 pipes at present upon my hands which I hope to make a very considerable advance on them according to their quality. Though yours in Chalk were miserable trash, yet I hope to advance you £50 upon that small parcel.

108b. I have paid your Spanish bills [of exchange], £100 and £90 unto Mr Fernando Body, and £50 unto Mr [John] Thomas. I wonder you would draw so on me knowing I am next month to pay above £1,100 for Chalk's [the *Mary*'s] fish and about £400 for his 6 months' freight, when as I have not received a penny to this day of all the goods he brought home, besides the goods which I bought for you to go in [Capt. Matthew] Smith [the *Prosperous*] which lie now upon my hands for your account. So that I shall be in disburse for you, which, in regard you are my old friend, I cannot stand for small matters. I have spoken with Mr [Abraham] Lee who is not worth the clothes on his back. If possible, I'll get his bond for your debt and advise you what passeth.

I have received a memory of what freight you expect from Mr Chalk last voyage, which comes far short of what you writ at Mr Chalk's arrival there. Pray get a paper under his hand what goods he received and then I'll make him allow for it. When he arrived, I knew not what he brought so I was fain to take his word in regard had no particular from you.

As to your skin of sylvester at Rouen which should be damnified, I have in my possession at present a certificate by a public notary which certifies the same which I writ you and the abatement. And for my part, I have that confidence in my correspondent there [Humphrey Wilkings] that the thing is real. And for the chest of campechena which fell in the sea at Santa Cruz [de Tenerife], you need not wonder at its being damnified, for Mr Standish saw it in my warehouse and did once cast a lot for it in regard he had 2 chests in the parcel; but it fell to you for to have it, and he said before we cast lots it was not reason that same chest should be put upon him, being damnified. So that he might have satisfied you of that doubt if he had been pleased, seeing you so much question my information. I wonder he did not blush when he writ the letter which you dictated. I have not time to write him 2 lines at present about it, but he must acknowledge his error else I shall scarce be in charity with him. My carriage to him here deserved no such acting, neither do I value any man's malice a rush in that way. With comfort I may say it, to you nor no man else I never writ a lie as to the sale nor quality of their goods. Neither would I have Mr Clerke nor no friend else to make use of me an hour longer than he shall find me derivate [sic] from the truth or act those things which becomes not an honest man.

Other things there are in your letter of 5 July which I should answer, but time will not give me leave at present, this ship being in the Downs before ever I knew of her going. So crave your excuse and in my next shall give full answer thereunto. ...

109. to William Clerke   9 Oct. 1655

These are chiefly to give you notice how I have written you at large per Mr Owen who goes over in this ship. Which letter I sent into the Downs with another for my father-in-law which I have notice was delivered, and accordingly you may be pleased to demand it of him. I knew not of this ship's going till she was past Gravesend.

Here are several ships come from Malaga without any lading. And Mr Chamlett and 2 ships more, which went from hence for Bilbao laden with pack-goods about a month since, are now returned back again with their lading they carried out, with much difficulty in that the Spaniards used many tricks to betray them. So I know not what Mr Chalk [the *Mary*] will do when he arrives there. I hope you have given larger orders than those you sent home by him. ...

110. to William Clerke   14 Dec. 1655

a. I have not written you a long time for want of conveyance, neither have I heard from you since the unhappy [Spanish] embargo, understanding you were then in Gran Canaria. I wish your absence from home at that time tend not to your prejudice. I am now to give you notice how about a month since Mr Chalk [the *Mary*] arrived into the harbour of Plymouth with his lading of fish, having been 4 days in Santoña road where he put his son ashore to give notice unto Lazaro de Ormacho how his father was there waiting his order, though at that time there was an embargo. But his son not returning, being kept prisoner for some days, he came away with 6 ships more. And since, his son that was left ashore is now come home in a Fleming, with whom I have had some discourse, who told me that he was with said Lazaro de Ormacho and delivered him a letter from his father, and said Ormacho answered nothing but patience, never so much as endeavouring to get the fish ashore. Nor did he make any reckoning of the business, very much slighting it. So that I know not what to do in the business. The ship lies upon charge and the fish decaying, and I have no order where to send her. And if had, I know not of any market within or without the Straits. Never was there such loss upon codfish designs as this year. Notwithstanding a war, at Cadiz it's sold at 27 *Rs plata* per kt, and here fish is not worth 18 *Rs* per kt. Neither will the owners abate me a farthing of the freight, so I expect they will sue me in the Admiralty Court. I thank God all the business that I have in the world does not trouble me so much as this. Neither do I know which way to act. If should send her for the Canaries, I doubt she will not be admitted pratique, being the commodity will discover she is an English ship.

Here is arrived Mr Charles Saunders empty, per whom I was in hopes to have heard from you. Seeing Mr Chalk was not arrived there [at Tenerife] at his coming away, you might well imagine that he had some impediment in his dispatch at Bilbao. Your too much confidence of Lazaro de Ormacho will tend much to your damage. It was ever my counsel to you for to desist meddling in a perishing commodity, especially in uncertain times. But what will it avail now to hint these passages? It will rather add affliction to affliction. So I shall forbear insisting on this particular.

110b. The last week our Lord Protector ordered that a price should be put on all wines, which we expect will come out next week at 8d per pint of Canary and 4d French wine. The noise of which hath made wines fall 50 per cent here, so that the poor merchant is ruined abroad and at home. I hope the next ships will bring me some lines of yours that I may know how to dispose of Mr Chalk. Hides, 10d per lb; cochineal, 26s per lb; campechena 7s [per lb]; sylvester, 3s 4d [per lb]; indigo a drug, 4s per lb; Campeachy wood, £35 per t; good new Varinas tobacco, 8s per lb.

We have now 40 sail of gallant men-of-war going to lie off the Spanish coast to wait the *galeones'* coming. Gen. Blake goes Commander-in-Chief. No hopes of any composure. Our peace with France proclaimed last week in great pomp, so I fear the Spaniard will down apace. There go 10 sail men-of-war to Jamaica to join with the rest there already, and it's conceived we shall land some forces in Flanders this summer, being in confederacy with the French.

Amongst all the ships at the Canaries I cannot hear what the *Prosperous*, Mr Smith, doth. I hope you will not let it come home dead freight, being so small a quantity of tonnage. I am informed my very good friend Mr George Jennings is arrived in Santa Cruz [de Tenerife] from Havana with a large parcel of hides. If it be your chance to see him, pray present my kind respects unto him and that I much rejoice at his good success and safe arrival. If I hear not from you per next ship, I shall resolve to send you Mr Chalk with his fish, not knowing where else to send him. Therefore, you may do well to make some kind of provision. West India goods will be in better esteem than wines by far. ...

111. to William Clerke   29 Dec. 1655

a. ... Three days since I received yours of 9 present per your servant Thomas Leigh, where I expected to have received from you an ample order for the disposing of your fish aboard Mr Chalk's ship [the *Mary*] or to what place should send it, which in reason you might have done. Considering that you had no news of him at the writing of your letter, you might very well conjecture all was not well at Bilbao. But your overmuch confidence of Lazaro de Ormacho did, I fear, drown your reason else surely you would have fallen in better account of the business than you did. But opening your letter and finding nothing what in reason I expected, I found myself in a worse condition than before, wishing that I had never had a hand in the business, being like to prove so unfortunate. And perusing of your letters, I find, per Mr Chamlett and others, you forewarn me not to act anything but what you shall order me, which was a sufficient caveat for me to sit still till had your order. But considering how the ship lies upon charge and her lading a perishing commodity and how highly it did import you to have this ship at the Canaries as affairs now govern, I have resolved with myself to run the hazard of receiving from you another check by acting contrary to your order and to send her unto you with her lading of fish, which is 1,710 kts as per bill of lading will appear, though no man besides myself would do it. And for the better carrying on the design, I have sent down your servant Thomas Leigh post to Plymouth to go upon her, who hath received from me several instructions whereby at his arrival at Orotava he order things in a right way, a copy of which you may please to order him to send you ashore. I have made a passport for the ship in a very ample manner with a seal and firm, calling the ship the *St Peter* of Monnikendam, whereof is skipper Peter van Bruge, burthen 60 lasts, consigned to *Sr* Diego Pereyra, the Customer, for the accounts of *Srs* Don Luis Pereyra and Don Rodrigo Gomez Dias of Antwerp, which I know to be Diego Pereyra's correspondents and great friends. I have ordered the Dutch master to declare he brings but 5 or 600 kts of fish and that it was brought into Monnikendam as prize. Said Diego Pereyra hath a formal letter and bill of lading for 1,700 kts for account of abovesaid of Antwerp which the skipper is to carry ashore at his first arrival with the passport. So I have done my part. Pray God give good success thereunto, and hereafter you may not be so strict in your orders to such as you know and have had experience of, as you have had of me. I hope the fish will come to a very good occasion, there having none gone this year. But you must give order that it be carefully landed else they will spoil, it having been so long aboard. I wonder the ship could take in no more at Newfoundland, but I fear the master and company have too large a proportion, of which you may take notice thereof and advise me.

111b. You days past sent me a memory of all such goods and monies as were laden aboard Mr Chalk [the *Mary*] last voyage, which is more than I received freight for here. Therefore you may do well to adjust there with him and send it me under his hand, else he will deny it here. I have ordered my cousin John Paige to get 4 Flemings at Plymouth to go in the ship, which are to row the boat ashore at their first arrival. So I hope for a small composition you will have her admitted; after which is done, my earnest desire unto you is that you will immediately, without the loss of any time, unload the ship and likewise endeavour her speedy dispatch for the several reasons which I shall give you. First, you may take notice that there are from several places, to my knowledge, 4 ships bound that way which in all probability may arrive there within a week of this ship. Secondly, Mr Breton advises me from Madrid of 2 current how there's a new General going for the Canaries, which may be there as soon as this comes to hand, who is a rigorous man and a great enemy to our nation.[1] And thirdly, Gen. Blake is now ready with his fleet bound for the coast of Spain whence undoubtedly he will do acts of hostility, upon which the Spaniards will put to public sale all the embargoed goods and take stricter courses with you. All which things considered, it more than ordinarily concerns you not to lose an hour's time; and if possible can get a chapman, sell your codfish, though under the assize.

Now as in my former, so I confirm it again, our Lord Protector had ordered no Spanish wines shall be sold for above £26 per pipe or butt and French wines, £20 per t. So that in regard there are 2 West Indiamen arrived there and hides so great a commodity here and in Rouen, 40 per cent higher as per the coranto I here send you which came this day to my hands, you will do well to load as many of ditto commodity as you can, and, on the other side, as few wines as can. And if it should so fall out that you load not all the ship, pray let my father-in-law have the refusal of it. I shall make some insurance outwards upon this ship and likewise homewards for your account. Campeachy wood, £30 per t. In regard of our fleet's lying upon the coast of Spain, I believe you will have store of West Indiamen at the Islands, but the first goods that arrive here will come to the only market.

I have furnished your servant Thomas Leigh with about £20 for your account per clothes, postage and provisions, which he may give you an account thereof. The owners of this ship and I am like to have a suit in law about Mr Chalk's coming away from Santoña, except some honest men end it by way of reference [i.e. arbitration], [which] I think better than going to law. During Mr Chalk's being with you, have a care what you do. You may write Thomas Leigh what you will have done for he and the owners are upon the ketch with me and have been all along. You be confident I shall not see your interest any way left for want of diligence. What you may write Chalk is that you are much damnified by his coming from Santoña and that you will not pay for his lying at Plymouth.

All the ships that loaded this vintage are arrived, God be praised, though none come into the river. Only [the *Endeavour*], Mr [William] Jop, was taken by 4 men-of-war 30 leagues off Tenerife, supposed to be Frenchmen bound for the East Indies which went out of Nantes 2 months since, before the peace was made.

The enclosed for my father-in-law pray deliver with your own hand. No person else hath any letters in the ship. If, with the effects you have in the Island and the proceeds of this ship's fish, you could load 2,000 hides, you would make a brave business, which I hope you will be able to accomplish very well.

Mrs Leigh was yesterday at my house, who made a very great complaint unto me of you concerning the money you received of Mr [John] Turner for her account and would fain have me to have paid her £50 or £100 for your account. I told her had no order, but that would not serve till I told her you had no effects in my hands. Pray per this ship give her order of payment, for I have partly engaged my word you shall do it. Thus, with my kind respects to yourself, hoping to see you here speedily, I commit you to God. ...

[P.S.] I shall not send Capt. Russell [the *Katherine*] nor any other ship from hence. Therefore you may expect no tonnage, neither do I know how shall send your goods or pipestaves at present.

1. Breton's report was ill founded. Don Alonso Dávila y Guzmán had become the Capt. General in 1650 and served until 1659 (Viera y Clavijo, *op. cit.*, ii, 786).

112. to William Clerke   1 Jan. 1656

I have written you at large per this ship [the *Mary*], to which crave reference. These are chiefly to confirm my former advice how this day the Spanish merchants have been with our Lord Protector again about the price of wines but cannot any ways find relief, so that they are absolutely put at £26 per pipe, which is, as we gave them to understand, of greater prejudice and loss to the poor merchants than the embargo in Spain. But all will not avail, but we must suffer.[1] God give us patience to undergo so great a loss.

So that except it be to get in some debts that are owing you, I would advise you as a friend to load as few wines as you can and to buy most part West India goods, as chiefly Caracas and Havana hides and Campeachy wood. And if the Caracas tobacco be new, to buy some of it, but if old, meddle not with it upon no terms. But what you do must be presently upon receipt hereof, for that from hence and by via of Holland, etc., there are at least 6 ships bound for that Island, which at their first freighting were merely intended to load wines; but now upon this unhappy business of the putting prices, all have contradicted their orders not to meddle in any, if can get West India goods. So that if you can buy a good parcel, though more than you can well compass or intend to load, yet upon their arrival you cannot want to sell the over-plus upon what terms you please. I look upon hides as there will be 40 per cent cleared by them as now worth in Rouen.

I trust in God your codfish will come to a good occasion. ...

[P.S.] Mr Throckmorton and Mr Cocke in 2 great ships are now in the Downs ready to depart, so that in all probability they cannot be 2 days' sail astern this ship, which may serve per advice. I very much fear that Dunkirk and Ostend men-of-war will disturb Mr C[halk, the *Mary*] in the road [of Puerto de la Cruz, Tenerife]; therefore it behoves your speedy dispatch of him from thence.

1. In Dec. and Jan., 1655–6, Paige twice joined other merchants to petition Cromwell concerning wine prisage. The first petition, receipted by the Council of State on 5 Dec. 1655, asked the Protector to suspend execution upon a declaration of 4 May 1655 reviving Henrician statutory powers to set wine prices (P.R.O., State Papers 18/102/7; *C.S.P.D.*, *1655*, 151). The second petition, calendared among the Thurloe papers at 7 Jan. 1656, asked that the limit of £26 per pipe for Spanish wines be suspended 'until midsummer 12 months' (*State Papers of John Thurloe*, ed. T. Birch (1742), iv, 396–7). Cf. **114**, **117**.

113. to William Clerke   20 Jan. 1656

These are chiefly per covert to the enclosed bill of lading for 5,760 pipestaves, great tale, which were the 6,000 that were aboard Mr [Matthew] Smith [the *Prosperous*], so that either him, the lighterman, or the master of this ship, the *Irish Merchant*, Robert Hunter, have the 240 wanting. And of whom to demand them I know not. I am in hopes they are all aboard this ship, which may easily be seen for she carries none but this parcel. The bill of lading says you are to pay freight according to charter-party, which signifies nothing, they going upon Don Alonso de Molina's tonnage and consigned to his brother, Don Francisco de Molina, unto whom I have given order they may be delivered you. I had sent your goods in this ship but that I sold it [i.e. the goods] unto Mr Arnold Beak and company before your advice came, who sent it for Holland in a ship they have going for the Canaries, which now gives over their design. So yesterday they proffered me the goods again for the money it cost them. ...

[P.S.] You are to pay no freight for the pipestaves. This letter is for their delivery.

114. to William Clerke   24 Jan. 1656

... [T]he *Mary* frigate ... departed from Plymouth with a fair wind some 16 days since, which hath continued ever since so that I trust in God she may be safe with you ere this time, of the which I should be right glad to hear thereof in regard I have advice she went alone. I have made insurance upon her outwards for your account for £800 at 3½ per cent and do purpose, God willing, to make the like homewards for a greater sum for your account. I am very much condemned by my friends and those that wish me well in sending the ship in this manner without your positive order, in regard you gave me in your former letter a hint to act nothing for the future without your order. But I am more confident in you than it seems you have had of me; and I hope however things succeed you will account it as an acceptable piece of service done you, for had I not done it all the fish would have perished, it not being worth here 18 *Rs* per kt merchantable fish, which would not have produced anything considerable.

Mr Chalk [Capt. of the *Mary*] like a knave hath passed bills of exchange upon me to pay the men's wages, which I would satisfy provided the owners would make allowance for his coming from Santoña and lying at Plymouth. But if must have a suit in law, I had rather might be for all than part. You cannot imagine what a deal of trouble I have daily about it. Never did man meet with such a pack of malicious owners as I have of this ship.

Since my last the Spanish merchants have been with our Lord Protector several times, and I think through mere importunity we shall have Michaelmas next allotted us for to sell our wines as we can, and after that time the assize to take place [Cf. **112**, **115**], which will not much avail us, the vintners having many old wines upon their hands at present and combined together to bring us down.

All wines from Garachico and Rambla prove very bad this year. Orotava very good, only a great many mixed with *vidueños* which makes them foul. As for West India goods, I have writ you the needful in my former. Only Campeachy wood rises, worth at present £35 per t. Mr [Matthew] Smith [the *Prosperous*] will not abate one farthing of this freight as per charter-party, so now are in law. No hopes of peace. ...

115. to William Clerke   21 Feb. 1656

... I hope long ere this time you have dispatched Mr Chalk, upon which ship [the *Mary*] I have insured £1,300 for your account at 4 per cent and resolve to insure more if possible, there being abundance of Dunkirk men-of-war abroad with commissions against English, and all the Brest men-of-war are now entertained at San Sebastian where they have brought in Mr Jop.[1]

Wines, except very rare, are very drugs. Our Lord Protector declares that as soon as the Spaniard prohibits our manufactory he will do the like here by all kind of Spanish goods. But that will not advantage at all the wine merchants for that after 1 Dec. next no wines shall be sold for [more than] £26 per pipe.

Gen. Blake is now at Portsmouth ready with 60 sail men-of-war and fire ships to lie upon the coast of Spain. He carries many soldiers so 'tis thought he will land somewhere. If once they draw blood on each side, I fear your person there will not be secure. I long much to hear from you. ...

1. Cf. **111b**. Cromwell claimed that Jop's ship, the *Endeavour*, was taken to the East Indies by French privateers who captured her off Tenerife and disembarked 14 of her crew in Guinea. And by his letter of 26 Sept. 1656 to Louis XIV, he sought restitution of the ship and damages on behalf of Richard Baker and his partners. *Writings and Speeches of Oliver Cromwell*, ed. W. C. Abbott (Cambridge, Mass., 1937–47), iv, 294, 828.

116. to William Clerke   14 March 1656

These chiefly serve per covert to the enclosed from Mr Richard Baker where he sends you the best dispatches that he hath now at this present in England and withal hath given order to Mr Breton [at Madrid] long since, to my knowledge, to send you such papers as you shall need, which I doubt not but go per Don Balthazar de [Vergara] Grimón who, I suppose, may be in Tenerife long ere this.

I have received yours per Mr Owen and Mr Standish, which shall answer tomorrow per this bearer, Don Alonso de Molina, who is a very honest young man. I am hearty glad to hear of Mr Chalk's [the *Mary*'s] arrival at Orotava, and the more in that he comes to so seasonable occasion with the fish. And I question not but you will act your part. As to his dispatch home, I have now insured £1,600 upon him for your account home at 4 per cent. ...

[P.S.] I sent you 6,000 pipestaves in the *Irish Merchant* consigned in forma to Don Francisco de Molina y Lugo. Hides worth 10d per lb; logwood, £35 per t; wines a drug. This bearer, Don Alonso de Molina, is witness unto Mr Baker's papers, if anything be doubted.

117. to William Clerke   15 March 1656

Yesterday I writ you a few hasty lines which I here enclose, where goes a packet from Mr Richard Baker to you, who remits you copies of several papers attested by a notary public. I have been very earnest with him to send the originals, this being a good ship. And in time of war I question where a notary's fee will be valued; I'm sure it's not here from Spain. But by no means I cannot persuade him to it. All my hopes is that Don Balthazar de [Vergara] Grimón's arrival will clear you with such papers as Mr Breton will send [from Madrid]. Had you writ me of this business in time, I should have solicited Mr Baker here and Mr Breton with letters as that you need not have been imprisoned, which does much impair your credit here as well as your great hindrance there. Many that are ignorant and know not the original conceive you are in for your own debts, which some of your back friends here are subject to possess people so.

By a letter which I received from my father-in-law, I perceive Mr Chalk [the *Mary*] was arrived at Orotava with his lading of fish, which seems comes to a very good and seasonable occasion, at which I much rejoice at as if it did wholly appertain to myself as being instrumental to my good friend's happy success. For you well know I did it upon my own head, having not a tittle of any such order from you. Now you may please to take notice that I have insured for your account homewards on the *Mary* frigate £1,600 at 4 per cent; if possible, shall get some more done. I hope you will load her with West India goods home. For wines, they are a very drug at present; except very rare, you will lose a great deal of money by them. I should be hearty glad to hear of your coming home in Chalk, which I doubt neither you nor my father-in-law will not be so good as your words in that.

Here is aflying news that the *galeones* should be arrived at Cadiz, but I find no ground for it, so look upon it as a flame. If they should not arrive, Campeachy wood will be worth here at least £35 per t all this summer, but if otherwise it will be lower in price. Hides are still a great commodity in Rouen. As yet there's 4 chests of your Campeche grain [campechena] unsold and your wines and sarsaparilla in Chalk.

I have received yours per Mr Standish as likewise per Mr Owen, to which have not time to answer at present. In case you should remain there till vintage, as I hope you will not, then, and in such case, pray let me hear from you per all vias, and what West Indiamen arrive there and what they bring, and what expected. I verily believe there will great many come there in regard they know our fleet will lie off Cadiz so it will be dangerous for them to proceed there. So that in such occasion there may be good done. For wines, there's no thoughts of any next year except they may be bought for 20 Ds per pipe. We have till 1 Dec. next to sell our old wines, I mean of this year, which cannot be done though had given us 6 months longer. So that after that time we must not exceed £26 per pipe for the best, as per the enclosed order appears more at large. So that for my part I am sure shall suffer deep by those I have, they not proving so well as I could wish, having yet 150 pipes unsold. ...

118. to William Clerke at Plymouth   27 Dec. 1656

In the first place, I congratulate your welcome home, being joyful to hear of your arrival at Plymouth, from whence I received your welcome lines of 23 current with another from my father-in-law, which is more good news than I have been accustomed to receive this many years. The Lord make me truly thankful for it.

I perceive you received my letters by the vintage ships where I advised you what passed between me and Mr F[rancis] C[larke]. Whereupon I perceive you are partly resolved to go for Holland until you have better settled your affairs. But seeing you are pleased to make use of my weak judgement, I shall in brief impart what I conceive most convenient, although by yours I cannot very well perceive how business stands. But be it how it will, it's my opinion on receipt hereof you take post and come for London where you may be as private as you please, no place like unto it. And then you may the better communicate your business to your friends and transport your person from hence where you think fit better than from any place. But if the wind should continue easterly and that you remain at Plymouth when all the rest of the merchants come up, it may

141

breed a jealousy in some here and so trouble you there. Now in case you are resolved to pass the other side and not come hither, it's my opinion you go for Flanders, for if you go for Holland you will be as subject to be molested as if you came here. I have acquainted your brother Mr George Clerke of your arrival, from [whom] the enclosed goes. He is of my opinion that you come up post and that you send us notice by a porter where you are. I live in Bishopsgate Street. However, I shall write you 2 lines for Dover to lie at Mr Michael de Haze's house. Both to him and my cousin Mr John Paige [of Plymouth] I have written to furnish you with what money you have occasion of.

Mr Chalk's business is now upon arbitration, and the last day of our bonds is 30 instant. I would fain renew them for a longer time, as have done twice already, but they will not yield to it. You writ me Chalk [the *Mary*] was to have gone to the Palma to take in 30 ts of goods upon freight when he was in trouble about the silver. [Cf. **103**, **104**.] If you have any such letters from thence, pray send them me up or an affidavit by oath from yourself how it was so, else it will go against you. Thus you might send up the next post without any delay. I shall not enlarge for present, being suppose shall have you here. ...

[P.S.] Here is no news as yet of George Webber and that fleet's arrival [from the Canaries]. God grant they be well.

119. to William Clerke at Antwerp   6 Feb. 1657

I received yours, 28 past, from Gravesend, being very glad to hear the business succeeded so well that you had no interruption, considering the many pretenders against you. The news was upon the Exchange the next day. It seems there was a person at Gravesend that knew you who came up that tide and reported saw you embark upon the Flushing pink, which was told Mr Bradick who immediately told all that knew you. Who, with James Cowse pretends you owe them 16,000 *Rs*, who seem to be vexed at your going away and affect their pretence. They brought a sergeant to make an attachment in my hands for goods and monies of yours, but your release did soon cool their courage. Whereupon seeing that, they desisted. So that it was well you did it, otherwise I should have had many more of the same nature.

According to your desire, your brother [George] and I went to your cousin Francis Clarke's and delivered your letter to him which did not so much satisfy him as other reasons we gave him. Give him his due, I find him a very fair, conditionable person. We told him, as understood by you, that conceived little or no balance due to him, which made him break out into some passion. And in conclusion he proposed that would refer all the whole business to your brother and myself, so that we fear there may be more than you were pleased to discover to us. To which end he hath now given us a copy of all such goods as sent you, with their costs, as also of what received in returns. So that against post you will have a more particular relation of this business. Pray in your next omit not to write Mr Richard Lant and above all Mrs Leigh, and if you think convenient, the widow [of Stephen] Slaney or Mr Robert Lant. Ten days being past, the great wonder of your sudden departure is almost buried.

As to what you writ about what communicated at your departure, I gave you then my answer that if you please to send me over that paper which promised would, I shall comply with my promise in giving a final determination thereunto with all expedition, which is my earnest desire and request you fail not thereof, whereby each man may distinguish his own. However, for what you shall have occasion to defray your journey charges all along and something to defray your charges of what you go to pretend, I shall be ready to disburse.[1] And as I have been so, I shall desire a continuance of love and friendship between us. And when you have tried all your friends, none hath nor shall be more affectionate and real to you than I. What passeth in your affairs I should be very glad to hear of its good success. And thus with mine and my father-in-law's kind respects to you, commit you to God. ...

1. Clerke intended to apply to Spanish officals for licences which would have allowed him to resume his trade at the Canaries.

120. to William Clerke at Antwerp   13 Feb. 1657

I have yours from Middelburg and 13 current from Antwerp, being glad to hear of your safe being in those parts. In my last, writ you at large so shall be brief at present, only to acquaint you that have of late spoken with Mr [Richard] Lant, your master that was, who does seem to condole your condition in regard of the weakness of your body to travel, expressing much of affection towards you. And as to Mr Francis Clarke, your brother and I have perused over his invoices and demands which he now sends you. We could wish you to give us an estimate a little more or less what they might there produce, also what the returns you sent him come to, and what debts remain for his account, that so, if possible, it might be adjusted. For neither he nor Mr Lant does not require at your hands, for ought I can see, a perfect or exact account considering your books and papers are taken away [by the Canarian officials].

Thanks be to God, our ship *Posthorse* from the Canaries, in company with Mr Casby, is now arrived in the river, who bring us a strange relation that you and the rest of our nation were turned away merely by the importunity and bribing of them which you accounted your friends. For which they gave the [Capt.] General [of the Canaries], etc. 3,500 pieces of eight. The junta was Don Balthazar [de Vergara Grimón], Don Cristóbal [de Alvarado Bracamonte], Don Jerónimo, Don Melchor, Don Benito [Venia y Vergara], Nicolas Alvares, Pedro Fernandez, Pedro Flaniel and others. So that you may see which way the game goes. If you could get licence to return there, it would be of more importance by far than your books.

There's arrived a ship or galleon at Santa Cruz [de Tenerife] which came last from Puerto Rico and brings for the King and particulars 1,000,000 pieces of eight and 12,000 hides, some sugar and ginger. The plate is landed in Santa Cruz castle.

As for the £110 you writ of, shall be remitted the next post. Had I been well, should have been this. I am sorry Mr [Baldwin] Matthew's friend did disappoint you, but it's no fault of mine. ...

121. to William Clerke at Antwerp   20 Feb. 1657

In regard I received none from you this post, shall be brief, these being only to acquaint you how per this post I have remitted a bill of exchange unto Mr John Shaw [Paige's correspondent at Antwerp] for your account for £110 sterling, to be paid at Amsterdam, being could get no good bill for Antwerp.

The enclosed is from Mrs Leigh who, I suppose, will be upon the old strain, never contented. I told her she had no reason to have anything back again in regard her son [Thomas] had cost you much money and gained sufficient experience, so the loss was yours more than theirs. Upon which she seemed to be discontented with me. So, I pray, order your brother [George] to talk with her for I shall not, having but ill-will for what I have done hitherto. ...

122. to William Clerke at Antwerp   13 March 1657

I have yours 7 current with an enclosed for Mrs Leigh which I shall deliver, wishing you had remitted her unto your brother Mr George Clerke. But since it's your pleasure to remit it unto me, I shall to the best of my capacity make good your lines written her, although you have left out one of the main arguments in your favour, which is that he [Thomas Leigh] hath of late made a voyage for the Canaries without any order of yours, as if he had been no man's servant but at his own disposal, and, by the experience which gained being your servant, by the investment of £350 here got clear £250. Which in some manner they may thank you, either for his education, or at leastwise for your permission therein, which I shall hint unto them, seeing you have omitted it.

I am sorry my letter with the bill of exchange did not come according to course. What might be the reason I know not. Sure I am there was nothing wanting in me. But I admire, seeing you carried Mr Jollife's credit, that you could want for such a sum whereby to prejudice your affairs. But it seems that proved like Baldwin Matthew's credit, otherwise you could not have wanted.

I would wish you not to rely too much on courtiers' promises for too much modesty with them never takes. You had best go yourself where the person is and not to delay it. What you pretend is obtained by several English as I am informed, so that it's common [knowledge] your namesake Leonard [Clerke] is now in Flanders about it, who writes confidently is to go for the Canaries with much freedom, which I desire you not to take notice as came from me.[1]

Mr Francis Clarke and your brother with myself met days past when we made some kind of entrance into the business. The next time I hope shall go further. You calculate the 800 kts Campeachy wood [at] 28,000 *Rs* when as he presents your own invoice where you make it to be 22,000 odd *Rs*. As to this particular, shall be more larger after our next meeting. In the interim I cannot but let you know that by what hitherto I find Mr Francis Clarke to be a very civil, reasonable person.

Pray in your next let me know how you find yourself as to health in those parts. My father-in-law thanks you for your care in his commission and desires to be kindly remembered to you. ...

1. Clerke was seeking licences which would have allowed him to resume his trade at the Canaries. And, as is suggested at the end of this letter, Paynter hoped to obtain, through Clerke's good offices, the same permission.

123. to William Clerke at Antwerp   3 April 1657

I have yours 1 and 7 current, having perused the contents. I take notice what you writ touching your affairs with Mr Francis Clarke which I communicated unto your brother [George]. Likewise he did the same with me with another letter which you wrote him. And having consulted together, we met this afternoon with Mr Francis Clarke with whom we had a very large discourse. To give you the particulars would be too tedious. Your brother made him a proffer of £400 which he very much slighted as a thing at high matters. By what I can perceive £1,000 will scarce content him. I gather he hath taken too much counsel of some of your back Canary friends whose counsel in the end I told him would prove pernicious to him. I was with him at the tavern an hour after your brother parted from us, where I endeavoured to convince him of his large pretence and found him a little better pacified at last. So that I believe it may beget another meeting, desiring him to consider well of the business and to waive all passions. I should be hearty glad that we might beget a true understanding between you both, that so all differences may be ended, although I would not have you purchase your peace at too dear a rate, of which you may rest confident I shall have as tender a regard of your interest as though you were present yourself.

Per this post from Genoa they writ there's a ship of London arrived there from Barbados laden with sugars who 140 leagues off the Canary Islands met with 12 great ships steering for the Islands, which they say were Spanish ships. So it's supposed they are the *flota*, which for my part I cannot believe to be true. Said ship afterwards met with Gen. Blake's fleet and acquainted them of what had passed, so that a short time will produce the truth of this business.[1]

Mr Body's business is ended with Mr Hart, who is now awarded to pay Mr Body £2,040 sterling. If you intend to come for [Middelburg in] Zeeland to go with the convoy [for Bilbao], pray carry it privately and make no sh[ow] there. ...

1. Captain David Young of the *Catherine* interrupted his voyage from Barbados to Genoa on 19 February to tell Blake, his old commander, that 12 galleons were steering for the Canaries (J. R. Powell, *Robert Blake, General at Sea* (New York, 1972), 296).

124. to William Clerke at Antwerp   17 April 1657

I have yours of 11 current, being glad to hear you have all your dispatches for Madrid. God grant you no worse success there than have had at Flanders.

As to Mr Francis Clarke's business, I refer the relation to your brother's [George's] letter, who hath promised me to give you advice at full. We have by his desire met him again, but our labours reap no success, so shall forbear to advise you any more about it.

This day is come an express from the Downs which brings news that 2 of

145

our frigates have brought in a Spanish prize which came from the West Indies, Cartagena, being about 300 ts, 20 guns, laden with hides, indigo, tobacco and some silver, supposed to be worth £50,000 sterling. She met with 5 of our frigates off the Groyne. The news of the *galeones* at the Canaries is looked upon as nothing.[1]

I am now labouring about your account. I shall not be quiet till see an end of it. Mr [Robert] Turner hath promised me will do his part, which, if he do not, shall be no impediment to you though it will make my task harder. [Cf. **66c.**]

If Mr Millington be in that city, pray present my service to him and acquaint him of the news of the Spanish ship. ...

1. Three days after this letter was dated Blake's fleet burned the galleons at Santa Cruz de Tenerife.

125. to William Clerke at Madrid   8 July 1657

a. I have received your welcome lines of 16 June, being glad at last you are got to your journey's end. Since your departure from Zeeland, I have not writ you, not knowing how or to whom to address your letters in Madrid, neither have you now given me any directions, at which I admire, which makes me write with fear. However, having received one from you, cannot omit to answer it.

Here hath arrived of late 4 ships from Tenerife which came away since the burning of the *flota*. For West India goods they have not bought a *real*'s worth. The [West] Indians hold that which is left at such excessive rates that no man durst meddle with it, saying we must pay for that which is burnt. They ask 66 *Rs* per hide; 8 *Rs* per lb for indigo; 120 Ds per ruff [?rove] for cochineal. For logwood, that little which came is burnt in the ships, so that there's no meddling with them. For here those very commodities are low, as hides 8½d per lb; indigo a very drug, not worth 4s per lb, besides great custom and charges on it; cochineal, 28s per lb; campechena, 8s per lb; logwood, £80 per t; Varinas tobacco, if right sort, 6s per lb. I have notice there's 1,000 chests arrived at Santa Cruz [de Tenerife] of a right sort in a ship called the *Rosario* which came from Cartagena, which came in there 3 days after the *flota* was burnt. If a parcel of that could be bought at a *real* per lb, would turn to account.

They advise me from the Canaries how that English and French goods is not scarce worth the first cost, that the vineyards for *malvasía* are like to be scarce this year, so they expect higher prices than last year. And to help all, the Parliament of England have made an act that after 15 Aug. no Spanish wines shall be sold for above 9d per pint.[1] And to help all, they have laid 3 general impositions on them more than formerly which is Argier duty, 2s per pipe, and a new custom of 15s per pipe, and excise over and above the former 30s per pipe.[2] All which being well considered, I think to all judicious, knowing men in the trade I take it to be a prohibition. But there will not want some madmen or fools that will be doing, though they burn their fingers. Much good may it do them.

1. 'An Act for limiting and settling the price of wines', 9 June 1657 (Firth and Rait, ii, 1057).

2. 'An Act for the continuing and establishing the subsidy of Tunnage and Poundage', 26 June 1657, continued the Argier duty and raised customs on Spanish wines from 30s to 45s per pipe (£4 10s per t). 'An additional Act for the better improvement and advancing the receipts of the excise and the new impost', passed the same day, raised the excise on Spanish wines from 60s to 90s per pipe (£9 per t) (Ibid., 1123, 1186).

125b. We are not engaged for one pipe, neither will we charge a t for vintage. And if you have engaged for any, if by any means you can, break off the contract, for assuredly you will come to lose above 30 per cent of your principal although they prove good. If bad, lose all. There's no commodity that I would meddle withal except logwood, campechena grain, or Varinas tobacco. Thus, I have given you the best advice I can whereby you may the better govern yourself. Besides all this, our friends at Tenerife, Don B. and Juan de O., write us positively they will not receive a pack of goods nor meddle in the dispatch of any ship for future. So it's high time for any to give over when the natives forewarn. There's several others write the same to their correspondents here. Since their loss at Santa Cruz they are so enraged that they have embargoed 3 English ships and given one Thomas Yardley, whom you know, the rack in a most sad manner, which makes me tremble to think of trading there. You write me the island of Santa Catalina is taken by the English. There's now a ship arrived from Jamaica in the Downs which brings no such news, so that I doubt where it may be so.

Mr Baldwin Matthews [at Middelburg] hath drawn on me mere £58 6d which he furnished you withal. I have 3 weeks since remitted Mr John Shaw [at Antwerp] £150 more for your account which, with the abovesaid, makes above £200 which he writ me was accepted. I would have remitted it sooner, it had been all on to me, but I considered it with your brother [George] it was not convenient until we did hear of your arrival at Bilbao, not knowing but you might allot the said money to be paid Mr Francis Clarke, seeing you gave us no answer about it before you took shipping at Zeeland. But I find you were straitened with time, as per Mr Millington's relation. However, [Mr] Francis Clarke now begins to murmur, complaining that you and I have drawn him into an inconveniency in regard that he hath [not] his half money nor his obligation for the other moiety, which pray send per first, else he will have just cause to complain of you as you have of me about the account, though in the end you will find it's [to] my prejudice.

Since your departure God Almighty hath been pleased to lay a great affliction upon me in that hath been pleased to take away my son Gowen the 24th last month, which hath caused no small grief in our family to lose such a jewel as he, which hath made me unfit for my business above these 7 weeks. So that I must crave your patience in not complying with my promise. And now I have my other child [John] very ill. God knows what will become of him. I know the backwarder I have been in the business makes [you], Mr Clerke, think of great matter, but in the conclusion you shall have no cause to complain.

What passeth in those parts pray let us hear from you. Mr Benjamin Barron, I suppose you will find him those parts. Beware of him for he is a knave and hath cheated me in Mr Mourton's [the *Agreement*'s] lading of

147

pilchards in an unreasonable manner; is gone and never leaves me an account nor sends me satisfaction and owes my man £60 for goods sold 12 months since and never remits him a penny nor affords him nor me a line what intends to do, only gave out at Bayona was gone for England. ...

126. to William Clerke at Madrid   8 Sept. 1657

I have yours 8 and 15 past where I find you still complaining of your unhappiness in that cannot receive a line from your friends, at which I admire that mine of 8 July was not come to hand when your last letter was writ. It went under covert Mr Whitt of that city. And as for other letters, I fear they may be intercepted because they go immediately directed to you, which in mine and most men's opinion that know that place apprehend a danger. As for the £200 you so much complain of is not come to hand, I do admire at it, seeing I remitted Mr John Shaw [at Antwerp] 19 June £150 sterling with order to remit it you with expedition, which was 20 days before I received any letter from you of your being in Madrid. The other 50 odd pounds I paid Mr Baldwin Matthews [at Middelburg] for the value paid you in those parts. Your news of the island of Santa Catalina proves contrary, as per late advice from Jamaica.

In my former I gave you notice how Spanish wines were put at 9d per pint and 45s per pipe new custom and excise put on them. At which rate they are now sold at to the half undoing of the poor vintner and no good to the merchant, which very thing hath utterly undone the wine trade. From the [Canary] Islands they writ 15 Aug. how the tithes are auctioned at the highest rates as ever was known, and yet like to be but an ordinary vintage, insomuch they expect higher rates than last year. Much good may it do them. We have charged 50 ts this year to load wines if reasonable, but if bad, not a pipe ordered. In such case to put aboard the proceeds in cochineal.

In our small vessel I have permitted your brother [George] to send some small things for Juan Goncalis. Here have of late days arrived in Holland 6 ships laden with rich goods from the Canaries, which came the back side of Ireland, and daily more expected, insomuch there will remain but little West India goods in the Islands. And now they begin to fall very much.

In your formers you were pleased to advise might have 50,000 pieces of eight delivered in the Islands to pay in those parts [i.e. Spain] 4 months after with 20 per cent premium [for Castilian money in terms of Canarian]. To my knowledge, from Seville and Cadiz they writ this post, 12 past, how they deliver money there to be paid in the Islands at 20 days' sight for 10 per cent premium, which is a great difference.

They writ from Santa Cruz [de Tenerife] there arrived 3 San Malo ships with permission [i.e. licences], which brought 1,500 bales linens, etc., not knowing of the *flota*'s burning, which hath made such a glut that the Islands need no more of that commodity this many years. One of which ships is now arrived back to San Malo worth 500,000 pieces of eight, as per advice. So you may see which way the horse is curried.

There will not go so many ships to the vintage as usual. Mr Stephens is going in a ship of 150 ts, not to abode. George Webber is now gone with

Mr Bennett, formerly of Seville, in a frigate of 30 guns and pinnace with £15,000 cargazon for to trade in the West Indies, at Portobello and Cartagena, who have Spaniards aboard. I wish him good success, but it's much feared. There's many Spanish and Canary merchants in the design. We refused it. ...

[P.S.] If any news, pray advise us and which way you intend to steer your course. Your friend Mr George Clerke seems to be angry. Pray afford him 2 lines per first opportunity.

127. to William Clerke at Madrid   22 March 1658

a. My last unto you was of 12 Jan. where I gave you notice what passed between your brother [George] and myself with Mr Francis Clarke and how I paid him £125 for your account. The rest was paid by your brother. Since which time I have received none from you until this of 16 Feb. Neither indeed have I written you, which hath not been for want of respect but rather want of subject. I wonder mine of 12 Jan. was not come to hand, whereas your brother had answer of his of the same date.

I take notice what letters you have from the African Islands [i.e. the Canaries]. We have now some of 16 Feb., and for corn they will have enough, there having gone from hence, France and Holland near 1,000 ts, and so many ships for a second vintage as I never saw the like, which carried good quantities of goods with them. That trade is spoiled. Those rogues which do our business cheat us and take all the gains to themselves. We have a ship gone with 300 hhds pilchards and £1,000 in pack-goods, but she will not return except can get some of our effects invested in cochineal, campechena, Varinas tobacco or Campeachy wood, which I much doubt. For wines, this time a year we will not have a pipe. Perhaps others may load her upon freight with wines.

I take notice what you writ about A[braham] Lee [of San Lucar]. It's true he hath had a little business this year, but he hath so abused his principals by giving them such a parting blow as that they will scarce come there again. So that I look upon him now as in a very bad condition. However, according to your order, I here remit you 3 bonds of his which are all due and attested in the form you desired. Of the first bond I have received in part of Mr [Christopher] Boone £121, so there remains £79 of that, and the other 2 entire, not a penny paid on them. Had I known he would have served you thus, he should not have gone hence. Here he hath not a penny, rather owes great sums of money. If your leisure would permit, perhaps it might be worth your time to go and speak with him. And when this will not take, tell him I shall make all his principals to know who he is and that one word of my mouth in that nature may take all his business from him by showing the bonds, which as hitherto I have been private.

127b. This winter hath been so sharp as that for 3 months we had nothing but frost and snow, at which time no man could endure to sit and write an hour. So that you may not so much admire your account is not finished. True it is I have failed of my promise in it several times, and I think you or another may be as guilty of that as myself. Neither do I urge this as an argument of excuse, nor hath it been delayed out of any prejudice intended by me to you. But rather you will find it's [to] my own [prejudice] and that you may be taken of your opinion of having a farthing in my hands of yours. For every pound that I have of yours in my hands I'll be bound to give you double interest for its detainment, provided you will but oblige yourself to pay me but single interest for what you may owe me. I have not been 4 days abroad this fortnight to comply with your desire, neither shall I take that pleasure intended this spring, being now posting up my books and to give a period to your account. In the meantime I cannot but resent your over-earnestness. Did it come from a stranger, I should not so much admire at it. ...

APPENDICES

128. [Enclosure in letter of 1 Sept. 1649 to William Clerke (**9**).] A list of
ships bound for Tenerife to load wines, with their burden and to whom
they go consigned   ts

Mr Gilbert Crane to Mr Kilvert and yourself	190
Mr Barber to yourself and Mr Paynter	100
Mr Murwill to Mr Casby and Mr Turner	200
Mr William Chalk to Mr Paynter	120
Mr Henry Toope to Mr Bradick etc.	230
Mr Crampe to Mr John Turner	210
Mr James Blake to Mr John Casby	210
Mr Young to Mr Bonfoy	160
Mr Crispe to Mr Lambell and others etc.	250
Mr Joy to Mr Fowler and Mr Lambell	150
Mr Starling to Mr Throckmorton and Proud	190
Mr Jenkins to Mr Phillip Ward	150
Mr Sheere to Mr Campion and Lee	150
Mr Humphrey Holcomb's ship to Mr Body	150
Mr Hedgethorn to Mr Bonfoy	240
A Fleming to Don Alonso de Lugo	200
Mr Button from Naples with hoops	250
Mr Brookes from New England	140
Mr Pyle for Mr Lambell	250
Mr Smith from Nantes to Mr Benjamin Barron	160
Mr Izaack's ship from Topsham to Mr Body	100
Mr Robert Rinett from Lynn	140
Mr William Hayes to Mr Cowling	110
Mr Read from Colchester to Mr Paynter most part	120
A Bristol man as I hear to go	90
Mr Thomas Warren's ship	80
Mr Bennett from Barbary to Mr Fowler as I am told	200
Mr Bulkley's ship from Newfoundland	100
Mr Fowler's ship from Newfoundland	80
Mr Colquist from Newfoundland to Mr Paynter	100
A Fleming from Bilbao to Mr Body	220
Mr Jop from Bilbao to Mr Body	120
A New England man from Bilbao to Mr Body	160
Mr Hussy from Bilbao to Mr Turner	160
Mr Fishman to Mr Pearson and Webber	150
Mr Webber from Galicia with pilchards	70
Mr Sidrake Blake, I make account, must load	220
Mr Steward for Mr John Turner	200

Mr Humphrey Isham for Mr Wild and others   250
A collier now freighted for several men   120
In all 40 ships   6,490 ts
Of all these ships I am confident there will not fail 2, God sending them in safety. Rather, I doubt there may be some I know not of, besides Hollanders which I make no question but will be some. I thought this a very necessary thing to send you, whereby to govern yourself accordingly. ...

(B) JOHN PAIGE'S INSTRUCTIONS TO RICHARD JEWELL, SUPERCARGO ON THE *ELIZABETH*, FOR A VOYAGE TO THE BARBARY COAST AND TENERIFE

129. to Richard Jewell   2 Aug. 1650
    In the first place, I desire the Lord to give a blessing to your lawful endeavours in this our design.
2. You are to sail directly from hence to the Road of Safi upon the Barbary Coast.
3. When pleases God that you arrive at Safi in safety, you are to endeavour to get pratique and to make sales of the goods for our most advantage and to invest the proceeds as here underwritten.
4. In case that you cannot put off all or part of our goods at aforesaid port, then you are to go directly for Mogador and there to dispose of them. And when you cannot meet with a market fitting at Mogador, then you may go for Santa Cruz [de Berbería, i.e. Agadir] or any other crick or port thereabouts.
5. When you have disposed of the cargazon of goods, then you are to invest the proceeds thereof in good wheat and to load the ship with ditto commodity.
6. What monies shall remain, besides the ship's lading of wheat, employ it in good beeswax and 2,000 goatskins.
7. After you have made sale of our goods and laden the ship with wheat and wax, etc., then you are to sail directly for the port of Orotava in Tenerife, there to deliver your corn and other goods unto my good friends Mr Gowen Paynter and Mr William Clerke, unto whom I have given orders to receive it.
8. Pray take notice though I limit you to go for Santa Cruz yet I would be loath that you should trust to that port, being far to leeward. Rather, if possible, load the ship at Safi or some part at Mogador. The first port will be the only place for wheat and sales of the goods.
9. I make no question but you are very sensible that you go somewhat late of the year and that foul weather usually falls in upon that coast the middle of Sept. Wherefore, I earnestly desire you to make all the speedy dispatch you can to lade the ship whereby you may be at the Islands to load home the first wines, which you know imports very much.
10. Be sure to keep an account of the ship's days.
11. You must endeavour to keep a fair correspondence with Mr [John] Clarke, the pilot, because otherwise he will be cross and advise you nothing that you shall desire, which may prejudice you much.
12. Remember that you carry for Mr Paynter and Mr Clerke 100 hens.

13. You may buy for me a barrel of 150 lbs weight of the best dates you can.

14. Be sure when you are at sea to examine the master and company [of ships you meet] where they have any letters for Barbary.

15. Let me hear from you per all vias and especially how the ship proves.

16. I pray a care that you do not trust the Moors or Jews with any goods ashore except they first bring their corn.

17. Mr Clarke will partly advise you the prices of goods formerly there, but I would not have you to trust altogether upon his judgement.

18. I pray charge the master [Christopher Shadforth] that the ship be in readiness always to defend herself in case of French men-of-war.

19. When you sell the iron and guns, be sure you put off your goods assorted peradventure you will find a Jew that will cut a price for the whole cargazon.

20. If upon your first arrival you meet with a reasonable good market, let not slip the opportunity. Commonly the first is the best and repair not in a small matter.

21. I should enlarge some other particulars, but I hold it needless in regard I know you understand the business you go about, not doubting but that through God's blessing and your care and diligence the design may prove beneficial. ...

(C) GLOSSARY

average: apportionment of loss caused by intentional damage to a ship (e.g. cutting away of masts or boats, or sacrifice of cargo) to secure the general safety of the ship and cargo. In which case contribution is made by the owners (or insurers) of the ship, cargo, and freight in proportion to the value of their respective interests.

Campeachy wood: also known as *logwood*, the dyewood originally exported from Campeche in Yucatan.

campechena: see *cochineal*.

cochineal: red dyestuff composed of dried carcasses of insects gathered from the topal in Mexico. Also called *grana* or *grain*. Cochineal (or *grana*) *mesteque* was the finest grade and was cultivated for export, especially from Veracruz. Less valuable were the uncultivated *campechena* and *sylvester*, also known as 'wild cochineal'.

coranto: news-letter, often containing commodity prices.

cuarto: see *real, Spanish*.

ducat (D): see *real, Spanish*.

ell: linear measure, 45 inches.

encomiendas: goods commissioned for a special purpose.

fanega: also *hanneck*, Spanish measure of dry-weight capacity, equivalent to 1.75 Winchester bushels.

first penny: prime or first cost, before taxes or other charges.

flota: Spanish merchant fleet. In theory, if not always in practice, two Spanish fleets were to be sent to America each year. The *flota*, or *Nueva España fleet*, left Cadiz in May or June bound for Veracruz and also included ships bound for the West Indies. The *galeones* (galleons) left Spain in August bound for Cartagena and Portobello and also included ships destined for Venezuela. After wintering in the Indies, the two fleets were to assemble at Havana for the return voyage, but again this was not always the practice.

galeones: see *flota*.

grain, grana, grana mesteque: see *cochineal*.

hanneck: see *fanega*.

hogshead (hhd): large wooden cask which, when filled with wine or pilchards, was accounted as 500 lbs for the purpose of calculating freight.

hundredweight (cwt): also *quintal* (kt), measure of weight, 100–112 lbs.

leña noel: see *lignum rhodium*.

lignum rhodium: also *leña noel*, rosewood native to the Canary Islands.

logwood: see *Campeachy wood*.

malvasía: sweet white dessert wine vintaged in Tenerife. A drier Canary wine was known as *vidueño*.

maravedí: see *real, Spanish*.

memory: memorandum, especially as a list of goods to be shipped.

mil (m): 1,000, but as a count of fish or pipestaves usually 1,200.

milréis: see *real, Portuguese*.

Nueva España fleet: see *flota*.

orchil: red or purple dyestuff prepared from the lichen *roccella tinctoria*, also known as Canary weed.

panele: brown, unpurified sugar inferior to muscovado.

piece of eight: see *real, Spanish*.

pipe: wooden cask for wine and other goods. According to most sources, the pipe held 126 gallons, but testimony from the mid-seventeenth century suggests that the pipe used in the Canary trade was smaller, holding perhaps 112 to 120 gallons. For calculations of freight and taxes, two hogsheads of wine equalled one pipe, and two pipes equalled one ton.

plata doble: see *real, Spanish*.

premium: see *real, Spanish*.

puesto: stall from which wine is sold.

quarter: measure of grain equal to eight bushels.

quintal (kt): see *hundredweight*.

Ram Alley: or Hare Place south of Fleet Street, a place of sanctuary in the seventeenth century and hence a resort of debtors.

real, Portuguese: pl. *réis*, Portuguese monetary unit of the seventeenth century. A *milréis* (1,000 reis) was worth *c.* 9s 5d in terms of silver equivalencies from 1643–63 and was rated at 10s in an account Paige received in 1654.

real, Spanish (R): pl. *reales*, Spanish monetary unity equal to 34 *maravedís*. Silver coins in denominations of more than one *real* were known as *plata doble*, for example, *pieces of eight reales* or *ducats* (*ducados*) of 11 *reales*. *Cuartos* worth 4 *maravedís* were *vellon*, i.e. copper-based coins. Canarian money was a mixture of Castilian and Portuguese coins. Because of this, Canarian *reales* were not accounted as equivalent to Castilian *reales*, and it was necessary to pay a *premium*, at times from 8 to 16 per cent, in terms of Canarian *reales* for a given value in Castilian *reales*.

réis: see *real, Portuguese.*

rove: *arroba*, Spanish measure of weight, *c.* 25 lbs.

sack: ship which carried fish from Newfoundland to various English and European ports and especially to southern Spain where wine (sack) was often laded for the return voyage to England.

seron: crate or hamper.

stiver: silver coin from the Low Countries. Twenty *stivers* equalled £1 Flemish.

sylvester: see *cochineal.*

ton (t): as a measure of weight, from 2,000 to 2,240 lbs depending on the commodity. A veteran shipmaster of the Canary trade testified in 1650 that in freight calculations a *ton* was accounted as equivalent to 42–3 hides, 2 pipes of wine, 13–14 kts of ginger, 3 chests of sugar, 20 kts of logwood, or 8 chests of tobacco.

uzance: time conventionally allowed by merchants for the completion of an exchange operation, for example, between London and Antwerp, one month, or at *double uzance*, two months.

vara: Spanish linear measure, *c.* 33 inches.

vellon: see *real, Spanish.*

vidueño: see *malvasía.*

INDEX

References in Roman numerals are to pages in the Introduction; those in Arabic numerals are to serial numbers in the text. Items marked by an asterisk are explained in the Glossary (Appendix C).

PERSONS AND PLACES

—, Don Carlos, 60d, 64c, 66a, 73a–b
—, Don Melchior, Canarian winegrower, 52a, 120

Ackland
    Arthur, English merchant at Bilbao, xxvii, 33, 36, 40a, 76a, 77c, 81c
    Lewis, English merchant at Nantes, 84c
Agadir (Santa Cruz de Berbería), Morocco, 63d, 129
Algiers, xi
Alicante, Spain, 66b
Alvarado Bracamonte, Cristóbal de, xxxiii, 73a, 96d, 120
Alvares, Nicholas, xxxiii n., 120
Amboina, 61c
Amsterdam, Netherlands, xv, xviii, xxi, xxxiv, xxxix, 6, 25b, 35, 37, 40a, 41, 44, 48, 49, 53b, 56b, 59a, 71a
Andrews, John, English merchant at Terceira, 74, 76a, 77c, 78a, 81b, 84c
Antilles, Lesser (Caribee Islands), 97, 100b
Antwerp, Netherlands, xviii, xix, xxxi–xxxii, 31b, 111a, 119–24, 126
Aponte, Juan de, Canarian winegrower, 71b
Arras, siege of, 89f
Arundell, William, merchant at Fowey, 13a, 17, 89e
Ascham, Anthony, agent of English government at Madrid, 19a, 21
Asia, trade with, xxxvi–xxxvii
Asilah, Morocco, 89c
Audley, —, shipmaster, 30a, 31a–b
Avery, —, shipmaster, 23b
Ayscue, Sir George, 53b, 58a, 61d
Azores, xxi, xxix–xxx, 64c, 66b, 72 n., 78a

Baker, Richard, English merchant at Madrid, xxiii, 6, 10, 22d, 31b, 40a, 42, 43 n., 44, 47b, 115 n., 116–17
Balcarsel, Lorenzo, Canarian winegrower, xxxiii n.
Bankes, —, shipmaster, 29
Bantam, xxxvi–xxxvii
Barbados, xxiv, 63a–b, 65, 78a, 83b, 89d, 96c, 100a, 123 n.; agent from, 28; ginger from, xvii; fleet to, 25b, 27b, 30b–31a, 33, 37, 53b, 58a, 61d, 94b, 97, 99b, 103; royalists in, 25b, 27b; slaves to, 86; sugars from, xv, 35, 40a, 44, 61d, 106a, 123; wines to, xiv, 25b–26a, 28, 31a, 54, 61d, 89d, 91b, 93b, 95, 99b, 100b
Barbary Coast, xx–xxi, xxv, 10, 23b, 25a, 25b–26a, 27a, 30a–b, 32, 34–5, 39a, 40b, 61e, 128–9
Barber, Thomas, shipmaster, 1, 3–4, 6–7a, 8–12b, 15, 18, 19b, 128
Barron, Benjamin, merchant at Plymouth, 125b, 128
Bayona, Spain, 125b
Beake, Arnold, London merchant, 113
Bean, [Humfry], shipmaster, 54–55a, 60a, 80
Belle-Île, France, 7a
Benin, Bight of, xxiii, 46, 47b, 52b, 61e
Benítez de Lugo
    Diego, Canarian winegrower, 6, 30a, 51b–52a, 53a, 64b, 66a
    Luis, Canarian winegrower, 50, 71b, 81a
Bennet, Sir Henry, xxxii
Bennett
    —, merchant, 126
    —, shipmaster, 128
Berkeley, William, London merchant, xxiv, 68a, 77a, 78b, 81b, 84b, 89e
Best, Richard, London merchant, xiv
Bewley, John, London merchant, xi, 83b
Biafra, Bight of, xxiv, 63a
Bilbao, Spain, xviii, xx, xxvii, 11a, 13b, 27b, 29, 34, 39b, 42–3, 81c, 83b, 91a, 96c, 125b; convoy for, 123; Newfoundland fish to, xxvi, xxxi, 11b, 14, 19b, 21, 23b, 26b, 96d, 97–8, 102, 104–108a, 109, 111a; ships from, 128; ships to, 31c–33, 35–6, 40a, 75
Biscay, Bay of, 39b
Blaeu, Simon, Dutch mariner, xxxiv
Blake
    James, shipmaster, 13b, 17, 22a–b, d,

Index: Persons and Places

Shaw, John, English merchant at Antwerp, xix, xxxii, xxxvii, 52b, 57–58a, 121, 125b–126

Sheere, Henry, shipmaster, 11a, 29, 128

Shorton, —, 64b, 66a

Showers, —, shipmaster, 1

Skinner, Daniel, London merchant, 53b n.

Slaney
    Humphrey, London merchant, xxii
    John, London merchant, xxii
    Stephen, London merchant, 2, 5a, 26b, 31a, 31c, 46, 47c, 52a, 55a, 57, 60b, 67b, 69–70; 74; widow of, 119

Smith
    —, shipmaster, 11a, 12b, 14, 128
    Matthew, shipmaster, xxx, 107–108b, 110b, 113–14
    Robert, 106b

Smyrna, Turkey, 93a

Smyth, —, shipmaster, 82

Southampton, 37, 44

Spain, xvii, 31c–32, 39b, 52b, 75, 83b; American goods from, xvii–xviii; bribing officials of, 111b; coinage of, 27b n., 30a–b, 31b–c, 51b, 58a–b, 60c, 61a–b, 63c, 75, 81c, 84a, 126; commercial monopoly in America, xix, xxxvii; 'Consejo' of, xxxii; credits in, xxvi–xxvii; dearth in, 77a; *donativo* of, xxvii; embargo against English trade in, xxx–xxxi, 53b, 63c, 96c, 99b, 106b, 108a, 110a, 111b–112, 115; English merchants in, xxx, 106b; fears of war with, xxx, 12b, 26b, 65, 85, 89c, f, 94b–95, 96c–d, 97, 99a–b, 100b, 104–5, 106b, 108a, 109; iron from, xx; sickness in, 5a, 6, 8, 10, 32; silver of, 63c, 91a, 103, 118, 120, 124; war with France, 89f; war with England, xxv, xxx–xxxiv, 110a–b, 111b, 114–15, 125a, 126

Spicer, Michael, London merchant, 77b, 88, 89a, d

Standish, Ralph, English merchant in Tenerife, xxxi, 63b, 89d–91a, 93a, 96b–d, 108b, 116–17

Starling, —, shipmaster, 128

Steniquer, —, shipmaster, 73a

Stephens, David, English merchant in Tenerife, xix, 32, 61d, 68b, 84c, 126

Steward, Peter, shipmaster, 5a, 9, 11a, 17, 22d, 23b, 26a, 27a, 29, 30a, 32, 60a, 61a, 80, 83b, 128

Stoke Fleming, Devon, x

Straw, Nicholas, shipmaster, 65–66a, 73b

Sumatra, xxxvi

Surat, 99a

Sweden, 63c, 71a; King of, xi

Sweeting, Robert, 90, 91b

Sydrakeson, —, shipmaster, 29

Taylor, —, shipmaster, 47a, c, 49–50, 55a, 64b

Tenby, Wales, 65

Tenerife, x–xxxix *passim*; 1–129 *passim*; assize of fish at, 111b; rain in, 32, 61d, 83b; slaves imported into, xxii–xxiv, 25b, 42, 44, 46, 47b, 48, 51b, 52b, 63a, 125a, 126; vintage at, 25a, 47c, 49–50, 61d, 75, 129

Terceira, 67b, 74, 76a, 77c–78a, 81b, 84c

Texel, 78c; battle off, 77c

Thames, River, xii, 39b, 89c, 94a, 96a, 111b, 120

Thomas, John, 103, 108b

Thomson
    Maurice, London merchant, x, xxxvi–xxxviii, 53b
    William, London merchant, 53b n.

Thorne family, of Bristol, x

Throckmorton, William, English merchant in Tenerife, 68b, 91a, 112, 128

Toope, Henry, shipmaster, 1, 9, 128

Topsham, Devon, 20, 23b, 41, 46, 58b, 128

Trinidad, xxxiv

Trinity House, Masters of, 50

Tromp, Lieutenant Admiral Martin Harperszoon van, 68b, 71a, 76b; death of, 77c

Truxillo, xxxiv

Turner
    John, English merchant in Tenerife, xiv, xvi, xviii, xxi, xxv, xxvi n., xxvii, xxxix, 11a, 17, 22d, 23b, 27b, 30a, 37, 39b, 43, 49, 59a, 61b, 83b, 84c, 96b n., 111b, 128
    Robert, 66c, 100b, 124

Venia y Vergara, Benito, xxxiii, 71b, 120

Veracruz, 97

Vergara Grimon, Balthazar de, Canarian winegrower, xxxiii, 50, 81a, 83b, 116–17, 120

Vigo, Spain, 87

Waight, Thomas, shipmaster, 64c, 72, 75–76a, 78a, 81b, 84b–c

Walker, Dr Walter, civil lawyer, 77a; Judge Advocate of the High Court of Admiralty, 19a

Wall, —, shipmaster, 79, 82, 84b

Ward, Phillip, English merchant in Tenerife, 128

Warren
    Nicholas, London merchant, x, 106a
    Thomas, London merchant, x, 27a, 30b, 39a, 44, 52b, 67a–b, 80, 128

Webber
    George, London merchant, 19a, 80, 118, 126
    John, English merchant in Tenerife, 17,

SUBJECTS

LONDON RECORD SOCIETY

The London Record Society was founded in December 1964 to publish transcripts, abstracts and lists of the primary sources for the history of London, and generally to stimulate interest in archives relating to London. Membership is open to any individual or institution; the annual subscription is £7 ($15) for individuals and £10 ($23) for institutions, which entitles a member to receive one copy of each volume published during the year and to attend and vote at meetings of the Society. Prospective members should apply to the Hon. Secretary, Miss Heather Creaton, c/o Institute of Historical Research, Senate House, London, WC1E 7HU.

The following volumes have already been published:

1. *London Possessory Assizes: a calendar*, edited by Helena M. Chew (1965)
2. *London Inhabitants within the Walls, 1695*, with an introduction by D. V. Glass (1966)
3. *London Consistory Court Wills, 1492–1547*, edited by Ida Darlington (1967)
4. *Scriveners' Company Common Paper, 1357–1628, with a continuation to 1678*, edited by Francis W. Steer (1968)
5. *London Radicalism, 1830–1843: a selection from the papers of Francis Place*, edited by D. J. Rowe (1970)
6. *The London Eyre of 1244*, edited by Helena M. Chew and Martin Weinbaum (1970)
7. *The Cartulary of Holy Trinity Aldgate*, edited by Gerald A. J. Hodgett (1971)
8. *The Port and Trade of Early Elizabethan London: documents*, edited by Brian Dietz (1972)
9. *The Spanish Company*, by Pauline Croft (1973)
10. *London Assize of Nuisance, 1301–1431: a calendar*, edited by Helena M. Chew and William Kellaway (1973)
11. *Two Calvinistic Methodist Chapels, 1743–1811: the London Tabernacle and Spa Fields Chapel*, edited by Edwin Welch (1975)
12. *The London Eyre of 1276*, edited by Martin Weinbaum (1976)
13. *The Church in London, 1375–1392*, edited by A. K. McHardy (1977)
14. *Committees for Repeal of the Test and Corporation Acts: Minutes, 1786–90 and 1827–8*, edited by Thomas W. Davis (1978)
15. *Joshua Johnson's Letterbook, 1771–4: letters from a merchant in London to his partners in Maryland*, edited by Jacob M. Price (1979)
16. *London and Middlesex Chantry Certificate, 1548*, edited by C. J. Kitching (1980)

All volumes are still in print; apply to Hon. Secretary. Price to individual members £7 ($15) each; to institutional members £10 ($23) each; and to non-members £12 ($28) each.